While I Have Being

While I Have Being

Winterreise (Winter Journey)

KENNETH L. VAUX

WIPF & STOCK · Eugene, Oregon

WHILE I HAVE BEING
Winterreise (Winter Journey)

Wipf & Stock
An Imprint of Wipf and Stock Publishers
199 W. 8th Ave., Suite 3
Eugene, OR 97401
www.wipfandstock.com

ISBN 13: 978-1-62032-337-3

Manufactured in the U.S.A.

Deep thanks to Melanie Baffes,
valued theological colleague and editor.
Thanks for your thorough and excellent work.
Pass it on.

Contents

I

Midwinter Reflections

I will sing unto the Lord the Lord as long as I live:
I will sing praise to my God while I have my being. (Ps 104:33)

November 23, 2010

"Being" is a song that is much of what I think and write about. Though moving toward retirement, I still dream and imagine vast horizons ahead, luring me on with exciting new ministries now at hand. Was it Aristotle who said that one should not have the audacity to write a book before turning 60? Well I'm ready!

This journal, I project, will cover my last year of teaching, which includes a sabbatical season in Europe and concludes with my final classes and the presentation of a *Festschrift* to honor our Northwestern colleague, Garry Wills.

The focus of my work at present is major reflection on my two academic assignments, Doctrine of God and Moral Theology, expressed in manuscripts from which I teach: Teaching God and Teaching Good. As if "knowing the unknowable God" was not enough, I also keep a running autobiography that focuses variously on a medical crisis, the Tucson Ordeal, an interfaith analysis of the uprising in the Middle East, a sabbatical in England, Belgium and France and the concluding months of my tenure in Evanston. My sabbatical projects beyond this diary are *The Ministry of Vincent Van Gogh in Religion and Art* and *Horror of War and Hope for Peace: Essays in Honor of Garry Wills.*

In method, I aspire to be a Talmudic thinker, cut from the mold of my small book, *Prophètes Parisienne* (Ch VII). The public intellectual I emulate most is Parisienne Emmanuel Levinas. I wake each day following the inspiration of the theologian on whom I cut my teeth, Karl Barth, who, as dawn broke each day in his Safenwil Parish or Basel study, put on the music of Mozart and held the Bible in one hand and the newspaper (*Basler Zeitung*) in the other. "What God was doing in the world" became the ground-plan of contemplative action for self and any collective, nation, corporation, or church. My Paris research would eventually settle on Paul Ricoeur as I came to contemplate the requirements of a hermeneutic for interfaith studies.

Levinas takes specific scriptural texts, looks at them in their rabbinic setting, their hermeneutical context, especially in light of existential philosophy, Heidegger/Husserl, and upon that basis offers ethical (pastoral) wisdom and action. He offers this in the unique mode of a French public intellectual in the mold of Derrida, Ricoeur, Levy, Levi-Strauss, Camus, de Beauvoir, Irigaray, et al.

On the theme of this diary ("Praise, while I have being") Levinas offers this wisdom: "The a-Dieu (bidding one farewell in God) is not a finality." It is not about the Hegelian/Heideggerian alternative between being and nothingness that falls short of the "ultimate." "The a-Dieu greets the other beyond being, in what is signified, beyond being, by the word Glory."[1]

For 50 years, I have delighted in the fog of non-comprehension in that I have tried to decipher the meanings of thinkers like Derrida and Levinas (both in French and English) even as I have followed their example of Sephardic/political and pastoral address. I emulate the thrust of this intellectual tradition in seeking universal and interfaith currency for ideas and convictions. "What God is doing in the world" is the criterion for authentic theology. I seek to be a public intellectual from within the bosom of the Church. In the American setting, I set my standards by Cornel West.

I also know, and I have taught this my whole life, that being an heir to the grace of life also involves the acceptance of limitations and of finitude

---

1. Emmanuel Levinas, quoted in Jacques Derrida, *The Work of Mourning* (Chicago: University of Chicago Press, 2003), 209.

and that pain "is God's megaphone."[2] Pain is the lot of every person and all of life. The fathoming and transformation of suffering therefore, is close to the secret of existence under God. Approaching morbidity and mortality is also a sacramental mystery in the beginning of new and culminating life.

I believe even more strongly in the resilience and vitality of another body—that of the Church and of our local parish church. Last night, I made it to a meeting at Terry Halliday's home, a working group on making our congregation a more responsive "university" church. In Barth's words, I wish to practice a *Kirchliche Dogmatik.*

Thinking of yesterday, I heard last night on the radio that two others died on that fateful 22nd of November in Dallas so long ago, C.S. Lewis and Aldous Huxley. I remember our pastoral colleague John Calvin Reid, in Mt. Lebanon in his memorial sermon saying, "JFK died today in Dallas . . . so did 'Jack' Lewis in England and an unknown child in India, in the eyes of God . . . they were all the same."

One hymn for Christ the King and First Advent that I wish our congregation knew and loved is "Christ is the World's Redeemer" [Latin c. 590].

> Christ is the world's Redeemer, The lover of the pure,
> The fount of heavenly wisdom, Our Trust and hope secure;
> The armor of His soldiers, The Lord of earth and sky;
> Our health while we are living, Our life when we shall die.
> Christ hath our host surrounded,
> With clouds of martyrs bright,
> Who wave their palms in triumph,
> And fire us for the fight.
> Christ the red cross ascended,
> To save a world undone,
> And suffering for the sinful,
> Our full redemption won.
> All glory be to the Father,
> The unbegotten One;
> All honor be to Jesus,
> The sole begotten Son;
> And to the Holy Spirit, The perfect Trinity.
> Let all the worlds give answer, Amen. So let it be.

2. C.S. Lewis, *The Problem of Pain* (New York: Harper One, 2001), xxxiv, 226.

(Columba, "Christ is the World's Redeemer," c. 590)

Fascinating words: Christ the "red cross" ascended. Our minds travel to the Red Cross and Crescent, to the Star of David, to relief agencies par excellence. The agency logos are also symbols of persistent agony in the world: the Crimean War, Verdun and Fort Vaux, Haiti, Afghanistan, Israel-Palestine. The signs also stand for the unfathomable enigmas we call theodicy, human vicissitudes that are woven into the very mysteries of God. Teilhard de Chardin said, ". . . in the eyes of a mere biologist, it is still true that nothing resembles the way of a cross as much as the human epic."[3] Yet these symbols are also tokens of help, symbols of proffered care and first aid.

November 24 (Thanksgiving eve)

"He is called the Pope's Maestro and strangers now are friends."[4]

Twenty years ago, Sir Gilbert Levine, the American maestro, and Pope John Paul II collaborated on a series of concerts broadcasted internationally from the Vatican. The concerts broke new theological ground and reaffirmed the revolutionary accomplishments of Vatican II. It was an expression of repentance for the deep complicity of the Catholic Church in the two millennia-long Christian genocide against the Jews and an affirmation of God's eternal *Berith* and covenant with the Jews as the fraternal, indeed parental, faith to Christians. As a young seminarian and priest in Krakow, Karol Wojtyla, like leaders of Vatican II, although intensely conservative, yearned for Christendom to find rapprochement with the Jewish people. A hardy lad, he had Jews among his close camping and mountain-climbing friends. Like John XXIII, and all deeply-Christian Judaophiles, he sought forgiveness, atonement, and reconciliation with the great olive trunk into which Christians and Muslims are grafted branches.

The two Poles were from Krakow, a site of the disgraceful *Shoah*. Levine, the Jew, whose wife's family had been exterminated at nearby Auschwitz-Birkenau, became the conductor of the Krakow Symphony.

3. Pierre Teilhard de Chardin, *The Phenomenon of Man* (Sussex, U.K.: Sussex Academic Press, 2003).

4. "The Pope's Maestro," on *Chicago Tonight*, WTTW Chicago/PBS, November 23, 2010.

The young priest, Wojtyla, a professor who ministered and taught at the university, became Pope. Levine had promised his wife that he would go to Birkenau and say a prayer for her murdered family, and his appointment at the symphony became known to the Pope.

Levine visited Auschwitz and viewed the grotesque exhibits: the heaps of eyeglasses ripped rudely from faces, the piles of hair brutally cut off, suitcases piled in anonymous mountains, each case telling its story. He knelt at the crematorium and took a handful of ash and dirt, still mingled with fragments of bone.

At Krakow, he conducted the music of two geniuses of that Austro-Hungarian empire: Mozart's "D minor Piano Concerto" and Mahler's "Fourth Symphony." The last movement of Mahler strikingly depicts a child's vision of heaven.

The date of the inception of this interfaith brotherhood was 1987. Russian tanks were still in the streets of Krakow. After the Mahler, Levine saw the noted Polish composer Krzysztof Panderecki leap to his feet in applause. It was a *kairos* moment of beauty, truth, and justice.

Levine soon met the Pope and began an intense friendship, one where each man's faith was deepened by the other. As "others" were united and strangers and even enemies became friends, redemption ensued and from the ashes arose the resurrection phoenix.

The Vatican concert series was envisioned to heal the estrangement of Catholics and Jews. It achieved so much more. In this age of interfaith and international strife, it seemed to heal the deep wounds of alienation between the three Abrahamic faiths. Two tenderhearted souls, shaken by circumstance and encounter, rose to deeper understanding and more profound faith.

November 28, 2010 (First Advent)

"With Heart and Voice," a 6 a.m. program of sacred music ends with John Rutter's arrangement of one of my favorite hymns. It is said that Queen Victoria's organist once changed the tune from Helmsley and before all six verses were finished, a note appeared on the console: "You will never again drop Helmsley from 'Lo He Comes with Clouds Descending.'"

> Lo! He comes, with clouds descending,
> Once for favoured sinners slain;

Thousand, thousand saints attending
Swell the triumph of His train:
Alleluia!
Christ appears on earth again.
Every eye shall now behold Him,
Robed in dreadful majesty;
Those who set at naught and sold Him,
Pierced, and nailed Him to the tree,
Deeply wailing,
Shall the true Messiah see.
Those dear tokens of His Passion
Still His dazzling body bears,
Cause of endless exultation
To His ransomed worshipers:
With what rapture
Gaze we on those glorious scars!
Now redemption, long expected,
See in solemn pomp appear:
All his saints, by men rejected,
Now shall meet him in the air:
Alleluia!
See the day of God appear.
Yea, amen; let all adore thee,
High on Thine eternal throne;
Saviour, take the power and glory;
Claim the kingdoms for Thine own:
Alleluia!
Thou shalt reign, and Thou alone.
Yet with mingled hope and fearing,
Wait we still our Judge to see;
In the day of Thine appearing.
Spotless blameless may he be!
Ever watching,
Teach us, Lord, to welcome Thee. Amen.

(Charles Wesley, "Lo He Comes with Clouds Descending, 1758)

Advent: A strange season. Internally as discordant as the bizarre secular season that unfolds in the malls beginning with shopping stampedes on Black Friday, the frantic day following Thanksgiving. As the skies change from sunny to grey, Advent changes with the vestment colors, now Christ the King red becomes the Sarum blue and violet, Van Gogh's colors of passion, pathos, suffering and victory. "Lo He Comes" is gently sung on First Advent by the King's College Choir. "Deeply wailing . . . O come quickly" plead the boys' voices with scarcely a dry eye.

The orthodox Christian creed asserts that Jesus came as visitor, to reign as vicar, and will come again as vindicator: *Munus Triplex*, prophet, priest, and king. Various human schemes, juridical and judgmental, have been added to the long, vengeful history of the church and religion more broadly. The first and final coming, portrayed in the disturbing yet sublime texts of Advent, need to be carefully pondered so that they can transfigure our lives in justice and peace through the unfathomable love of God, here and now and into all eternity.

The inner meaning of Advent is found in the paradoxical truth of scripture: that God's judgment is His mercy and His mercy is His justice. Love comes out into the world in the Messianic faiths of Judaism, Christianity, Islam and even "natural (primordial) religion" in this hauntingly feminine presence called *Logos*, Word, Wisdom, Instruction, Way, Messiah, *Christos*, "the second God in heaven." The center of this revelation is God with us, *Emmanuel*, "to all who receive Him, He gives power to become the children of God" (John 1:12).

December 5, 2010 (Second Advent)

The dawn cracks on a snow covered Chicago with heart and voice at six a.m. The themes that hit home to this struggling soul seeking peace of body and mind were: 1) The silent mystery of the season, the Russian liturgy with its *Hospodi Pomili* and the Spanish *O Magnum Mysterium*; 2) the meditation on "*est ist ein ros entsprungen*" (a rose has sprung up from Jesse's trunk), emphasizing the gentle organic gift of divine wisdom; 3) Orlando Gibbons' Advent masterpiece, "This is the record of John," recalling the years when this genius, who would become the composer/organist of the Royal Chapel, was a chorister at King's College, Cambridge. The mood I sought and celebrated during Advent and Second Advent, coming and coming again, was expressed in a Gospel song sung by our church choir, "I hear the Prophet Callin.'" One verse is based on Isaiah 35: "then will the eyes of the blind be opened."

The Advent texts, a unique body of legendary material that has always fallen short of full acceptance as having historical and even faith-valid substance, has achieved a boost of credibility through the work of

Raymond Brown in *The Birth of the Messiah*.5 The material includes: the visit of an "angel of the Lord" to the pregnant Mary and her dreaming, concerned betrothed Joseph in Matthew 1; the wise-men (Magi); the star; Herod and his infanticide; the birth in Bethlehem; the diversion into Egypt; Luke's narrative of the Priest Zachariah in the Jerusalem Temple and his wife Elizabeth and their late-in-life, Abram/Sarai like-conception of the Prophet *par excellence*, John the Baptizer; Mary's greeting of Elizabeth; again Mary's angelic visitation; the *Magnificat*; the births of John and Jesus; the shepherd's field vision and visit to the manger; Simeon's prophesy and blessing of the baby at the circumcision; the prediction of the child's future and destiny *vis à vis* the nation; and 84-year-old Anna's prophesy. To this might be added the prologue of John's Gospel and then the telling reference to John the Baptist: "and this is the record of John" (John 1:19), although this text is of a quite different genre and meaning.

While acknowledging the historical difficulties, Brown has shown convincingly the indispensible theological purpose and content of this material. His contention, in sum, is that, while the texts are similar in format to the star-child birth of Julius Caesar, in form they arise out of the very structure and substance of the Gospel. Brown's view is in accordance with the ancient English and American Advent hymn, "The Cherry Tree Carol." Note the profundity of the commonplace:

> When Joseph was an old man,
> An old man was he,
> He married Virgin Mary,
> The Queen of Galilee,
> He married Virgin Mary,
> The Queen of Galilee.
> As Joseph and Mary
> Walked through an orchard green,
> There were apples and cherries
> Plenty there to be seen,
> There were apples and cherries
> Plenty there to be seen.
> Then Mary spoke to Joseph,
> So meek and so mild,
> "Joseph, gather me some cherries,

---

5. Raymond Brown, *The Birth of the Messiah: A Commentary on the Infancy Narratives in the Gospels of Matthew and Luke*, Anchor Yale Bible Reference Library (New Haven: Yale University Press, 1999).

For I am with Child,
Joseph, gather me some cherries,
For I am with Child."
Then Joseph flew in anger,
In anger flew he,
"Let the father of the baby
Gather cherries for thee,
Let the father of the baby
Gather cherries for thee."
Then Jesus spoke a few words,
A few words spoke He,
"Let my mother have some cherries,
Bow low down, cherry tree,
Let my mother have some cherries,
Bow low down, cherry tree."
The cherry tree bowed low down,
Bowed low down to the ground,
And Mary gathered cherries,
While Joseph stood around,
And Mary gathered cherries,
While Joseph stood around.
Then Joseph took Mary
All on his right knee:
"Oh, what have I done, Lord?
Have mercy on me.
Oh, what have I done, Lord?
Have mercy on me."
Then Joseph took Mary
All on his left knee:
"Oh, tell me, little Baby,
When Thy Birthday will be,
Oh, tell me, little Baby,
When Thy Birthday will be."

"On the fifth day of January
My Birthday will be,
When the stars and the elements
Shall tremble with fear,
When the stars and the elements
Shall tremble with fear."

(Anonymous, "The Cherry Tree Carol,"
1820, celebrating the flight into Egypt)

In Gian Carlo Menotti's words, the baby born is "the color of earth and thorn, the color of wheat and dawn" (Gian Carlo Menotti, "Song of the Magi/Amahl and the Night Visitors," 1951). Earth and humanity, heaven and divinity are in the genius of Brown's Christology.

Father Raymond Brown, as Dean of modern New Testament scholars, was the first tenured professor from the Roman Catholic Church to teach at Union Theological Seminary in New York City. His work navigated carefully the way from the historic catholic view of verbal inspiration of scripture to the new horizons of Vatican II, where scripture was to be understood as accessible to reason while rooted in revelation. The document, *Dei Verbum (Pope Paul VI, November 18, 1965),* held that scripture is the vehicle by which sacred writings convey the message of salvation. Inerrancy had been replaced by a new criterion of efficacy as scripture and was witnessed to and conveyed salvation and redemption.

Brown's Christology focuses on this doctrine of the Word, where Jesus is understood to stand in the Jewish tradition of the primacy of God and the *Shemah/Hashem* (the oneness of God and the prohibition against having other gods), all the while refusing to call himself God. Even in the highly theological and Christological Gospel of John this is the case.

A trained and observant rabbi ("... not one jot or tittle will diminish from the law," Matt 5:18), Jesus did not presume to call himself God, although this was his right (Phil 2). God declared and delivered Jesus to be this beloved and only begotten Son (*agapetos, monogenos*) (Gen 22, John 3:16); "God was in Christ, reconciling the world to himself" (2 Cor 5:19); "God has made Him Lord and Christ" (Acts 2:36); Messiah (*Christos*) is a "taken up," bestowed office. Therefore we cry with Thomas, "my Lord and my God" (John 20:28).

For these theological reasons, Brown resists the magical aspects of the nativity narratives in favor of the mystery and down-to-earth wonder. In my own view, I assert that the self-ascription of Jesus is yes: "I am the son of ABBA" but it is most often the "Son of Man," that is strikingly like the Hebrew Bible's designation of *Yahweh*. Think of the closeness of Exodus 24:10 and Ezekiel 1:26: "And above the dome over their heads there was something like a throne, in appearance like sapphire; and seated above was the likeness of a throne was something that seemed like a human form."

Brown taught in the tradition of Thomas Aquinas, where reason and revelation are inextricably interrelated as the twin gifts of God. This theological standpoint, benefitting from Thomas' reading of the two doctors, Maimonides and Avicenna, both Semitic biblical exegetes, recapitulates early Christianity's appropriation of Neo-Platonism and Aristotle, and, in order to protect both the immanence and transcendence of God, seizes again the handmaiden of philosophy. This move, focused in Medieval *Al-Andalus*, has become the presupposition of all subsequent theology, Catholic, evangelical, even Jewish and Muslim.

His renderings, therefore, of the nativity materials is thoroughly Semitic (worldly) and theological. Fundamentalism and literalism as alternate philosophical systems are replaced by an evangelical agenda. Rather than being hopelessly mythic and magical in structure and substance, these narratives are at the heart of biblical theology. Here we find the glory of God fully manifest. Although a critical scholar of the birth narratives without peer, he is a churchman and herald of the Gospel. He thus bridges the scholarly and salvific Gospel. Mary is no longer a girl disgraced out of wedlock, but the preeminent theologian in the early church. James, Jesus' brother, is not some fraternal pretender but, with mother Mary, Bishop and creative thinker.

December 9, 2010

The reader of this diary senses that my being and my perception of well-being are threatened at this point in life as I reach three score years and 12. My Van Gogh research trip to Belgium and Holland has been cancelled and the sabbatical temporarily delayed. Surgery awaits me on January 3rd. My good wife Sara is off to Antwerp to carry on holiday celebrations with our family there.

To speak as a philosopher, I know that non-being lies under the fragility of being in this world (Tillich after Heidegger), although I take my comfort from theology like the Heidelberg Confession, within which my family stands: where "I trust my faithful savior, Jesus Christ, my only hope in life and death" and Psalm 104 with which I headline this diary. I also believe, to continue Tillich's formulation, that "true" or "authentic" being is found as "new being" transfigures the non-being threat of mortality into the light and immortality of the Gospel. With Paul, we can say that we no longer live but Christ lives in and through us. We live as one with Him, being made like Him in death and that if possible we might attain with Him the resurrection of the dead. I write and speak of this conviction often but living it out in ultimate circumstances is another story. The reader will forgive the like minded error of rendering life and death as fuzzy abstractions.

December 11, 2010 (Saturday a.m. men's group)

I find a strange camaraderie in this motley association, which is one of our church's bulwarks. The home congregation is a great strength at this time. At this moment, it is better to have grass-roots "inner strength" bodies than outer distinctions of body. The congregation loves the "evangelical Christ," conversion based ministry and, above all, this church, First Presbyterian Church of Evanston and its pastor, Ray Hylton, whom I will follow against the gates of hell to support.

My mind today is on China. Our morning speaker was a 20-something Chinese woman from Beijing, whence my long-standing colleague, K.K. Yeo has just returned. I offered a prayer for the great people of the nation of China. I gave thanks for the Nobel Peace Prize winner, 54-year-old Liu Xiaobo, who has been 11 years in prison for his work to reform human rights in the post-Tiananmen-Square period. An empty chair stood in Stockholm as actress Liv Ullman read Liu's final statement: "Hatred cannot rot away at a person's intelligence and conscience." I thanked this great people for doing more than any other nation for clean energy and for cautioning North (and South) Korea from its recent saber-rattling.

The young woman serves as an evangelical worker to organize Chinese students at Northwestern into bible study, church visits and, living out her new life- passion, to "bring them to the Lord." I concur with this yearning that I have learned from K.K.—who combines this evangelical impulse with a respectful appreciation of traditional Chinese faiths: Buddhism and Daoism, Confucianism and even Maoist communism. In these synergies, he has argued that American and Western Christianities have much to learn from China. Christianity is not exceptional to America. All nations in the world have their own particular divine destinies (Acts 17:26) within the overarching providence of God.

E. Stanley Jones has written a masterpiece called "The *Christ of the Indian Road*.6 Is there also a Christ of the China, Korean, African and Arabic roads? Jones found deep sacredness in each of those indigenous roads with their holy, pre-Christian traditions. Is that where we start today?

In dialogue over many years, I have expressed appreciation for the positive effects of the "Peoples Revolution," especially the upsurge of general welfare and health care. Of course, I have regretted the atheistic Leninism and the political suppression of rights such as those inflicted on Liu Xiaobo. The religious mystery I ponder is the fact that China welcomes Buddhism when persecution ensues in India only to then turn its own persecution on Tibet and the Dali Lama, forcing him into the 15-day trek over the Himalayas back into India. The nations of China, India, Brazil and others together with the world faiths of Christianity and Islam, Judaism, Hinduism and Buddhism convey hope and love, justice and peace into this dark, yet God-visited planet.

December 12, 2010

Advent III takes a turn toward serenity with its Old Testament scripture:

ISAIAH 35:1–10 (NIV)
1 The desert and the parched land will be glad;
  the wilderness will rejoice and blossom.
Like the crocus, 2 it will burst into bloom
  it will rejoice greatly and shout for joy.
The glory of Lebanon will be given to it,
  the splendor of Carmel and Sharon;
they will see the glory of the LORD,
  the splendor of our God.
3 Strengthen the feeble hands,
  steady the knees that give way;
4 say to those with fearful hearts,
  "Be strong, do not fear;
your God will come,
  he will come with vengeance;
with divine retribution
  he will come to save you."
5 Then will the eyes of the blind be opened

6. E. Stanley Jones, *The Christ of the Indian Road* (Nashville: Abingdon Press, 1925).

and the ears of the deaf unstopped.
6 Then will the lame leap like a deer,
and the mute tongue shout for joy.
Water will gush forth in the wilderness
and streams in the desert.
7 The burning sand will become a pool,
the thirsty ground bubbling springs.
In the haunts where jackals once lay,
grass and reeds and papyrus will grow.
8 And a highway will be there;
it will be called the Way of Holiness;
it will be for those who walk on that Way.
The unclean will not journey on it;
wicked fools will not go about on it.
9 No lion will be there,
nor any ravenous beast;
they will not be found there.
But only the redeemed will walk there,
10 and those the LORD has rescued will return.
They will enter Zion with singing;
everlasting joy will crown their heads.
Gladness and joy will overtake them,
and sorrow and sighing will flee.

You are here:

PSALM 146

¹ Praise the LORD.
Praise the LORD, my soul.
2 I will praise the LORD all my life;
I will sing praise to my God as long as I live.
3 Do not put your trust in princes,
in human beings, who cannot save.
4 When their spirit departs, they return to the ground;
on that very day their plans come to nothing.
5 Blessed are those whose help is the God of Jacob,
whose hope is in the LORD their God.
6 He is the Maker of heaven and earth,
the sea, and everything in them,
he remains faithful forever.
7 He upholds the cause of the oppressed
and gives food to the hungry.
The LORD sets prisoners free,

8 the LORD gives sight to the blind,
the LORD lifts up those who are bowed down,
   the LORD loves the righteous.
9 The LORD watches over the foreigner
   and sustains the fatherless and the widow,
   but he frustrates the ways of the wicked.
10 The LORD reigns forever,
   your God, O Zion, for all generations.
Praise the LORD.

JAMES 5:7–10

⁷ Be patient, then, brothers and sisters, until the Lord's coming. See how the farmer waits for the land to yield its valuable crop, patiently waiting for the autumn and spring rains. ⁸ You too, be patient and stand firm, because the Lord's coming is near. ⁹ Don't grumble against one another, brothers and sisters, or you will be judged. The Judge is standing at the door!

¹⁰ Brothers and sisters, as an example of patience in the face of suffering, take the prophets who spoke in the name of the Lord.

MATTHEW 11:2–11 (NIV)

²When John, who was in prison, heard about the deeds of the Messiah, he sent his disciples ³ to ask him, "Are you the one who is to come, or should we expect someone else?"

⁴Jesus replied, "Go back and report to John what you hear and see: ⁵The blind receive sight, the lame walk, those who have leprosy are cleansed, the deaf hear, the dead are raised, and the good news is proclaimed to the poor. ⁶Blessed is anyone who does not stumble on account of me."

⁷As John's disciples were leaving, Jesus began to speak to the crowd about John: "What did you go out into the wilderness to see? A reed swayed by the wind? ⁸If not, what did you go out to see? A man dressed in fine clothes? No, those who wear fine clothes are in kings" palaces. ⁹Then what did you go out to see? A prophet? Yes, I tell you, and more than a prophet. ¹⁰This is the one about whom it is written:

"'I will send my messenger ahead of you,
   who will prepare your way before you.

> [11]Truly I tell you, among those born of women there has not risen anyone greater than John the Baptist; yet whoever is least in the kingdom of heaven is greater than he.

There is a magnificent power in this set of texts. Serenity and an awesome annunciation of a creating, coming, caring, and consummating God. Is something new happening theologically in the world? The "Birth of the messiah" texts find something new coming out of something old. Something has been set to work in the world that is now coming to fulfillment. Is this some new God or new clarity about God?

This is the most challenging reflection afforded by the season to this Jacob-like wrestler with a wound in the flesh and a struggle with the faith. Jesus' Advent is spoken of as the hope of Israel and the yearning of all humankind. But in this very messianic vein, it is sometimes seen as a misdirected hope for a conquering and vanquishing military King, a warrior-Messiah. Jesus seems to disown this identity that his mission is to overthrow the Roman Empire.

There is also something hauntingly unprecedented and novel in Christian Advent. A new dispensation? Maybe this King of Kings is destined to dethrone all worldly powers and empires, all pretenders to self-deification, from Rome through all predecessors and all posthumous aspirants up to the huge financial empires, the money cities of the 21st century, described in *The New York Times* today (December 13, 2010). Tottering in the West and America, but thriving in Riyadh, Dubai, Rio and Beijing, even formidable still in London and New York, these modern towers of Babel continue to rise on the earth and beneath them are buried in obscurity the tiny steeples, domes and minarets, tributes to the "Living God" who holds all these powers subject in his hand.

What indeed sways the future, these new empire cities of finance, law, and business with all the necessary accouterments—education, health care, political and military machinations and maneuvers? Or is it the news of Bethlehem and Golgotha? And how does the herald of that new-news place it within the old, old story of Eden, Sinai, and Moriah?

In world history today, efficacy and power seem to be forthcoming from these new dynamos with traditional spiritual/ethical loci of meaning and energy found to be devoid of liberating and saving credibility and force.

Yet, at the same time these principalities and powers, East and West, financial and military, seem to come up empty. They do not heal, liberate, and save. In many spheres of our life on earth, the passion for prosperity seems to tinge and color faith, and justice is often left to incapable structures of order and restraint.

But some new enthusiasm seems to be afoot in the world. President Obama accedes on tax cuts for millionaires and billionaires, including a $26 billion gift of the people's money to some 2000 very successful entrepreneurs.

The Isaiah, James, and Matthew texts (above) seem to relate wellness and wholeness to physical, social and economic realities: "God (Messiah) sustains "the widows and orphans." The "farmer waits patiently for the Spring rains and the valuable crop" and ". . . blind see, the lame walk, the lepers are cleansed and the poor receive good news." Here and now? Where? Only in potentia? Up to us to deliver? And so at day's end, unbelieving, we trudge home with mountains of packages made in Shanghai, bank-rolled in Riyadh. And by sheer grace we wonder as we wander, for a bloodhound stalks.

December 16, 2010

The day is marked by a national review of the progress in the now near ten-years of war in Afghanistan. The surge seems to show some promise but the promised beginning of the troop draw-down next summer draws skepticism. The theatre is now Afghanistan and Pakistan with the obvious loss of Ambassador Richard Holbrooke leading to doubts about the efficacy of anti-terrorist efforts in Pakistan. The last words Holbrooke had were with a Pakistani doctor as his aorta was giving out: "take care of Pakistan." The Taliban and *al-Qaeda* have seen their consolidations disturbed but the confidence in the Afghan government is still lacking.

My own contribution to this matter has been to look at the broader issue of "war in the world: the theological enigmas of wealth and war." I see the broader fabric of war in this arena having etiology in the unending Israel/Palestine crisis. The challenge is also related to religio-political factors. I propose a matrix of two intersecting vectors: Theology and Ethical options. Theological loci of God, good and evil, sin, ethics and end-purposes intersect with four possible options of action: pragmatic, democratic, theistic (humanistic), and apocalyptic. I proceed then to analyze selected nations of the world: Indonesia, India, China, Brazil; Afghanistan and Pakistan, Israel/Palestine, Africa; America, Europe, Russia, and broader Asia. As these peoples contribute to the religious/political milieu within that, this concrete money/military crisis in the world is taking place.

Within this field of factors, certain personalities arise as actors: Buffett, Gates, Soros, and the other thousand billionaires in the world; the International Monetary Fund (IMF) and World Bank; Obama and world political leaders; David Petraeus and world military leaders; and above all the populations of the nations. The global economic crisis, precipitated by financial carelessness and recklessness in this country, has yet to disclose its full impact. It now is evident that Gandhi was correct to suggest that war will become monetary and money will become the new form of war. Creative imagination will be called on within politics, education, religion, and the populace itself to manage, ameliorate danger, and cause the world's people to prosper once again, the work of secular redemption.

Key players in this world drama include Dominic Strauss-Kahn, the managing Director of the IMF, presently involved in shoring up vulnerable European economies. Ireland and Greece have hit rock bottom. Spain, Europe's fourth largest economy, is heavily top-loaded with debt. The Euro-zone experiences slow growth after the economic collapse of three years ago. In his view, the G-20 must develop a comprehensive policy where the economies that are doing well allow strength to flow in and through struggling economies so that a win-win situation occurs. The strength of the whole is the strength of all. Here we see, in secular guise, the theological premise where the whole global body allows vitality to flow to all members of the body responding to the head, who is God and who wills the well-being of the whole so that all shall flourish while suffering is ameliorated and the weak are lifted up. Reciprocity and responsibility is therefore called for from all members. The IMF is in good hands as the French Socialists now command 65 percent support of the French for President in 2012.

James D. Wolfensohn, former president of the World Bank, is also one of these notable world-historical individuals. An accomplished cellist, tutored by Jacqueline DuPres and her husband, our friend in Chicago, Danny Barenboim, he also was a track star.

From Australia, Wolfensohn is acquainted with the "down and under" and by personality and commitment his overarching concern is with the poor of the world. He was the architect who designed the debt forgiveness program for African nations where live most of the 2 billion desperately poor of the world, the bottom one-third, the failed nations whose populations are living under $2 per day, struggle for survival. In his book, *A Global Life,*[7] he pleads that the only persons with power and efficacy in the world, leaders of the G-7, now G-20, take to heart and will the "poorest segments of humanity" not only because it is right and just but because there will be no stability in this world while inequality continues to advance rapidly.

America remains situated at the top of the world's economies, generating 31 percent of the world product but China, India, Brazil, and Europe are on the move. The world has witnessed a dramatic upsurge of improvement of the lot of the impoverished and poor in recent decades, but the gaping inequality burgeons even more rapidly, overshadowing grace and hope with the disgrace of injustice. My book, *America in God's World*, documents this perplexing double edged-sword.[8]

December 18, 2010

Pastor Ray's text from Hebrews 1 intrigues me. Perhaps it belongs with the nativity texts as we suggested for the Prologue to John's Gospel:

> **Listen to this passage : Hebrews View commentary related to this passage in Hebrews 1.**
>
> In the past God spoke to our ancestors through the prophets at many times and in various ways, [2]but in these last days he has spoken to us by his Son, whom he appointed heir of all things, and through whom also he made the universe. [3]The Son is the radiance of God's glory and the exact representation of his being, sustaining all things by his powerful word. After he had provided purification for sins, he sat down at the right hand of the Majesty in heaven.

---

7. James D. Wolfensohn, *A Global Life: My Journey among the Rich and Poor, From Sydney to Wall Street to the World Bank* (Philadelphia: Public Affairsä/Perseus Books Group, 2010).

8. Kenneth Vaux, *America in God's World: Theology, Ethics, and the Crises of Bases Abroad, Bad Money, and Black Gold* (Eugene, OR: Wipf and Stock, 2009).

[4]So he became as much superior to the angels as the name he has inherited is superior to theirs.

[5] For to that of the angels did God ever say,
"You are my Son;
today I have become your Father"?

Or again,

"I will be his Father,
and he will be my Son"?
[6] And again, when God brings his firstborn into the world, he says,
"Let all God's angels worship him."
[7] In speaking of the angels he says,
"He makes his angels spirits,
and his servants flames of fire."
8 But about the Son he says, "Your throne, O God, will last for ever and ever;
a scepter of justice will be the scepter of your kingdom.
9 You have loved righteousness and hated wickedness;
therefore God, your God, has set you above your companions
by anointing you with the oil of joy."
[10] He also says,
"In the beginning, Lord, you laid the foundations of the earth,
and the heavens are the work of your hands.
11 They will perish, but you remain;
they will all wear out like a garment.
12 You will roll them up like a robe;
like a garment they will be changed.
But you remain the same,
and your years will never end."
[13] To that of the angels did God ever say,
"Sit at my right hand
until I make your enemies
a footstool for your feet"?

The text, with Paul or Luke associated in authorship, is written for the Jewish Christian community and is steeped in Hebraic wisdom such as we find in Paul's contemporary, Philo, and in Hellenistic wisdom such as is found in the Mandean literature such as the Acts of Thomas or the Odes of Solomon. Christ is the King of Israel, The Wisdom of *Logos*, God, and Lord, lower and higher than the angels, human and divine. Larry Hurtado of New College, Edinburgh has captured the essence of this doctrine of the elevated and exalted Christ. His book, *Lord Jesus Christ*,[9] shows that this high Christology, typical of Hebrews, grows naturally out of contemporary Judaism as it does out of the Jesus devotion of the primitive Christian community.

At Saturday men's group yesterday, I reported on the return of K.K. Yeo from Beijing. With the help of our Great Commission mission budget in the church, he is activating a multifaceted program of Christian Studies approved by the government in this premier university of the nation. He trains undergraduate and graduate students in biblical and theological studies. He trains ministers who, in turn, influence their congregations. He also prepares the literature that will be necessary for the education proposed. At present he is translating many Christian classics into the Chinese (Mandarin) language. He also trains leading scholars from mainland China as doctors in bible and theology who will take up the tasks of an indigenous teaching force.

This is a theological development of historic meaning. A Christian community has been rising within the 1.4 billion person nation for many decades. The Catholic and mainline protestant (Three Self) churches have official status. When the unofficial house churches are added, we may have a Christian community of close to 200 million persons. Large communities of Buddhists and Muslims make China a remarkably diverse nation and apparently thriving in the face of an official atheistic secularism.

To my prayer, Pastor Ray added a prayer for K.K., as he continues to struggle with an issue in the cervical region of the spine. "Help K.K. to be aware that his every experience and condition is enfolded in His Lord and His good will for K.K.'s healing and ministry." God's only Son brought this all into being and will bring it through to completion. As I type this Fourth Advent opens with Bach's organ prelude "Lord Jesus Christ, God's only Son."

December 19, 2010 (Fourth Advent)

Songs of Mary. A 15th-century carol, "Maria Mare," prompts me to sketch out a miniature in my rose breviary. I ask today to be given courage to live with grace so that my life betrays to all only *soli dei gloriam*. Don't let

9. Larry W. Hurtado, *Lord Jesus Christ: Devotion to Jesus in Earliest Christianity* (Grand Rapids: Eerdmans, 2003).

me become so stammering that I'm afraid of my own shadow, like a new King George VI in the 1930's (Hitler-time). In the good film, *The King's Speech*[10] (which I predict will win the Academy Award), the sketch of the lake is after Delacroix' boats by the sea, which becomes the motif for Van Gogh's pieces of fishermen on the Sea of Galilee. Ascriptions abound as we move toward Christmas: "Mary had a baby; what did they call Him? King Jesus, Everlasting Father" (Jessie Norman). Then again he will be called "Wonderful Counselor, Mighty God, Everlasting Father, Prince of Peace." And again, "*Adonai, Radix Jesse*, David's king." And again, "He is God and Lord of all" (*Once in Royal David's City*, 1884). At Christmastide, we seem to blur the humanity/divinity equation; accent on one side seems to call forth the opposite emphasis. I find myself with Larry Hurtado, believing that God is fully honored when ascriptions of "fully God" are made to Jesus.

December 20, 2010

The S.T.A.R.T. Treaty, the "Dream Act" "Don't-Ask-Don't Tell," "Extension of the Bush Tax Cuts," "Virginia Judge declares 'Obama-Care' mandate unconstitutional," "North Korea threatens 'Holy War' if the South continues its provocations," public policy challenges persist as the congress tries to make travel plans home for the holidays. Perhaps surprisingly, the birth-of-Christ texts are also characterized by the same mingling of personal, existential, and political considerations. Biblical believing, therefore, requires that, just as Herod's infanticide and "O little Town of Bethlehem" are concurrent and intertwined, so are the issues of immigrant justice and Christmas candle-light faithfulness. Vexing indeed. No retreat into sheer quietism or activism is allowed for biblical believers. God's cosmos is organic, at-once and at-where, divine and human, spiritual and worldly. Take your pick from the old hymn classic: "blessed assurance, Jesus is mine" or "blessed disturbance, I am His."

This hymn seems to announce the day of nativity, which is ever-now, yet so long ago:

> In the bleak midwinter, frost wind made moan,
> earth stood hard as iron, water like a stone;

10. *The King's Speech*, Tom Hooper, dir., U.K. Film Council, See-Saw Films, The Weinstein Company, 2010.

snow had fallen, snow on snow, snow on snow,
in the bleak midwinter, long ago.
Our God, heaven cannot hold him, nor earth sustain;
heaven and earth shall flee away when he comes to reign.
In the bleak midwinter a stable place sufficed
the Lord God Almighty, Jesus Christ.
Angels and archangels may have gathered there,
cherubim and seraphim thronged the air;
but his mother only, in her maiden bliss,
worshiped the beloved with a kiss.
What can I give him, poor as I am?
If I were a shepherd, I would bring a lamb;
if I were a Wise Man, I would do my part;
yet what I can I give him: give my heart.
(Christina Rossetti, "In the Bleak Midwinter," 1872)

The same contrite greeting of the sublime Lord of life in the *kleines Kleckerdorf* (a no-place of the world) called Bethlehem is the theme of the David Wilcox arrangement of the Service of Readings and Carols from Kings College, Cambridge that, for hundreds of years has greeted the "Day of Days."

Once in royal David's city
Stood a lowly cattle shed,
Where a mother laid her Baby
In a manger for His bed:
Mary was that mother mild,
Jesus Christ her little Child.
He came down to earth from Heaven,
Who is God and Lord of all,
And His shelter was a stable,
And His cradle was a stall;
With the poor, and mean, and lowly,
Lived on earth our Savior holy.
And, through all His wondrous childhood,
He would honor and obey,
Love and watch the lowly maiden,
In whose gentle arms He lay:
Christian children all must be
Mild, obedient, good as He (overly Victorian!).
For He is our childhood's pattern;
Day by day, like us He grew;
He was little, weak and helpless,

Tears and smiles like us He knew;
And He feeleth for our sadness,
And He shareth in our gladness.
And our eyes at last shall see Him,
Through His own redeeming love,
For that Child so dear and gentle
Is our Lord in Heav'n above,
And He leads His children on
To the place where He is gone.
Not in that poor lowly stable,
With the oxen standing by,
We shall see Him; but in Heaven,
Set at God's right hand on high;
Where like stars His children crowned
All in white shall wait around.
(Cecil Frances Alexander, "Once in Royal David's City, 1848)

December 24, 2010 (Christmas Eve)

The Vaux family gathers for Christmas at three poles: Midwest, West, and Western Europe. Ken and Bill Murphy hold down the Monastery "into the silence" in Evanston. We're both struck by the contemporaneity/antiquity of Christina Rosetti's *"In the Bleak Midwinter."* Sean, Cat, Aislinn, and Ehrin are with sister Megan and the Curries. We'll do the Christmas Pageant together at First Presbyterian, Evanston.

Christmas in San Diego is fighting rains, mud-slides and those boring 70-degree days. Keith and his clan seem to have no need for Midwest sleigh-rides any more than we feel need for the Deutsche *Tannenbaume* and *Stille Nacht*.

In Antwerp, Bert, Sarah, Kris, and Mom-Sara will celebrate somewhere near some of Peter Paul Rubens' Nativity Scenes and will keep alive the last vestiges of Eurocentrism.

Au passant, another part of the family will gather on the East side of Long Island. My brother Richard, his wife, Sandra, son Joe Vaux, Trish, and the two children will gather, although Russian Orthodox Christmas lags by one week.

The several epicenters of this Vaux diaspora may hover near the wireless this morning for the Ceremony of Carols and Readings from King's College, Cambridge waiting to see if some nuances are noted. Will a new John Tavener work call to mind the Orthodox liturgy of Russia, Syria, and Ethiopia? Will the sound of minarets be suggested from Egypt or Iraq or some new offering from the Silk Road?

What of these strange rumblings from North Korea? A "Holy" or "sacred" war, if South Korea persists in her provocation? By this surprising theological language, father and son in North Korea seem to be pointing to the themes of persecution, apocalyptic, end- times, martyrdom, and sacrificial solidarity, a kind of secular eschatology. The South, we must not forget, is a Presbyterian plantation, Syngman Rhee, the first president (1948–1960), was a graduate of Princeton Seminary, my alma mater. His strong-man and anti communist policies had much to do with the Korean War, partition, and yet another example of "unending war."

Another development I'm watching having to do with pop-culture is the "Christmas film" releases. Of particular note is a work of the Coen Brothers, a remake of the classic John Wayne Western, *True Grit.11* Noted for their sardonic (satire, irony, Jewish, sarcastic, mocking) humor, once again they are chosen in the U.S. and Europe to be among the select "Christmas" films that have Oscar and Palme D'Or written all over them. The Charles Portis novel is a classic. Matt Damon found it irresistible. The sound track, much like *O Brother Where art Thou?* itself,[12] is country Gospel: "Leaning on the Everlasting Arms," "Hold to God's unchanging Hand,""What a Friend we Have in Jesus" *and* "Talk About Suffering."*13*

The portion of the Coen brothers' *oeuvre* challenging to my taste recalls Berlin, Paris (between the world wars) and the Catskills after 1950, where humor as iconoclasm and a "cry for justice" and "l'chaim" itself is born in the anguish of Jewish existence in a world ("my people") so love before a prosecutorial Christian history, [also mine] and a God who has a lot of explaining to do: *Barton Fink* (1991); *Fargo* (1996); *Big Lebowski* (1998); *O Brother Where Art Thou?* (2000); *No Country for Old Men* (2007); *A Serious Man* (2009); and now, *True Grit* (2010).

One wise consultant on the Coen *oeuvre* says that the work "is about finding a way to heaven" through the decisions and crises that confront us. In my framework, this might be seen as finding the power to know and do the good amid the temptations of life: choosing life, justice, and

---

11. *True Grit*, directed by Ethan Coen and Joel Coen, Skydance Productions, 2010.

12. *O Brother, Where Art Thou?* directed by Joel and Ethan Cohen, Touchstone Pictures, Disney Studios, 2000.

13. "True Grit: Original Motion Picture Soundtrack," Carter Burwell, Producer, 2010.

care for another, salvation in other words, rather than the way of damnation that is death, injustice, and self absorption.

The Coen canon is part and parcel of my Christmas devotion of readings and carols. The new film, *True Grit*, resonates with the theme of this winter diary. I am thankful for *life*, which is the provisional bequest of breath and soul, of water and thought. I'm still an old man in this country, one whom, in the words of an aspiring colleague, is walking into the sunset with clenched fist. I must remember that though being occurs within those structures and substances we call body and blood, the gift is not of flesh and blood, but of God and Spirit, "In Him was Life and His Life was the Light of Men" (John 1:4, NIV). Birth is of the will of God not of the will of the flesh.

December 24, 2010 (Readings and Carols from Kings)

Stephen Cleobury's commission from Finland is simply a Christmas Carol. The early reading stands out ever new: "Because you did not withhold your only son . . . I will bless you . . . your seed will be as the stars of the sky and the sands of the seashore . . . by your seed you shall possess the gate of your enemies, and in your seed all the nations of the earth will be blessed" (Gen 22).

I'm not sure what to make of this. I know what Constantinian Empire, Crusading Europe, Colonial England, confident globalizing-America and contemporary Israel do with it and I stand in shame and am resolved to search out salutary meaning from this obviously abused text.

> DET är en ros utsprungen av Jesse rot och stam.
> Av fädren ren besjungen den står i tiden fram,
> En blomma skär och blid,
> Mitt i den kalla vinter i midnatts mörka tid.

> Lo, how a rose e'er blooming from tender stem hath sprung!
> Of Jesse's lineage coming, as men of old have sung.
> It came a floweret bright amid the cold of winter,
> When half spent was the night.

> (Theodore Baker, "Lo, How a Rose E'er Blooming," 1894)

Isaiah 11 is more comfortable in its symbolism and its elusiveness. Allow me the German rendition, "a rose shall spring from the stem of

Jesse (David's dad) . . . branch shall grow out of his roots . . . and the Spirit
of the Lord will rest upon him, the spirit of wisdom and understanding,
of counsel and might . . . with righteousness he will judge the poor and re-
prove with equity for the weak of the earth . . . and for them he will smite
the earth and the wicked...and the wolf shall dwell with the lamb . . .
and a little child shall lead them . . . and they shall not hurt or destroy in
all God's holy mountain . . . For the earth shall be full of the glory of God
as the waters cover the sea."

I wonder who the middle-east voice was who read a later reading on
the wise-men and the Holy Family. I once auditioned to read in the same
service, this one at Christ Church, Oxford, many years ago. The 12 or so
readings started in complete darkness outside the cathedral, in dialects
edgy and remote: pidgin, Scots, Cockney, Gaelic, Aussie, and, of course,
the noisy and raucous American English. Here was my trial and I didn't
make the cut, I think they chose an American Rhodes Scholar who spoke
a cross between "Spanglish" and "black English." As the readings moved
from the ancient anticipatory texts of Genesis and the prophets, the
Garden and the *Akedah*, to the sublime Gospel texts culminating in the
Prologue of John, the voice became London, then Cambridge, and finally
purified Oxford English. One forgot for the moment that none of the sacred scriptures originated in English, let alone Oxford or Cambridge.

December 25, 2010

Believe it or not, a "white Christmas" is rare, yes even in Chicago—once
every ten years or so, on average. The "tinies" (our two- and three-year-
olds) enjoyed the Christmas Pageant last evening as the snow started. This
was their first experience of angels, shepherds, kings, "baby Jesus." They
stood amazed for a few seconds now and then, which is about their limit.
The laypersons in the church put together a great effort: Mary and her
family were especially convincing, as well as a real live new baby with siblings. For the diverse company of families, blacks, Asians, some homeless,
lots of young struggling couples, unemployed, and discouraged, church
is the touch of the infinite, of neighborly care, of the love of God through
our own poor approximation.

December 27, 2010

Pastor Ray's message was on the central Christology section of Paul's Letter to the Philippians: "All things that were gain to me I count as loss (*Zamian*), (*Schaden*: Luther), for Christ . . . for the excellence of knowing Christ I count it all as 'dung' (*skubala*), (Rot, *merde*) . . . for whom I have suffered the loss of all things, that I may win Christ and be found in Him . . . That I may know Him, the power of His resurrection, the fellowship of His sufferings, even being like Him in his death . . . if, by any chance, I might attain the resurrection of the dead" (Phil 3:7–11).

We are still in the season of the Christ Mass. Understandings of the life and teaching of Jesus of Bethlehem, Nazareth, Galilee, Judea, Jerusalem abound. Discernments of Jesus as the Christ are also embedded in every text and song, prayer and greeting, even in the malls and city sidewalks. In alluding to the Prologue of John, we have added to the literature of "the Birth of the Messiah." We have not dealt with Paul's "Christ," although it is the most pervasive, weighty, and influential. It is even traced in the Gospels, although most evident in Luke-Acts and, of course, John. What is the meaning and problematic of this "Christ?"

For Paul, "to live is Christ, to die is gain (Phil 1:21 and numerous texts throughout the epistles). The literature on the life and message of Paul focuses on this singular notion: "*en Christou.*" James Stewart's *A Man in Christ*14 is the classic of the New Testament scholar/preacher. In the second century, a theologian whom we are just beginning to discover, Marcion of Synope, decided that Paul was basically the whole story. The Hebrew Bible and even the rest of Christian scripture were spurious, indeed dangerous to the faith of Christ. His Gospel was narrowly rejected by the nascent Church. Walter Bauer, in his studies on early Christian orthodoxy and heresy, and others, have argued that Marcionism was the earliest form of Christian orthodoxy and that it nearly won the day.

My main Christmas-tide reflection is now whether the church, especially the "evangelical" movement, lives out this ancient "Gnostic" heresy. I have explored throughout my writings whether we have forgotten that Jesus was a Jew and that the covenants with Israel, and even Hagar/Ishmael, are still seen to be in force in Genesis and in Paul (i.e., Galatians). "*En Christou*" is certainly the two-edged sword doctrine of the Christian

14. James S. Stewart, *A Man in Christ: The Vital Element of St. Paul's Religion* (Vancouver: Regent College Publishing, 1935).

Faith. Heresies flare out of both sides of the question: "Who do you say that I am?" On the one side are the near-truths of Ebionism, Arianism, Adoptionism, and Unitarianism. On the other side are the exaggerations of Christo-monism, Tritheism, and Polytheism. My own thought is shaped by the Cambridge school of scholars in Jewish-Christianity, including Judith Liu, and mediating Paul scholars, Bob Jewett, K.K. Yeo, and Larry Hurtado. I am also deeply influenced by Osvaldo Vena, a liberation Gospels scholar who sees Jesus as Bonhoeffer's "Man for Others," the first true and authentic "disciple of God."

Paul's martyr credo melds these key aspects of genuine faith. It is the life song, death song, suffering song of a servant disciple/apostle, one commissioned to this "death-into-life" being already "hid with Christ in God," new being even while he takes with thanksgiving his being, "while we have being," and he offers praise.

Meanwhile, in the domains of the Three Kings, U.S. drones kill 17 on the Pakistan/Afghan border and our multi-trillion dollar homeland (Bethlehem) security budget has vitiated all our care for the weak and poor at home and abroad. In the same moment, a handful of suspected Pakistani "terrorists" (angels?) are imprisoned on suspicion of plotting holiday targets from Mumbai to Manhattan (will we ever learn as the Apostle did?).

December 29–30, 2010

All prepped and ready to go. Lab work yesterday, traipsing through the foot-deep snow. Today a 40-degree melt has taken it down to six inches and allowed Sara to slip into Chicago from Brussels. I feel hopeful about surgery on Monday (January 3rd). It comes from a background of gratitude that in 72 years this has been my first major health crisis. Like the Magi, we will hope for sure guidance of those who have given their lives across long years of training to serve the life and health of people in the world. As Al Caldwell, a seminary colleague, prophesied when he underwent this procedure some years ago, I too hope to sing, "Let justice flow down like waters and righteousness like a mighty stream" (Amos 8:11–12).

December 31, 2011/January 1, 2012

I was shocked and could only tremble at two pieces of news. In Northern Iraq, a Chaldean Catholic congregation was attacked by a suicide bomber killing large numbers of Christmas worshipers perhaps spelling the effective end of the Christian community in one of its most ancient sites in the world. Then, on New Year's Eve in Alexandria, Egypt, midnight mass was underway at All Souls Coptic Catholic Church in the Mediterranean seaport. Another suicide bomber offered sacrifice, entailing the gruesome death and injury of not only 100-plus innocents, but affecting our Abrahamic co-religionists as well.

As the words "this is my body and blood" are shared in liturgies, patches of the same flesh, bone and blood, are spattered on the front and sidewalls of the Church. Even the Mosque across the street was stained with blood as, we can believe would have been the neighborhood synagogue, had that community not been reduced to a remaining few Jews from a once vibrant and abundant community. *Terra Sancta*, the land of the Magi, is rapidly diminishing as Christian and Jewish populations and, in some cases, even Islamic peoples disappear from Israel/Palestine, Egypt, Iraq, Afghanistan and other sacred lands.

The Pope in Rome calls for courage, patience and the steadfastness of martyrs. Just nights before, 100,000 pilgrims sang "O Little Town of Bethlehem," in the very city around Constantine's ancient church of the Nativity, in full sight of the Apartheid wall of the State of Israel. One can only ask whether concurrent events in Iraq and Egypt, in the same crucible of Holy Lands where "peace on earth" was once heralded in the heavens "to those who proclaimed good will towards men," justified the disgrace of the apartheid wall.

In the Christian world, we now enter the realm and time of Epiphany. I have undertaken this season of manifestation in the Skokie Hospital as a very noncompliant and impatient-patient. Deep epiphany has been there with me from the receipt of Professor Bachir's blessing and prayer from Columbia University to the Prayer shawl presented by Belinda, the hospital chaplain, in Van Gogh's brilliant indigo. This story will unfold its way in the days ahead.

We need now remember, as Abraham's peoples of violence who have caused so much bloodshed in the world, Jews, Christians, Muslims, even Hindus, that as a season of light and life displaces the long season of darkness and death. Those cruel secular powers, posing as sacrosanct empires, dotted the skyline with crucifixions in that first Epiphany, so still today human demonic constructs like *al-Qaeda* and other pretentious powers feel commissioned to carry out the judgments that belong to God alone. The complex mood of Epiphany is captured in the 1899 hymn of Benson set to the old English tune by the music master of Down Ampney, Ralph Vaughn Williams.

> O sing a song of Bethlehem, of shepherds watching there,
> and of the news that came to them, from angels in the air.
> The light that shone on Bethlehem" fills all the world today;
> of Jesus" birth and peace on earth, the angels sing always.
> O sing a song of Nazareth, of sunny days of joy;
> O sing of fragrant flowers" breath, and of the sinless Boy.
> For now the flowers of Nazareth, in every heart may grow;
> now spreads the fame of his dear name, on all the winds that blow.
> O sing a song of Galilee, of lake and woods and hill,
> of him who walked upon the sea, and bade the waves be still.
> For though like waves on Galilee, dark seas of trouble roll,
> when faith has heard the Master's work, falls peace upon the soul.
> O sing a song of Calvary, its glory and dismay,
> of him who hung upon the tree, and took our sins away.
> For he who died on Calvary, is risen from the grave,
> and Christ, our Lord, by heaven adored, is mighty now to save.
>
> (Louis F. Benson, "O Sing a Song of Bethlehem," 1889)

January 6, 2012 (Epiphany)

Our spirits soar into high skies with the help of Vaughn Williams, "Sing a Song of Bethlehem," Bach's Cantata #65, "We have seen a shining star," *wir wirden da und stellen , und commen.* We greet Poulenc's, "We saw the star and the Magi rejoiced with great gladness, and they entered the house and offered to the Lord gold, frankincense, and myrrh" (Francis Poulenc, "Quatre Motets pour le temps de Noël," 1952).

January 8, 2011

My birthday has come and gone as the fog of post-surgical recuperation has yielded to the scary fog of the political shootings in Arizona. I wish I had the lucidity to address such issues in my present funk, but I must have the courage of deep patience out of the love of God, my creator and the derivative respect this body now needs.

Tavis Smylie interviews Jeff Bridges who sides with Tavis' project for children with his new film, *True Grit*, which has given him a special voice to advocate the needs of children in this exceptional period in world history of personal and public negligence toward children. A nine-year-old girl was gunned down in the political assassination over which we still grieve in Tucson. This year, we may ironically say we have 100,001 shootings in this Wild West country of ours, killing 30,001, mostly kids.

Tavis summarizes the concern that we who have been given a special voice in our world have, to use that advocacy to serve "the least of these." Bridges added that we need to create "rings around the Congress" with the children of this society whose chances for a good life are so constantly delimited by our public policy frugalities. In Dr. King's penetrating words, we only come up with "blank checks" and "insufficient funds." Yet the rhetoric is frightful and contradictory. "We need to do more for the mentally needy," say those who worked in Tucson where the 22-year-old assassin went on his troubled way, deeply disturbed, as the state cut its mental-health budget 50 percent in the last three years. Others say "no more spending" at any level, local, state, national, global. So we are left in a terrible ethical limbo.

My answer is the Gates/Buffet proposal of our 1000 billionaires or our 50,000-plus 100 millionaires giving over half their estates. Then we can meet all domestic needs, education, health care, and poverty, maybe even make a dent in polio, malaria, and HIV in the broader world.

My theological and ethical system has always called for a blending and complementary engagement of private and public sector commitments. Certain ministries pertain to public sources and structures, others are personal and private. Both are essential. As Sargent Shriver, who would die next week, would say, "We can't pour 60 percent of our national wealth into the Viet Nam war and into the war on hunger and poverty at home."

January 13, 2011

I read today from an inspirational diary as we begin this New Year—extracts from John Ruskin, "Day By Day," a beautiful first edition still housed in a 100-year-old box that I picked up in an Oxford Bookshop some decades ago. My birthday extract (January 8th) is from the Pre-Raphaelite's book *Modern Painters*. It reminds me of the subtleties of cold and warmth, of color and drab, of life and health, of pain and growth.

> About the river of human life there is a wintry wind, though a heavenly sunshine; the Iris colours its agitation, the frost fixes upon its repose. Let us beware that our rest not become the rest of stones, that so long as they are torrent- tossed, and thunder-stricken, maintain their majesty, but when the stream is silent, and the storm passed, suffer the grass to cover them and the lichen to feed on them, and are plowed down into dust.[15]

In Tucson, arrangements are ready for the funeral of a nine-year old girl accidently invited to attend the Shopping Center Rally this past Saturday, who has become an amazing symbol of hope and kindness in the vitriolic world that is present-day America. Her name is Christina Taylor Green.

Last night at his funeral homily, President Obama extolled her as a citadel of life and love by whom our thoughts and actions to come out from the Tucson assassination ought to be measured. If Tavis Smylie is correct and such little ones are the spiritual- ethical monitors of the civility and goodness of our world-in the making, and if his assertion *vis à vis* Jeff Bridges and "True Grit," that our "common life is judged by the way we care for "the least of these," then we might expect some arousal into greater holiness in our civil contract through her innocent sacrifice, some agitation of the Iris color against the bleak winter of our discontent.

To quote the President at Tucson:

> . . . In Christina, we see all of our children" (he trembles for a moment thinking of his own daughters). So curious, so trusting, so energetic and full of magic . . . here was a young girl who was just becoming aware of our democracy; just starting to glimpse the fact that someday she too might play a part in shaping her nation's future.[16]

15. John Ruskin, *Modern Painters*, Vol. 2 (Smith Elder, 1848), 5.

16. In the text, partially prepared by our own Northwestern University scholar in

A memorial book prepared in Christina's honor, as one of 50 babies born on September 11, 2001, offered the wish, "I hope you know all the words to the National Anthem and sing it with your hand over your heart. I hope you jump in rain puddles" (exactly the picture I see of my 3-year-old granddaughter).

"If there are rain puddles in heaven, Christina is jumping in them today. And here on earth we place our hands over our hearts, and commit ourselves as Americans to forging a country that is forever worthy of her gentle, happy spirit."

Christina is the measure by which the worthiness of our concern and care for children will and must be judged. As she skips through the rain drop puddles right into the presence of God and the rain drops in that new place where there are only tears of joy, there our mortal limitations are transfigured into a rainbow of heaven, her beauty refracted through the tears and raindrops which with God showers benediction on the creation. "Our democracy must be as good as she wanted it to be," the President concludes. [17]

The bleak mid-winter of Christina Rossetti and her colleague, John Ruskin, continues "snow on snow." If you accept Vaux's strange prolepsis chronology (then and now, here and there, "long, long ago," and yet ever present) promise and peril are ever with us as are hope and renewal.

On the dark side, we grieve that after the shootings in Tucson and the moving pleas for civility of speech and life, gun sales are up 60 percent and we are warned by a popular political figure not to begin another "blood libel" campaign as there were against Jews in 12th century Norwich, when they were accused of being "Christ killers" by crucifying a young lad named William in 1144.

Sarah Palin had Gabby Gifford's congressional district in her rifle-scope cross-hairs on her website and, through some set of associations, her attempted assassin had her and seemingly also the attorney John M. Roll, chief federal judge in Arizona, in particular in mind.

Yet the impulse of new healing and life is already felt, a crocus in the January snow. Her fellow Jewish congresswoman, Debbie Wasserman, believes that Gabby "woke up" to Barack and Michele Obama and to her own ministry to confound the targeted violence that had precipitated the

Journalism and Public Policy, "She had been elected to her student council, she was off to meet her congresswoman . . . (probably a good and important role model)."

17. President Barack Obama, speech on January 13, 2011, *Washington Post*, http://,

heinous act. How complex is our nightmare, our dream, our rhetoric, and our action. It devolves on our deepest personal and public beliefs and values. Here even amid the tears, "life and immortality come to light . . ." (2 Tim 1:10).

January 15, 2011 (Birthday of Bishop Ammons, his first in heaven, now at last at home, and Dr. King)

The last service I recall of this power was for a high-school runner who was killed in a freak shooting around the corner from our home near Evanston High School. At our home church, First Presbyterian, Evanston, we were joined by our sister congregation, First Church of God, for the service. As the procession began with more than a thousand students and community folk, a shout was raised, "Christ is risen, He is risen indeed."

In this service, we were thankful for the ministry of Edsel Ammons and for the heritage he left in all of us to live out thoughtful faith in dedicated lives. Resurrection, wrote William Stringfellow, was verified where strife against the demonic thrived. The bishop's life was about learned ministry in a world satisfied with the superficial. It was about racial diversity and cooperation in an age of segregation. It was about resisting corporate powers (in Detroit) when the church was expected to be silent and complicit. He was a pioneer of resurrection in a world and church that preferred the complacency of idolatry and anti-life. Thanks be to God for Bishop Edsel Ammons.

January 17, 2011(Martin Luther King, Jr. Day)

'Ho, Ho Ho, who wouldn't go." Now not "Ho" but Hu is coming to town and there will be click, click, click on the economic roof-tops of the Sino-American delivery of Santa Claus sledfulls of toys, trinkets, and all the other stuff of modern life, including debt purchase, which seems to keep the world spinning on its albeit torque-full axis.

Hu Jintao is thought of as the leader of the fastest growing national power in modern history. But is he an emperor with no clothes? He seems to defy the "great-man" notion of a world leader, no Stalin, Roosevelt, even Mao. He didn't know about big airplane contracts in a preliminary meeting last week. He doesn't even seem in control of his faction of the party (almost sounds like the U.S.). He speaks of himself as the servant of the people. It almost sounds like Obama, our M.L. King protégé now exulting in his Sephardic and pastoral ministerial tour de force, in Tucson. But here we go, anarchists and liberals alike tremble, a socialist and communist, deciding the fate of this agonizingly independent-interdependent world. Bring on . . . Hu?

January 18, 2011

The song of the season and this very weekend is this one each year: "Shall We Gather by the River?" (with Northwestern's own William Warfield and the arranger Aaron Copeland at the piano, a 1963 recording). It is a dreary yet expectant kind of eschatological season. Bach is all around, especially the Brandenberg Concerti. The old Baptist hymn belongs in the Coen brothers, *O Brother Where Art Thou?* or *True Grit* (sitting there excluded from the Golden-Globe Emmy nominations, edged out by *Black Swan*, another seasonal soiree).

I once asked Bill Warfield to sing at Second Presbyterian Church, Chicago, in which I was then serving as interim pastor. I knotted the deal with an appeal from church leader Etta Barnette, who was Bill's original Bess in "Porgy and Bess" on Broadway.

Here is the song written (words and tune) in 1865 by Pastor Robert Lowrie of the Hanson Place Baptist Church in Brooklyn. As he lay prostate in the new Prospect Park (Calvert Vaux), totally spent from frustrating ministry in abolition and other vexing matters, his spirit took flight:

> Shall we gather at the river, where bright angel feet have trod,
> With its crystal tide forever, flowing by the throne of God?
> Yes we'll gather at the river, the beautiful, the beautiful river
> Gather with the saints at the river,
> which flows by the throne of God.

> (Robert Lowry, "Shall We Gather at the River?" 1864)

Dr King loved this hymn nearly as much as the other "homecoming vision" of Tom Dorsey, "Precious Lord take my hand, lead me on, help me stand . . . take my hand, precious Lord, lead me home" (Thomas A. Dorsey, "Take My Hand, Precious Lord," 1932). He had "Haley" (Mahalia Jackson), sing this at his funeral. On this MLK day, we are reminded that it was Haley who stopped Dr. King mid-sentence in the 1963 March on

Washington, a march for "jobs and freedom," and said
the dream, Martin." This scissors and paste from an ear.
make history in this telling speech that convinced the cl
ger had to die . . ." See the new biography of MLK's lav
Dream.[18]

January 19, 2011

I marvel that such a sublime and otherworldly song as "Shall We Gather
at the River" (recall also the sound track from the Coen Brothers' *O
Brother Where art Thou?*) should pertain to such secular matters as the
Memphis garbage-collectors strike, Operation Breadbasket (food for the
hungry), the disenchantment with the Viet Nam War and the cry that we
"cease killing the least of these" at the other side of the world. On "The
Tavis Smiley Show" today, Professor Cornel West affirms the same, that
the index "of the least of these" will be that which must guide our policy
decisions in these days. Warfield also sang, with Copeland conducting,
the "Walls of Zion." God forgive me, but I can't help seeing the great Israeli apartheid wall running smack through the city of Bethlehem.

January 20, 2011

"It's a miracle"—this from, of all people, our secular son, the physician Keith. My surgeon said yesterday that a quite remarkable
rejuvenation had occurred. For two weeks now, I've enjoyed full
emptying of the bladder. I haven't known that for 10, perhaps 15
years. I exult in exuberance and thanksgiving. Now I've got to
tone myself up again and renew a less health-obsessed outlook,
reengaging with my ministry and set of intellectual projects. Keith
has been a strong support and medical guide through this entire
ordeal. More importantly he has been, as all our family has been,
an intellectual interlocutor for many years. We debate medicine,
healthcare policies, and politics, per se, the arts, literature, film,
and international affairs.

18. Clarence B. Jones and Stuart Connelly, *Behind the Dream: The Making of a Speech
that Transformed a Nation* (New York: St. Martin's Press, LLC, 2011).

Not only is the urinary system working as if I were a 12 year-old, last night I enjoyed the predawn sweep of ideas that worked as vividly as when I was a professor in the medical school and a pastor at Chicago's Second Presbyterian Church. At that time, I would envision entire articles, chapters in books, complete sermon passages or program ideas. I'm not sure whether it was the creative juices of REM sleep or Michelangelo's discerning a shape and specific form embedded in a block of raw material, which of course was the product of tough contemplation and preparation.

Here's how the dream went. I would stay with our dear friends in walking distance of the Texas Medical Center—the Allgoods, Cunninghams, Jirciks—and I would write a monograph on the miracle/ assassination patient. The last famous patient I worked with at Rehab was Communist Leader Marshall Tito when he came in for treatment in the 1960's. This event had some of the drama of waiting for Howard Hughes' flight from Mexico with the cadaveric eccentric, with great Medical Center plans, then in multiple organ failure. I had consulted regularly on the advanced neurological and spinal-cord patients. To this issue I now turn.

II

Tucson Ordeal: Intersecting Destinies

INTRODUCTION

It was a late afternoon, January 27th, in 1967. I awoke groggy from the anesthesia. We had just driven into Houston from frigid Chicago. The new Presbyterian campus minister at Rice and the Medical Center had experienced episodic bouts of appendicitis as he took his leave from the Presbyterian Church of Watseka, Illinois where the door had closed to effective ministry, at least in his mind. He had been arrested in 1964 in Hattiesburg, Mississippi for voter registration work and he had returned to Biloxi for an evidentiary hearing that would eventually proceed to the U.S. Supreme Court. Regardless of the justice of that event, a short-lived first ministry in a church of his own had drawn to a close and he was off to the Western edge of the old Confederacy, which had been headquartered in Mississippi, of all places. Now he must begin again.

As my mind slowly cleared in the bed on Fannin St. in a new hospital in the Texas Medical Center, the news was from NASA headquarters just east of Houston. A space capsule has just misfired and fire engulfed the launch pad with three astronauts aboard: Gus Grissom, Ed White, and Roger Chaffee.

Now, 44 years later, on my birthday, January 8, 2011, I wake from another anesthesia fog and hear a similar word from my physician son, Keith, who was a toddler when we drove into "Cowtown-USA," part of the weekly 10,000 migrations from parts north that would transform this place into one of the nation's large and great cities. Keith says that there has been a shooting in Tucson, Arizona. Apparently targeted is the Congresswoman of the eighth Congressional District, Gabrielle Giffords, the wife of astronaut Mark Kelly, and again I am heading to Houston.

Gabby is now receiving intensive neurological rehabilitation at TIRR (The Texas Institute of Rehabilitation and Research) where I served as a consultant in ethics, now 40 years ago. I will send her and her astronaut husband, Mark, a copy of *Ministry on the Edge*, an autobiography that traces some of this work.

Apropos the complexity of the Tucson ordeal, I recalled a conversation with Astronaut John Glenn, not only a colleague at the Presbyterian Church near NASA where I would occasionally preach and teach, but a fellow alumnus of Muskingum College in New Concord, Ohio. After the flame-out he said: "It is just a matter of time until a fire occurs, an explosion happens on ascent or in orbit, or a ship escapes from controlled orbit and drifts endlessly in remote space. Ken, we must know why we are doing this, you must help us." After the explosion in the Spacecraft Challenger in 1986, I took his admonition to heart and reflected on the metaphysics and meta-ethics in an Op Ed essay in the *Chicago Tribune*.[1]

The wheels in the mind of the old philosopher of medicine were again humming. "Why are we doing this again, we ask, the space project, the biomedical project, the social-reconciliation project?" I reflected in my winter diary:

Here's what flew across the mindscape: I was going to land at Hobby Airport, Houston with Gabby Giffords and her Astronaut husband, Mark Kelly, as they began rehabilitation in the Rehab Institute where I worked for many wonderful years when I was in the Medical Center in the 1960's and 70's. I would stay with our dear friends in walking distance of the Texas Medical Center and I would write a monograph on the miracle assassination patient. Among the challenging spinal-cord cases the last famous patient I worked with at rehab was Communist Leader Marshall Tito, a friend of DeBakey, when he came in for treatment in the 1960's. This event had some of the drama of waiting for another DeBakey spectacle, which occurred as we cleared a whole wing of Methodist Hospital to receive on the heliport Howard Hughes's flight from Mexico with the

1. For the *Chicago Tribune* essay, see Kenneth L. Vaux, *Ministry on the Edge: Reflections of an Interfaith Pioneer, Civil Rights Advocate, and the First Bioethicist* (Eugene, OR: Wipf & Stock, 2010), 44.

cadaveric eccentric with great Medical Center plans. Then in multiple organ failure, he died en route and all the transplant units and life-support paraphernalia were for naught and the Hughes Medical Center eventually located in Florida and Arizona. I had consulted regularly on the advanced neurological and spinal-cord patients at TIRR and many of my novel, then controversial, convictions about "Informed Consent," DNR's and like policies and procedures, now the law and clinical practice of the land, had their birth here at TIRR. Most of our Institute of Religion ethics staff—Moraczewski, Schooler, and me—served clinically with that splendidly attentive community of healers.

I had also written about two astronauts, John Glenn and Buzz Aldrin, both church friends. I would tell the story of the 1967 fire and the later Challenger Spaceship, with the unique edge of what the *Chicago Tribune* called a political-poet as one of my more than 30 Op Ed essays there and in the *New York Times* from the 60's to the 80's. Who knows, I may find myself back in the crucible of Bioethics before this is over, I mused.

My hidden agenda in calling Dr. Glen Cunningham, my long-standing interlocutor in bioethics, was to weasel an invitation to spend a short time in Houston in early February and return to my old haunts, TIRR, Methodist, MD Anderson, where I could write some material on Gabby Giffords and her Astronaut husband, Mark Kelly. Before I knew it the assignment was booked.

Now I had to ask, what can I say that will contribute? I'm not planning to report on the miracle/recovery unless that presents itself in a different light when I talk with her healthcare professionals. As I proceed to visit TIRR and Herman Hospital it is evident that the extraordinary healing continues; she is talking. The popular media will cover that spectacle as it has from day one in Tucson. I'm interested to see if the broader fabric of the case, the prevalent political ethos in the country, the theological factors, the aftermath of shame and suppression, suggests a thicker and richer interpretation. How will President Obama's eulogy in Tucson and his upcoming "State of the Union" address on January 25, provide revealing context? He acknowledged her empty chair to the still-grieving throng.

I'm interested in composing a universal and sacred history of this unfolding event. The best a theologian-pastor-ethicist can offer is some broader and deeper context, even though it comes from the "Twilight Zone." To borrow from great culture and literature, for all we know we may be witnessing the drama of Verdi's *Rigoletto* (with Monteroni's curse *"Maledictione"* as Gilda lies mortally wounded in a recent Opera from the Met) or the strange intruder on the streets of Seville raising the young girl from her funeral cortege as the Grand Inquisitor has him thrown in jail. Was it curse or blessing, salvation or damnation, good and evil, or was it just random misfortune?

Seeing the inter-human, interfaith, and transcendental aspects of this profound tragedy is found in one observer's sequence of the events of that day: a white catholic lawyer drops by the rally and was killed at the shopping center where his congresswoman, a Jewish woman, had her life saved by a gay Hispanic student and a Korean surgeon. Even in diversity and immigration-conflicted Arizona, we have witnessed a varied multi-ethnic "miracle."

In 1968, for example, the same year that Norman Mailer lived in Houston and chronicled the NASA space shot, writing *Of a Fire on the Moon*, I wrote my hermeneutic on the new space technology, *Subduing the Cosmos2* (foreword by Buzz Aldrin). Now, again, I've set a course as a public intellectual seeking some sort of epistemological and ethical universal cache for another particular cultural crisis, in my case, I attempt a casuistic (case-based moral philosophy in the tradition of Talmudic writer Emmanuel Levinas and semiotist Jacques Derrida), with a backdrop of interfaith wisdom.

Before sketching the intertwining and interacting destinies of Gabrielle Giffords, John Roll, Christina Taylor-Green, and Jared Loughner, we need to note some extant etiological (causal) and interpretive theories, which are already profuse in the land.

In this incessantly Puritan land, we would expect to find the normative theory of Thornton Wilder in the Bridge of Saint Louis Rey, to be alive and well. The Calvinist playwright, author of "Our Town" and "The Skin of our Teeth," tells of the bus accident on the bridge where a set of miscellaneous persons are killed in a seemingly meaningless, random tragedy until the accident is dissected in detailed retrospective examination of each life trajectory and destiny until each death becomes perfectly plausible, indeed providentially inevitable. Other theories in the air emphasize free-will factors and social, political, and psychological explanation. Sara Palin's website had the 8th district in the cross-hairs of

---

2. Kenneth L. Vaux, *Subduing the Cosmos: Cybernetics and Man's Future* (Louisville: John Knox Press, 1970).

the gun-sight. At least the biblical citation John 3:16 was not engraved on her sight. We'll leave that for Texas-Oklahoma football games. "Schizophrenia to be sure," certify a thousand therapists. If only we had kept the mental health coffers full, nothing of this sort could ever have occurred. This delusion is, of course, belied by the brute empirical fact that just yesterday the same sordid thing transpired among several hundred innocents in Karbala, Iraq and Moscow, Russia, even as our son-in law was hastening back to Belgium.

Another pet theory betrays the fact that we are also biomedical enthusiasts, as we extol Gabby's miraculous recovery, we vibrantly believe that Dr. Spock's frontier therapeutics in Star Trek will one day instantly heal wounds, injuries, genetic flaws, neuro-maladies, indeed all morbidities and mortalities, ever perplexing, to which flesh is heir.

I seek beyond the facile explanations to rather offer a unified and overarching analysis of this solemn event. This leads me to begin by taking a reading of the "Ultimate Being," the "Giver of Life and Death" (Job) who presides over the inception, procession and conclusion of all life, even that of a sparrow, yet is not the cause of such stupidities and shootings. As C.S. Lewis writes in the *Problem of Pain*, God cannot be blamed for rocks, knives, and guns; these are the instruments of human malevolence. As the Creator and Redeemer of all life in this world, God's knowledge and care is comprehensive. The Divine transcends our petty schemes to define Him, especially as one who boorishly prospers and punishes at sheer caprice. This is the God Kierkegaard condemns as the human reduction of "the God of Abraham, Isaac and Jacob," reduced to "ludicrous twaddle." The comprehensiveness of God is more about human responsibility and stewardship. My hypothesis in this essay will be that the comprehensiveness and enigma of *divinity* seek to enliven divine imperatives among *humanity*, justice, love and care for all life, especially the least of these and the "little ones." Theodicy is in order to anthropodicy. To recall another 50-year landmark inaugural remark of another fallen brother from the wild south-west, where even Matt Damon in *True Grit* is a Shakespearian, gun-slinging bounty-hunter, ". . . In this world, God's work must truly be our own."[3]

Let us first set forth some narrative data, albeit provisional, as a basis for our subsequent conclusions.

3. Robert F. Kennedy, Day of Affirmation Address, University of Capetown, Capetown, South Africa, June 6, 1966.

GABBY: AN "INTENTIONAL" TARGET

At the center of the list of *Dramatis Personae* is Gabrielle Giffords. Most analyses stress her centrality to the entire hatched plot. Since backing the Health Care Reform bill she had received a steady-stream of death threats, her Tucson office had been ransacked, and her husband, Mark Kelly, had been especially concerned at the "tone of the heated angry-rhetoric." She seemed to have become the central intended victim, *korban*, the sacrifice, to use the sinister symbol of today's assassinations and suicide bombings. Jared also, in this scenario, apparently had no plan to escape. He kept trying to load and fire until he was subdued. Was he a self-offering collateral to the *Akedah* of Gabby by virtue of his deliberate selection and targeting of the Congresswoman?

On this point Yvonne Sherwood, the Scottish biblical scholar, has shown how the September 11 suicide-bombers misinterpreted their own nihilistic acts on that fateful day in history in text and prayer as an extension of Abraham's sacrifice of Isaac.[4]

It has been conjectured that Gabby had several passing contacts with Jared before the Saturday morning at Safeway. He had attended a similar event of the Congresswoman in 2007, had received a letter from her thanking him for coming and had a file marked "Giffords" in his safe. Jared may have challenged, in his paranoiac thought, her counter-cultural views on issues such as gun control, immigration, healthcare reform, economic stimulus, and the like.

At the event of August 25, 2007 called "Congress on your corner," he had asked Gabby the somewhat bizarre question, "How do you know words mean anything?" He wrote in his file that Gabby seemed not to listen to him. He apparently had an independent streak that demanded that he be heard, at home, community, college and in public forum, where at all points he was always stifled, especially as his views became more bizarre. His tracking her had gone on for at least these four years before the Safeway incident.

On my Rubik's Cube of thought, will and act—the biblical momentum of existence—here is how I tag Gabby's Vita Activa: running, warning, overcoming.

---

4. Yvonne Sherwood, "Binding-Unbinding: Divided Responses of Judaism, Christianity, and Islam to the 'Sacrifice of Abraham's Beloved Son," *Journal for the American Academy of Religion* 72.4 (2004), 821-61.

From her days as a Sociology and Latin American History scholar at Scripps, continuing through the Master's in Urban Planning on a Fulbright at Cornell, she was running to make a point—the transformation of the social order. Studying in Chihuahua, Mexico as a Fellow of Harvard's Kennedy School of Government, she seemed to be the ideal follower of Eunice and Sarge Shriver: high idealism, concern for "the least of these," the preciousness of *l'chaim*, all life and breath, life, *Tikkun Olam* (to mend the wounded earth). As her husband Mark Kelly said to her in secret moments significant words for those dedicated to service, "with you I've never been closer to heaven." Kelly may remember John Glenn's retort to Yuri Gagarin's discovered heavens devoid of God: "I didn't expect to find my God there."

Gabby is a woman of God. Raised by a Jewish father and Christian Science mother, a sure recipe for secular sublimity and sheer spiritual worldliness, she is active at Congregation Chaverim in Tucson. She proudly claimed to be the grandchild of Akiba Hornsein, son of a Lithuanian Rabbi. She also belongs to a small circle of Jewish women politicians that includes Florida Congresswoman Debbie Wasserman-Schultz, of Florida's 20th District, is a life-long member of Hadassah, has taken as a high priority of her congressional work the direct talks between Israeli's and Palestinians. The National Jewish Democratic Council issued a statement after the shooting saying that "political rhetoric has contributed to the atmosphere in that this event transpired." We must ask the question therefore about an anti-Semitic dimension to the attack and to the enveloping atmosphere. From the dawn of this new millennium, Gabby's been running, and she's still going strong.

Political runners often run into walls. We think of Berlin and Bethlehem, South Africa and now even our own bastion of free movement and expression. Gabby rightly expressed concern over Sarah Palin's depiction of "the cross-hairs of a gun sight over our district. When people do that they've got to realize there are consequences to that. We might ask whether there will be. Right now she and Mark are on a mission of warning, watchmen on the wall, what our faith traditions call *euangeliol*, shouters of good news on the horizon, "watchman tell us of the night." On Gabby's watch, the warning light gleams gold.

Warning always provokes resistance. "Slow down" we are told, "keep the status quo." "If you're going to extend Bush tax cuts, extend them to everyone" and the 1000 billionaires receive 26 billion more dollars from the people's tax coffers. Gabby warned, Barack warns, even Warren Buffett and Bill Gates warn, as they plead with the *crème de la crème*, to give away half of their estates, to heal the sick, lift the poor, shelter the aging, feed the hungry—and many do. Our life-boat is still a luxury-liner and, as Tom Jefferson said prophetically, "I tremble for this country when I remember that God is just, his justice cannot sleep forever."

The final impact of Gabby's witness is "overcoming." The paradigmatic symbols of the Abrahamic faiths are suffering, death, and resurrection. Life is ever erupting in the face of threat in this cosmos, which has a Creator/Redeemer. Resurrection comes through inter-human expiration, *Tikkun*, throwing down your life for your fellows. Elisha came upon the seemingly-dead girl in 2 Kings 4 and gave her mouth-to-mouth resuscitation, Jesus came to the house of his best friends, and Lazarus had been dead as a doornail for some time. "I am the resurrection and the life," and he was. Judge John Roll threw himself on the body of his dear friend, Ron Barber, and saved his life, "greater love has no one that to lay down his life for his friends." And Daniel Hernandez, who can forget, there he is again last night at the State of the Union, Gabby's intern, Hispanic, gay.

How can we ever again turn our castigating murderous automatic pistol like Joel Osteen or missionaries in Uganda, on this most afflicted human cohort of church and state? How can we continue to crucify our Matthew Shepherds or defrocking our Gene Robinsons? Daniel ran into the fire, fell on Gabby and applied timely pressure on the forehead to stop the bleeding and made sure she didn't choke on her own blood. He saved her life.

She was an avid reader. Recent selections included *First Man: The Life of Neil A. Armstrong, The World of Diamonds, Deceit and Desire* by Tom Zoellner, Al Gore's *An Inconvenient Truth* and *The End of Faith* by Sam Harris. She is a probing, committed, critical, and life-loving person, as is plain for the whole world to see.

We cannot predict or control resurrection or Gabby's rehabilitation and as the French say in their creed, her *resuscitation*. All we know for sure is Lawyer William Stringfellow's creed at the East Harlem Protestant Parish, "resurrection is verified where strife against the demonic thrives." Gabby so thrives and passes the torch to us all.

JOHN: AN "INCIDENTAL" VICTIM

We may assume he was a Steelers fan and was looking forward to the playoffs. Steel girds strong and deep. Born in Pittsburgh, the 63-year-old seems to have been a faithful Roman Catholic, typical of the Irish and Italian immigrants of the scenic three rivers city.

His family had moved to Arizona where he attended Salpointe Catholic High School, then the University of Arizona and Law School.

I call his death incidental in that he had stopped by after Mass to see his congresswoman and have a word with her about the unmanageable case-load in the vast Western Federal Legal District. He was right down front. When Gabby was shot point blank from about three feet, he saved the life of Gabby's aid, Ron Barber, also his friend, by falling on his body to protect him. The eulogies at St. Elizabeth Ann Seton RC Church (the day after Christina's) emphasized his instinctive laying "down his life for his friends" (John 15:13). This was consistent with his reputed character as an eminently fair man, treating every person with dignity, which stemmed from an inner compass and conscience that saw each person to be of inestimable and infinite value.

Appointed to the Federal Bench by President G.H.W. Bush in 1991, he became Chief Judge in 2006. Here we note two cases that may reflect his judicial philosophy but are also colored by regional cultural factors. The matters now convey an eerie and haunting irony. Like Gabby, John may have had a conservative, even libertarian strain of view on handgun possession and cognate issues. He threw out a provision of the Brady Bill requiring a background check for persons seeking to buy guns. The U.S. Supreme Court upheld his ruling. He also ruled for an Arizona rancher who stopped immigrant Mexicans (the once indigenous people) at gun-point from crossing his land (their ancestral lands?).

The one complexity the Socratic-ironist in me would offer is one I submit when defending Methodist and Roman Catholic advocates of protection and granting sanctuary to so called "illegals" as priests and bishops who follow official Church teachings on protection and advocacy attempt to persuade their own reluctant and recalcitrant parishioners on the theology and ethics of the faith. "How can we reject and eject from our midst our own brothers and sisters in Christ?" I ask. The question is usually answered by stupefying silence.

John's witness also points to the overlying, complementary, and contradictory realms of law, biology, religion (ethics), and society in dealing with complex explanations and judgments of an event like the Tucson Ordeal. Michael Walzer of Princeton's Advanced Institute calls this realm "spheres of justice." I call it "ordeal" to convey the ambiguities and equivocations of temptation, justice, and forgiveness, which are all we are left with after the failure of all other parameters of explication, decision, satisfaction, and resolution.

His exemplary witness is honored today by naming a Law Center in Yuma after him as a tribute.

CHRISTINA: AN ACCIDENTAL INNOCENT

Christina Taylor-Green is the granddaughter of Dallas Green, well known in Chicago as the general manager for the Chicago Cubs. With Ryne Sandberg also at the funeral, Chicago was woven into a most poignant aspect of the Tucson ordeal. Born on the portentous date of Sept 11, 2001, the prodigious youngster was a budding political scientist, an "A" student, student-council member, the only female on a boy's little-league team, even while singing in the St. Odelia Roman Catholic Church choir. It seemed a perfectly fine idea to accept the invitation of good friend, Suzi Hileman, to attend the Safeway meeting.

Her profile was compelling to the world when highlighted by President Obama in his moving eulogy for the nine-year old girl at the Tucson Arena.

Part of the gravity of this compound situation is that it is becoming commonplace. It is estimated that just in this country (that seems particularly prone to shootings and child killing) 100,000 persons are shot with guns each year and 30,000 die. Most of the victims are young people. Surely one imperative, even in our "True-Grit," gun slinging culture, is that we should find sufficient sanity and simple humanity to ban assault weapons.

In this broader context, we should search out the broader sacrament (mystery) of Christina's differing and see that this "little child will lead them" (Isa 9:6, 11:6) out of the bloody boot-tracks into pathways of peace.

JARED: A "WILLFUL" KILLER

The jarring scene of the smug smile during the first court hearing to render an initial plea, gives the world alarming pause. With what manner and magnitude of wrong and evil are we dealing, we surely ask. Blending rage, revenge, frustration and acting out, an inexplicable enigma has arisen on the canvas of our dreams of the "better world we seek," turning our dreams into a horror-reel and transfiguring our building and healing efforts into a vast machinery of protecting ourselves from our worst nightmares. Day by day, we plead inability to create better conditions for human thriving, education, arts, music, and endeavors of the Spirit and of good conscience, because we have to invest all our resources into protection and security. Is the only answer to the Jareds, who repetitively jar our composure, constant surveillance of everyone and each of each other? Can we live in such perpetual suspicion? Is there not a better way?

His classmates have called him an "interesting character," "very philosophical," and a" politically radical loner." He himself exhibits patterns of sensitivity and engagement and autistic-like apathy. A technophile with computer, cell-phone and automatic pistol in hand, he texted "Good Bye" with little warmth and awareness that that contraction was a benediction, "God be with you." "Please don't be mad at me," he pleaded, as if totally incognizant that he himself alone had the power to make people glad or so, so sad. On his You-Tube video, he recorded the "final thoughts of JL on JL." "All conscience dreaming at this moment is asleep. JL is conscience dreaming at this point. JL is asleep." In mid-December, he wrote: "Now I'm glad I didn't kill myself. I'll see you on national TV. This is a foreshadowing. Why doesn't anyone talk to me? . . . you could call me a terrorist, employing terror on terrorism."

He resented government at all levels, believing it exerted mind-control and brain-washing on him. "I can't trust the current government (Giffords and Obama?)." I'm in a sleepwalk." We might wonder whether he was in the sleep walk when he went to buy the Glock-17, the semiautomatic pistol. Wal-Mart would not sell to him so he went to the next store. The sheriff claimed that he had made death threats on others. Suspended from Pima Community College for disrupting classes and the library, he could only get reinstated with a certificate of a health professional that "he was not a danger to himself or others." He couldn't or didn't get such a document and other plans began to hatch.

Regarding Gabby, he said that "the majority who serve District 8 are illiterate and hilarious." Mind control and brain washing on people was accomplished "by controlling grammar." "No," he said, "I will not trust in God." He seemed to be critical but not interested in faith. His life seems to be devoid of religious substance and experience.

His father had an altercation with him in the early dawn hours and chased him in the car as he dropped off the infamous "black bag" with 9 mm ammo packed inside, at a deserted patch near his home. One moment of grace for all the world to witness – much like the Pope forgiving his terrorist assassin or the Amish school parents forgiving and carrying dinner to the families of those who massacred their kids in the one room schoolhouse in Pennsylvania near Christina's birthplace—was Mark Kelly calling Jared's sobbing parents to assure them that they were not responsible and were forgiven. He would not extend the same to Jared.

A different shelf of books stood on his simple shelf. Some of the same stuff was on the shelf of the "Unabomber," the common lawyer of both might tell us: Marx's *Communist Manifesto*, Orwell's *Animal Farm*, Hitler's *Mein Kampf,* and Plato's *Republic*. He also had the touch of fantasy: Swift's *Gulliver's Travels,* Baum's *Wizard of Oz*, Barrie's *Peter Pan*, and Carroll's *Through the Looking Glass*. The difference between a prophet and a terrorist must be the substance of the utopias or dystopias conceived and the mania to take the measures of implementation, even violence, into one's own hands. Philosophers seek to understand reality, wrote Marx, we seek to change it. Fair enough, even noble, but verging on the fanatic.

My Rubik's cube has him questioning, stalking, and finally repenting. We meet him initially as one trying to find a voice, mentor-less, riddled with character and behavioral flaws, submerged in a system of neglect, cynical rudder-less, put off by the shallowness and perfunctory boredom of most lives he was intrigued by something unique in Gabby. Devoid of access to her or anyone who seemed to give a damn, he became a stalker. This movement of his already ominous journey will become clear as the months of vindictive and self-righteous machinations unfold. Finally, it is my guess, that the reality of his night journey, away from insight and maturity toward deeper confusion and dangerous freedom, will hit home and he will confront some redemptive presence, perhaps Gabby, perhaps the angel of Christina. He will be overwhelmed with grief and shame and will make amends. In one of the paradoxical bioethical absurdities of present-day juridical therapeutics, he may be treated intensively medically and institutionally so that he gets better in order that we might kill him as a competent person. Transpersonal anthropology will have at last become available so that we can rid the world of him.

Arizona state law does not allow the verdict of "not guilty by reason of insanity," which presents an interesting situation if that is his actual state. In does allow the verdict, "guilty but insane," the legal system seemingly concerned with political prejudices rather than any actual human conditions. Federal and state law allows the death penalty. As the case unfolds in coming months, along these lines or some other, two deceased and two yet-among us, will bear witness. Myriad other victims, vicarious observers and interested spectators, bread and circus folk, town-square-stoning enthusiasts, will offer further witness and testify. The ontological and ethical realities of the case seem doomed to be buried in political prejudice, proving again the judgment of the Apostle Paul that the law becomes the occasion of lawlessness.

The aforementioned four profiles will be greatly expanded, as will the interpretive matrix as the case unfolds. For now, I conclude with a sample set of conclusions as we all set our minds and hearts in that direction.

III

Recovery and Renewal

THEODICY/ANTHROPODICY

"GOD IS NOT MOCKED, whatsoever a man soweth that also will he reap" (Gal 6:7), is a simple summary of all biblical and extra-biblical moral wisdom. We humans speak of justifying the ways of God to man. The foregoing perennial wisdom is more concerned with justifying the ways of man to God, and to one another. The Tucson ordeal will cause us to ponder the enigmas of Job and Cain/Abel, Judas and Peter/Paul, Satan and Prophet. What we contemplate matters. What we will takes on irrevocable reality. What we say counts. Each human being who traverses the ordeal of existence can only confess daily what each of these exemplars in the dock, alive and now finally alive and at home, have taught us to confess, "Forgive what we've done and failed to do."

From this parameter of faith/ethics we might ask these questions: Why did this happen and how did its ominous directions and momentum escape notice? What kind of patterns in home, neighborhood, school, street, market, church, news media, patterns of recognition, affirmation, candor, admonition and advocacy of justice and mercy, expectation and kindness, might prevent such an ordeal, or allow us to help each other arise new and clean from the 40 days or years that each and everyone must inevitably face?

GUILT/GRACE

The dynamics of human and divine justice form the derivative dynamics of guilt and grace at the human level. For example, divine theodicy becomes the paradigm and pattern of judgment and allowance at the level of society and institutions. This, then, is mediated into the operational level of personal and interpersonal proffering, of holding responsible, and extending forgiveness. In other words, human life is configured within three levels of association: ultimate, intermediate, and immediate. At the level of the transcendent; of institutions: neighbors, families, work, structures, systems etc.; and of intimate associations, our life journeys take place and are imbued with meaning.

Another set of questions arise within this matrix: Where is God when it hurts? Christina's grandpa, Dallas Green, was manager of the Yankees, Phillies, Cubs, and Dodgers, one familiar with losses and disappointment, but this leaves him breathless, speechless, and impervious to the replete blanket of prayer, support, and monetary response. My precious 9-year-old granddaughter. Why? Don't even try to tell me. All that biblical faith can say is that though God receives His little child home, His sacred heart is wounded with us. Like the Auschwitz indictment, "God on Trial," He is there in the death camp, or as Elie Wiesel answers in response to the question in *Night* about where is God as the child is being executed. "He is there on the gallows." This question of ultimacy not only says, "I am with You" but also "what are you going to do about this?"

The interhuman questions abound in baffling complexity but frustrating in specificity and strenuous demand: "Who is my neighbor?," "Where is Abel, your brother?," "Write it on your door-post and your forehead," "Teach it to your children," "Don't forget that I delivered you when you cried from your oppression,""When did we see you hungry, thirsty, homeless, sick, imprisoned?," "In as much as you did it to one of the least of these, my brothers, you did it to me," "Revenge is mine, I will repay, says the Lord." So we work away on handgun policy, ameliorating education and moral-development endeavors, getting our own homes in order and the myriad *Torah* mandates, preventive and interventionist. And we try to relentlessly disabuse ourselves from the idolatrous and immoral displacements of righteousness with which we have filled the world.

And much of the transformative change called for begins at home, with me, and with the ships that transect our journeys in the night, and we alone are the warning and rescue vessel at hand and on watch.

BLAME/FORGIVENESS

Profound moral debate occurs about the relevance of these ethical principles to matters of social policy. Ethicists from Augustine to Reinhold Niebuhr have questioned the political applicability of sublime mandates such as "do not kill," "do not lie," and "do not steal," to decisions like Japan's attack on Pearl Harbor, Hitler's invasion of Poland, banks' exploitation of the poor in mortgages or credit-cards, or gun policies and the Tucson Ordeal.

Judaism and Islam, Israel and Tunisia, for example, might say that our faith does not commend forbearance and forgiveness. Especially, today Israel says "the wall is our response to terrorism." Young people in Tunis and Cairo shout *"Allah Akbar"* and insist that their yearning for freedom will not be discouraged by military dictatorship and oppression at home or abroad.

These antinomies characterize the tensions between blame and forgiveness. This nation's belief and value system has been shaped by contrary images on this overarching antinomy. On the one hand America has set itself since the events of September 11 on a policy of exacting the last ounce of revenge for the grievous mass assassination of thousands at the World Trade Center and the Pentagon. A budget and domestic-well being-vitiating military and security policy has followed for 10 years, first by mistake in Iraq, for a decade misdirected in Afghanistan, and most recently by drone technology and assassination activity in Pakistan. This revenge policy has set the peace of the world on edge for a full decade.

A different picture, totally in contradiction, is found in the Amish ministry of forgiveness and new-life that was their response to the gun shoot-up of their one room school-house. Immediately, this intensely fervent and very conservative people formulated their response, with their elders and wisdom-figures, largely women. Forgiveness was offered while their children were still being buried, meals were carried to homes of the killers and other neighbors, and the nation and world was stunned.

To summarize the import of this conclusion, I review a letter to the *New York Review* by Garry Wills, my colleague at Northwestern, Pulitzer-prize winner, for his Lincoln at Gettysburg. I am now editing a Festschrift in his honor that picks up not only on his Lincoln and generic presidential work but his classical studies and his important work on Augustine. We call the collection of essays *Horror of War and Hope for Peace: Essays in Honor of Garry Wills.*

In this new essay, he reviews Obama's speech at Tucson and calls it "His Finest Hour." Like Lincoln at Gettysburg, Obama went into a scene of great violence in Tucson. What do you say about the dead and the other fallen? Do you condone revenge or taking the law into your own hands either through rightist or leftist coercion? Wills comments, "Obama had to rise above the acrimonious debate about what caused the gunman to kill and injure so many people. (Like Lincoln) He sidestepped that issue by celebrating the fallen and the wounded." He praised those who gave their lives and those who came to their aid.

The "proper tribute" to the honored dead and wounded was to live up to their own high expectations of our nation. Lincoln gives the paradigmatic speech that we hear again at Tucson in the Second Inaugural. Wills concludes:

> Lincoln might have been expected in his Second Inaugural Address to trumpet the gains of the North and the setbacks to the South. Instead he invited all Americans to grieve for the tragic war and to share blame for the historical crime of slavery. God "gives to both North and South this terrible war as the woe due to those by whom the offense came. Death should forge a bond among the living. "The loss of these wonderful people should make every one of us strive to be better," Obama said, stepping around the obvious and divisive sifting of wrongs done, to urge the doing of right.[1]

Magnanimity in lieu of rage, concord in lieu of revenge is the response of forgiveness, not blame. If our sins were imputed to anyone of us, none could stand. All have sinned and fallen short of the glory of God. There but for the grace of God go I. Such underlying anthropology undergirds private action and is approximated, as much as is pragmatically possible, in the public order.

1. Garry Wills, "His Finest Hour," *The New York Review of Books*, February 10, 2011, 49.

RESIGNATION/HOPE

The final suggested conclusion of a fine-grained analysis of the Tucson Ordeal is that hope gain hold in the face of despair and resignation. Garry Wills concludes his essay with a reflection of Obama's Tucson speech with these words: "The loudest cheers . . . were for the news that 'Gabby,' as she was known to all her many friends, was recovering. Perhaps there was a sound, there, of a nation recovering."[2]

Humans tend to associate microcosm with macrocosm, nature with history, the finite with the infinite, the temporal with the eternal. Local events are viewed as ominous and portentous and God is engaged within time and space. By reason of this propensity of consciousness, which is not projection but mimesis, we live in the dialectics of resignation and hope. Tucson, we believe says something about America and about our particular philosophy and values. It reflects and shapes who we are and who we are becoming, individually and collectively. It condemns us and/ or offers a new chance for it mediates the Divine.

Psalm 104 captures this and the overarching dialectic we have pondered in this essay:

> Thou givest and they gather;
> thou openest thy hand, they are filled with good.
> Thou hidest thy face, they are troubled:
> thou takest away their breath, they die, and return to their dust.
> Thou sendest forth thy spirit, they are created:
> and thou renewest the face of the earth. (vv. 28–30).

2. Ibid, 49-50.

IV

Middle East Journal

THE HORIZON: TUNISIA

MID JANUARY OCCUPIED MY mind with the domestic crisis I label the Tucson Ordeal. By week three of this *Annus Horribilis/Terribilis*, the domestic microcosm had reverberated into international upheaval. America's violent state, 100,000 shootings per annum, had erupted in our client state, Egypt, along with our impulses of freedom and democracy. Now it was along that rim of the south side of the Mediterranean in Carthage where Hannibal's elephants rumbled and from where Augustine's silent words of *Civitas Terrena* and *Civitas Dei* radiated from Hippo where the stirrings were first felt. Here, toward the East, Paul the Apostle would weather storm and threatened shipwreck as he carried that sacred dispatch that would shake the world as no armies or armadas ever would or could.

Street unrest was unfolding in Tunis by mid January, followed by Algeria, Mauritania, Morocco, then January 25 in Cairo and January 27 when 15,000 marched on Sana'a, Yemen. The south Mediterranean, the Arab and Muslim world was quaking and few understood why, especially in London and Washington, D.C. Eventually the shock waves would reverberate to Morocco, Bahrain, Lebanon, Jordan, Saudi Arabia, Libya, Iran and countless other peoples, even the land where Gabrielle Giffords and Christina Green were shot in cold blood.

We should have known it was coming. In 2004, Condoleezza Rice, the little black girl whose life was indelibly marked by the killing of four

Sunday school girls in Birmingham, warned of an ethical Vesuvius, a suppressed volcanic power within an embedded formal structure, as she knew from her favorite Chopin nocturnes. Eruption was building pressure in the Middle East region and throughout the world.

From 2002 to 2005 President G.W. Bush, with surprising prophesy given his misadventures in Iraq and Afghanistan, as well as having the same troubling divine visions such as those that would haunt the Tunisian First Family, "I want you to invade Iraq." This "W" sought to nudge the regions monarchs and dictators, all his family friends, to wake up and listen to the people crying for freedom reforms. It was working. Then *Hamas* was elected in the Palestinian territories, our proclivities to support Israel kicked in and all was put off until this winter of discontent made glorious by the Spring . . . 2010–11.

Finally, President Obama warned the world in his June 2009 speech in Cairo what he had learned as a kid in Indonesia: that cruelty at the highest places created doomed dictatorial police-states (e.g., General Suharto).

In Tunis, to spark the flame it took a faith, a gesture, one unaccustomed in Abrahamic circles and more common in Buddhism, of self-immolation. The despairing provincial fruit-dealer and vegetable vendor who was struggling to support his widowed mother and seven siblings was disgraced by a slap on the face by a policewoman in the despised force. On December 17, he burned himself alive and ignited the revolution. His photo replaced that of President Ben-Ali throughout Tunisia. He became a folk-hero like Zena in Tehran, where the awakening was quenched and short-lived, though it still glimmers.

Before the president was exiled to Saudi Arabia, he had fashioned a police state, heard his Christian evangelical wife speak of her hearing God say he wished Ben Ali to rule this people. He concluded by increasing the force four-fold to 600,000 in the tiny nation. We are always called to make sanctuary states, bastion states; God requires the "mighty fortress," that is really the exposure of our insecurity. As Cairo would begin to unfold, new leadership reforms were already in place in this quite remarkable *etat Francaise.*

February 8, 2011 (Cairo)

The epicenter of the Middle East awakening waxes and wanes. After thrilling ups and terrifying downs during two full weeks of protests, more citizens have poured into Tahrir Square demanding that Mubarak go now, and more recalcitrant officials say "not yet." As of today, if my data is correct, 300 have been killed and 6,000 injured. Meanwhile in this region, the Arab Middle-East, 100 million are unemployed.

This pa and grandpa, called by his children and grandchildren "road kill on the information highway," did it again. He erased 14 days of diary entries from the beginning of Tahrir to the present. From my notebooks I share a few things I can remember.

Last night, Roger Cohen of the *New York Times* remarked that Egypt has been in a 30-year deep sleep from that she is just now awakening. [1]

A young professional in Tahrir Square says, "For the first time I feel alive. I now know that what I do matters. What I do has meaning."

Omer Suleiman, appointed vice president, seems to be falling under greater suspicion from the opposition, Mubarak's most trusted friend, head of the CIA, also military.

Notes on comparison with Indonesia, Obama's memory of his dad talking on General Suharto's cruelty has shaped his views on Cairo. Actually, the transition to a democracy went quite well in Indonesia.

February 5, 2011

The "Day of Departure," no one left from Government or the crowd in the square.

February 3, 2011

I stayed up all night on this ominous day, reporters, even Anderson Cooper (CNN) Nick Krystof (NYT) and old pro Christiane Amanpour (CNN) were shaken up, although Amanpour ended up walking right into Mubarak's office. Come morning it had not been a repeat of Tiananmen Square, as predicted. This revolution is as much about the intelligentsia and middle class as it is about the poor.

1. Roger Cohen, "A Republic Called Tahrir," *The New York Times*, February 6, 2011.

The fears that abound about an Islamic revolution are ill-founded. If anything, freedom would sink the Iranian ship. I still think it best to mute America's and Israel's voice. We have meddled enough, with the Shah, toppling Mohammad Mossadeq, etc. These are as unfortunate to our aspiration of being the harbinger of freedom and human rights in the region, as taking down Archbishop Romero and Salvador Allende in Salvador and Chile. Fearing communism or Islamism has always been counter-productive.

Early February

Fear of the Muslim Brotherhood was so intense that it kept the U.S. from welcoming one who would have become our best Islamic philosopher, Tariq Ramadan, who was to come to Notre Dame. He landed well at Oxford. England, like Germany and France, has become a different kind of interfaith culture than the U.S.

The main economic cause (grievance) underlying the Egypt uprising has been the "youth bulge," the fear of well trained and ambitious "under 25s," who can't get work, get married, or start a family. I wonder whether such desires for the "good life" can be realistically expected in the present world economy. Is the search for material prosperity an adequate impulse for social change that requires sacrifice?

February 10–11, 2011

Margaret Warner (PBS) interviews the foreign minister of Egypt. With all the other corrupt leaders, he feels that the U.S. has thrown him, them, under the bus, "After all I've done for you" he seems to feel. As doctors in white coats, lawyers in black robes, business leaders and academics in jeans and t-shirts call for decisive action, suspending emergency laws, and giving Mubarak a long vacation, the minister asks for time, lots of time, maybe another 30 years?

As evening fell in Cairo on February 10, one day before prayers and one week after the "day of departure," the lines have hardened, there is now only one possible conclusion: Mubarak leaves and the demonstration is over.

February 11, 2011 (Morning)

Stalemate, army supports Mubarak staying until fall. The government that America wanted and financially kept in power now turns against our finest democratic values and we are helpless to help.

This whole thing stirs the soul within me and shapes my conscience, as did the Civil Rights and Anti-Poverty movements and the peace movement.

February 11, 2011 (Mid-day)

Hallelujah, it is finished. Thanks be to God, the great blood-bath that could have been has been averted. Now the tough work begins!

AMMAN

The police state of Egypt is not replicated in Jordan, though in some ways Egypt is further along on the road to freedom. King Abdullah II has dismissed his entire cabinet in an attempt to diversify leaders and bring greater sympathy to the millions of disaffected youth who are quite discouraged by no jobs, restricted freedoms, exile from home (Palestinians) and little chance to marry and raise families.

The glimpse at Jordan gives us the chance to expound the "interfaith "thesis because the King and his uncle are among the world's leaders in the Common Word and Scriptural Reasoning movements.

The Super Bowl begins on February 6 with a recitation of the Declaration of Independence. Cairo provides a dramatic and ironic background to the readings by Colin Powell, soldiers around the world, players and ordinary workers and farmers. As Fox News presented the spectacle, one could only wonder at the words of its darling: Glenn Beck, that Cairo was about "a conspiracy for world domination by a leftist-Islamic Caliphate."[2]

Over against the stern division of opinion about the regicide going on, the words of the Declaration were sobering and inspiring:

"We hold these truths to be self-evident that all men are created equal . . . among (these truths) are the pursuit of life, liberty and the

2. "Who Didn't Beck Blame for Egypt's Unrest," Media Matters for America website, February 5, 2011, http://mediamatters.org/research/201102050001.

pursuit of happiness," (scarce chance in the "Caliphite," where 100 million are without work.)

"Whenever any form of government becomes destructive of these ends, it is the right of the people to alter or abolish it. When (a tyranny) seeks to reduce him under absolute despotism it is their right and duty to throw off such government." Today we witness that very abolition and renovation before our very eyes.

INTERFAITH INSIGHTS

In her salient leadership in the interfaith field (*History of God, Battle for God*), Karen Armstrong explains the derivation of "the Golden Rule," that along with Common Word (Love God with all your being, and your neighbor as yourself) is the pillar of interfaith wisdom. Such wisdom is the very power unfolding today in the Middle East, the crossroads of the world's faiths.

The first formulation of this proverb is ancient China in the sixth century b.c.e. In this period of "warring kingdoms," it was thought that battle "to the end," as with the Celts and Romans, was the only way to end disputes. The philosopher Mo Tse substituted the principle of *Jian Ai*, concern for everybody, down to the least of these, for the prevalent ethic of fighting one another to the death. Armstrong summarizes: "If you applied the Golden Rule, you would not invade another's state because you wouldn't like that done to you and your state. In war harvests are destroyed, expensive horses and weapons ruined, and there are thousands of causalities, so there is no one to look after the fields . . .[3]

RIIFS AND CARTS

The same wisdom is embedded in the interfaith centers, most of that have their base of operation in the Middle East. Established in 1994, the Jordanian Interfaith Coexistence Research Center was at one time directed by my predecessor, Fellow on the Cambridge Interfaith Center, Professor Aref Ali Nayed from Libya. Prince El Hassan bin Talal, brother of the former King of Jordan, is the patron of the center, which promotes

---

3. Karen Armstrong, "Why the Golden Rule is Key to Humanity's Future," *Shambhala Sun*, March , 2011, 57.

studies of Judaism and Christianity in interaction with the movements of Islam. RIIFS seeks to enhance the interfaith foundations of the wide-ranging and ever-raging civilizational issues of discord and hope for unity and progress. Whenever there is a conclave of international leaders, Kings Abdullah of Saudi and Jordan, Tony Blair of England, Benjamin Netanyahu of Israel and the President of the U.S., the event begins with a Common Word or Scriptural Reasoning project considering the scriptural heritage of the participants and ethical direction for the crises at hand. Big political events, it is believed, are too important to be left to secular whims. CARTS (the Cambridge Advanced Center for Religious and Theological Studies) has helped pave the way for cross-scriptural preparation of materials and discussion formats. We can only hope that the present meetings between the Mubarak government and the opposition coalitions are being convened with the same inspiration. Tony Blair usually carries this interfaith portfolio with that of his Quartet Liaison.

The Jordan Center publishes the Journal *Al Nashra* [the victory] that, like the Journal Muslim World (see Interfaith Manifesto in this document), includes materials for the present Muslim monarchies and dictatorships as they face restless populations. It becomes obvious that binding and reconciling litanies are required as a kind of *mizpah* benediction holding warring parties at bay, if not at peace. With Israel enjoying only the support of the American Jewish community and the U.S. and British Governments, and with the dwindling Christian presence in Israel and in Islamic states, Iran, Iraq, Afghanistan, even Palestine, such mediating structures and rituals are absolutely imperative.

At this point we can recognize what important states Lebanon and Syria become with their interfaith constituencies. One of the beneficial side effects of the freedom/democracy revolutions now gathering speed throughout the Middle East, is that the populations may again diversify, including the strengthening of the secular/humanist cohort. The concentration of faith communities in particular regions and the cleansing, targeted and inadvertent, of the others is a treacherous development.

Nayed, a Libyan businessman is the scholar most responsible for the document, "A Common Word," which has been widely used around the world and endorsed by Muslim and Christian leaders. My critique of it, recorded in "Christian Responses" on the Common Word website,[4] is that

4. Kenneth Vaux, "Comment on the Document 'A Common Word,'" October 21, 2007, The Official Website of A Common Word, http://www.acommonword.com.

the monumental and historic document, based on the Hebrew scripture from Leviticus, "Love God and your neighbor . . ." totally ignores the Jewish community and fails to enlist them in the triad, now become a dyad.

After leading the office of the Pontifical Institute for Arabic and Islamic Studies, Nayed assumed the post in Amman. His thought it a splendid example of interfaith wisdom for such a time as this.

Nayed's paper, *Duties of Proximity: Towards a Theology of Neighborliness*5 explores the meanings of proximity and neighborliness, key notions in the Abrahamic traditions of public ethics and in the kind of secular world these faiths (in concert) seek to fashion in the world.

Building on his helpful foundations for the document "A Common Word," he holds that the accidents of closeness and interdependent helpfulness are not accidents at all, but divine occasions and allotments, given to challenge concrete actions.

Today as even the streets of Libya, Nayed's home, resonate and reverberate with the expressions in Tunisia and Egypt, he seeks to search out the local and geopolitical ramifications of the telling scriptural question, "who is my neighbor?" Interfaith scholars immediately recognize the complexity of this teaching on the neighbor. Neighbor is a complex notion in sacred text, both my fellow Bedouin in the next tent, those from my family and tribe, but also he/she who is the stranger, even the adversary, belongs in this sacred company holding claim upon us. Any and all of these can be the God-provided neighbor, even those who sit now at the bargaining table with the establishment officials of the Mubarak regime. The events of the preceding months on the streets and squares of the Middle East are such a God-neighbor gift to the world.

To quote Nayed's important paper "as we gratefully respond to God's invitation to the eternal place of peace (*dar al-salam, dar al-Islam*/ Kingdom of God, Paradise), we are called upon to construct, maintain and grow environments of worldly peace." Exploring *Hadith* further, Nayed finds this to mean to visit our ill Jewish (and Christian) neighbor:

> Do you know what the right of your neighbor is?
> If he seeks your help, help him.
> If he asks you for a loan, loan him.
> If he becomes poor, support him.

5. Aref Ali Nayed, "Duties of Proximity: Towards a Theology of Neighborliness," paper presented at the "Mardin: The Abode of Peace" Conference, March 27–28, 2010, Artuklu University, Mardin, Turkey.

If he falls ill, visit him.
If he dies, participate in his funeral.
If a calamity befalls him, comfort him.
When you buy fruit, gift some to him.
Do not bother him with the aroma of your cook pot, unless you
share some of it with him.
Only a person blessed with God's compassion
    can realize the right of the neighbor.[6]

IVORY COAST, YEMEN, LEBANON

As the reverse, migrating geese fly, a few other regions are in view. Laurent Gbagbo in *Côte d'Ivoire* may be the prototypic propped up "strong man." His evangelical wife has inside *vox Dei* that he is meant to rule the country, so following the pattern, he rigged the elections. Despite U.N. monitors who certified that he lost, big, he refuses to "stand down" (the dignified French thing to do). His thugs still roam the capitol Abidjan and hassle the new president and the citizens; they seem to still be on payroll, reflecting the awesome power of the "hand-chosen" by God.

Yemen presents a more subtle and complicated picture. The real home of *al-Qaeda*, which increasingly mythic hoard of adversaries of the autocrats and their Western hegemony, she is one of the poorest places in the world. Thousands of pink-scarved youth have been protesting there for weeks. Ali Abdullah Saleh, former military strongman, has, like Mubarak, been president for 30 years. In preemptive concessions, analogous to Egypt, he has promised not to tamper with the constitution to allow himself another term or to allow his son to succeed him.

At the University of Sana, 40,000 have demonstrated demanding his resignation. It will not be as easy as Tunisia or as hard as Egypt. A classic north/south crisis (like Sudan), with the poor in the south and the ruling elite in the north, there is the chance to bring renewal via the freedom revolution to this small and poor country, badgered by American *al-Qaeda*-phobic, drone-driven hegemony, into a stronger citizen in the region, supplied by what my friends (Wycliffe translators) tell me is a wonderful, hospitable and gracious people.

Lebanon has been, and could be again, along with a justice-renewed Israel, the oasis in the wilderness, and the strong cedars on the snow-caps

6. Ibid., 7.

could rise again as a figurative Solomon's temple of wisdom would rise again in the world. Rich culture, truly interfaith history, splendid educational institutes, American University, (Hebrew University) and a highly sophisticated population hold great promise.

All would be hopeful but for one cloud on the horizon. Six years ago leader Rafid Gjairi was murdered along with 22 others. The U.N. asked for a tribunal, which is just now returning its verdict that may include evidence against Hezbollah leaders from the power that is now the ruling party. Syria was also implicated. For the interfaith population, justice must be done for the nation to be healed, so that it can move on. Israel must become a constructive economic and rebuilding support, rectifying the horrible devastation she wrought under Sharon with the bombing of the refugee camps.

Here's the hitch. *Shia* leaders are calling for the charges to be dropped, fearing the worst in the forthcoming indictment. The Druze leader, who may also be implicated, has also called the tribunal an American plot. Intrigue, not dictatorship, is the quandary of this historic free and democratic people. When I first visited A.U. 50 years ago, Beirut was the Jewel of the Eastern Mediterranean world. Mahmoud Ayoub, raised a Presbyterian in Beirut, now a leading Muslim scholar, a head of our international Muslim-Evangelical Dialogue Committee, represents the interfaith genius of this great people.

WHAT THEY REJECT

The template is clear and painfully repetitive: The witness of the people across the Mediterranean crescent is that there are some "ways" of life that they detest and will resist with their life's flesh and blood. They demand:

- The end to Western-planted and propped up dictatorships supplied by our own training in militarism, security surveillance, police states, and torture schools.

- The cessation of formation and rule of tiny elite states ruled by "strong-men," kings, shahs, dictators, with as much as 30 percent of the population living on stipends and government pensions (funded by Western foreign aid).

- The gnawing poverty robbing young people of the chance to work, to begin families, and thrive in free and participatory states.

- The *Muhabarat* (police state) is a recondite institution from Nazi and Communist era that has lingered on since the 1950's, since 2001 in America, now must be displaced by democratic, justice-driven forms of government where formal freedoms of speech, assembly, travel, and religion are enriched by the substantive freedoms of work, education, health care, shelter, food and clean water, and safety from danger and threat.

- The old anti-communist, cold-war saw, "domino effect," is not accepted, neither is Tony Blair and Hosni Mubarak's facile dichotomy that we must either have decorum and order or chaos. In Cairo, this school of thought betrayed its true totalitarianism when, as the force of order, it caused chaos by shutting down the media, the social-media networks, and sent in the chaos-makers on horse and camel-backs wielding machetes and whips. If anything should make the world insist that this regime must stand-down immediately, this is it. This is the Nazi state sending in the incendiaries to burn down the Reichstag, while accusing the "chaos" forces of communism. The antithesis of chaos is not repression but creation. The new order is only worthy if it is an order of Spirit, goodness, and creativity.

- The counsel of *New York Times* writer Tom Friedman is not always reliable, as when he says that all the world needs for peace is a McDonalds on every corner. But his word on Cairo and Egypt is right on when he calls for a vibrant, economic thrust for the nation, placing it not on the "just-getting-by" plateau but in the community of nations who are really pace-setters in developing economic vitalities and world markets. The Muslim tradition along with the Christian (Copt and Evangelical), has profound gifts to offer to this renaissance. If she were able to open some cathedra of her once rich synagogue community, it could only help.

WHAT THEY SEEK

This great and historic nation of Egypt seems poised not only to lead the Arab world into this modern world, but in contrast to the fabricated plastic worlds of Dubai, Saudi Arabia, The Emirates, Kuwait, and other recent gifts to world history from the oil boon, Egypt bears the glory of the Pharaohs, the sages and poets of ancient civilizations, The Alexandria

Library, the repository of the treasures of ancient literature and culture, the mythology and High religion, the axis point of monotheism and the ethical vision with along with the refinements of the peoples of Israel, Greece and Rome have laid the cornerstones of excellence, thought and beauty, truth and wisdom, on that the world establishes its honor and insight.

The protestors today throughout Egypt live on in the inspiration of this heritage. Three hundred dead and 6,000 injured attest to that ancient and ever-new strength. Young Turks, like *New York Times* writers, Nick Krystof, Roger Cohen, and the stalwarts of the Cairo Bureau excepted, call them "wired and shrewd,"[7]—fair enough, but their courage and magnanimity borders on the transcendental. When Wael Ghonim, the Google executive, emerged from two weeks in prison, his tearful recollection of now-deceased friends and his confession that he did nothing, except start the whole thing, inspired the world.

The fine and encouraging aftermath of the Jasmine revolution is that the architects and foot soldiers who made it happen will be the ones who work out its shape and success.

The best roadmap to a "new and better world" is to be found in interfaith consideration. The resident and diaspora Egyptian scholars and leaders will now be called on to envision and construct this environment. The same will be true of the Greek, Spanish, Irish, Iranian, Palestinian, Israeli, Syrian, Iraqi, and Lebanese peoples. This old and good world is the priceless heritage of the whole earth, not just the British Museum and the *Palais de Louvre*.

Lebanon will be key, along with Israel, Syria, Egypt, Holland, Morocco, Tunisia, and Turkey. The desperate states of Africa, the bottom echelon, and forgotten peoples of the earth, now also bear those inestimable gifts of intimate interfaith association. Like the ancient King of Somalia, who joined the other two wise men on the road to Bethlehem, carrying frankincense from this horn of Africa, such gifts will transform the world.

7. David D. Kirkpatrick, "Wired and Shrewd, Young Egyptians Guide Revolt," *The New York Times*, February 9, 2011, http://www.nytimes.com/2011/02/10/world /middleeast/10youth.html?pagewanted=all.

THE POSSIBLE CONTRIBUTION OF INTERFAITH WORK

We flew mid-day on February 11, from Chicago to Houston. When we left early in the morning, hundreds of thousands bowed the knees and head in the deep petition of morning prayers in Cairo. Many said that they might be called on this day to love God, their nation and their deceased friends, with *psuche (soul)*, one's life. In a most moving scene, as the tens of thousands of young people took to their knees in prayer, *Sunni* and *Shia*, secular and religious, hundreds of Christians circled around them in support, Copts and Catholics, protestants and evangelicals, hand in hand and arm in arm in solidarity. When we landed, jubilation abounded. Faith and prayer, peace and hope, and not just that of Islam, had played a major role.

Roger Cohen of *The New York Times* has just called for "truth and reconciliation" commissions, much work now needed to be done: disclosing the truth; who ran the prisons; the torture chambers; where did all the people's money go; the Suez revenues; the massive foreign aid from the U.S. and other nations; will there be war-crimes or crimes-against-humanity proceedings?

Was it our negligence to allow such corrupt states to come into being under our tutelage? Had we not had a hand in creating this set of dictatorship/ monarchies in the region? Weren't Mubarak, Iraq and Afghanistan, the Taliban, at least in part, creatures of our making? Where could we look for better and sounder guidance and wisdom? Wasn't there some hope in the new consultation where Christians and Jews reconciled into toleration and mutual recognition of redemption? And now, even with the suspect motivations of the events of September 11, could we not consider our sibling relationship with Islam, so that the whole Abrahamic family, two-thirds of the world's population, might live in creative synergy—"faithful unification rather than fateful trifurcation?"[8]

Faith and interfaith, perspectives that have been so helpful in the deconstruction crisis we have come through now, can help us in the formidable tasks of reconstruction.

8. Kenneth L. Vaux, *Jew, Christian, Muslim: Faithful Unification or Fateful Trifurcation? Word, Way, Worship, and War in the Abrahamic Faith* (Eugene, OR: Wipf and Stock, 2003).

In these months, I have written "an Interfaith Manifesto" that may provide some convictions and strategies for the process unfolding before us.[9]

This Interfaith Manifesto affirms that a universal covenant of reverence for life binds (God) to the whole creation; a humanistic covenant to the entire human family for now and for the future; a faith covenant with all of the religious communities on earth; a covenant of particular paradigmatic *Torah* faithfulness with the Jewish people for justice and truth in the world; a Christian evangelical covenant with the Jesus peoples of all persuasions and the peace-submission covenant of Islam.

This "divine initiative and human response, indicative and imperative" is the distinctive character in all biblical covenant, Edenic, Noahic, Abrahamic, (Israelite and Ishmaelite), Mosaic, Davidic, Prophetic, Messianic (Jesus), and Islamic. The covenant, in each wave of the development, guarantees divine blessing contingent upon human faithfulness. The stunning theological truth must therefore remain, unless invalidated by divine action, each covenant remains intact under God, therefore each is forever subject to human respect, honor, and reciprocal attentiveness, given the divinely grounded continuity. In light of the first passage of our Manifesto, the entire covenant, sacerdotal (with a specific faith community and scripture), monotheistic, humanistic and naturalistic is blessed by God, the Giver and Sustainer of Heaven and Earth.

When it comes to the biblical peoples, "Peoples of the Book," greater specificity and intensity is possible. It may be that the "Covenantal Humanism," embracing rational "choice theory" Kantian and Habermasian deontological moral theory, is a good place to start for formal ethical theory and process. This perspective can sketch out a legal and public-policy approach. The drawback is that concrete moral injunctions do not arise from such universal rational theory. John Rawls, in his late work, turned to "religious theory" to implement his "least-of-these" root imperative. Self-interest and even human-equality rational ethics cannot move to James Cone's "preferential option for the poor."

In her very latest work, Martha Nussbaum has asked whether respect for "the contemptible" of the world can be derived from a universal, rational, "capabilities theory." The right to vote and to receive fair employment practice may come for gays from rational, equality theory. But what about

9. See Kenneth L. Vaux, *Journey Into an Interfaith World: Jews, Christians, and Muslims In a World Come of Age* (Eugene, OR: Wipf and Stock, 2010).

deep care for humanity and solidarity amid the fury of persecution? Gays and gypsies went into Hitler's ovens with the Jews. Something more than technical, customary law, Heidegger's philosophy and Harnack's theology, was needed.

When we turn to Israel/Palestine, the epicenter of global justice and injustice, we explore this deeper current of justice and ethics. Here we find norms incumbent on all humanity, where the Noahic and Gentile rule pertains. This current of good and evil is unique to the "Peoples of the Book." I have summarized this as a "template" or "matrix" of biblical righteousness. It comes from the activity of Scriptural Reasoning. Judaism leads the Abrahamic faith family into what Muslim leaders, in the most important religious document of our time, call "A Common Word." Its essence is the call to the "love of God and neighbor." Hebrew texts formulate these synergistic two loves as a "redemptive complex," which Christianity and Islam take up in turn. This quintessence of faith and life is spoken of as a sprout, which springs up in the desert of the world. The composite Abrahamic tradition tells of God's healing messianic gift to the world and our responsive act of doing justice and care. In this way, the synergy, the Sophia of "loving God and neighbor" is activated. The activation of this reciprocal love creates in the world the extraordinary gift that can be called a "Template of Righteousness." This is the message of Jesus' inaugural sermon (Matt 4).

> The complex can be seen as divine indicative
>   yielding human imperative:
> The hungry are fed . . . feed the hungry . . .
> the thirsty are given drink . . . give the cup of water
> Homeless sheltered . . .
> Sick healed . . .
> Blind see . . .
> Lame walk . . .
> Possessed exorcized . . . exorcize the possessed
> Prisoners released . . .
> Oppressed liberated . . .
> Poor encouraged . . .
> "The least of these" honored . . .
> Sinners forgiven . . .
> And the dead are raised . . . raise the dead.

A cornucopia of grace. Jesus' claim to the lawyers is that God's righteousness, what Walter Brueggemann calls "God's goodness," is our faith/work. *Gabe and Aufgabe,* gift as task. God's proleptic action becomes our present assignment.

When we speak of the "Messiah," the three members of the Abrahamic family often resort, initially, before political reason, to eschatological language, which can make for strife rather than peace. Still, Isaiah 11 holds before us the salvific matrix in that "the wolf shall lie down with the lamb," "they shall not hurt or destroy in all my holy mountain." To ignore this for "Real Politik" discourse is as dangerous as misconstruing this eschatology itself as political speech. My friend Jon Levenson once responded to my good wishes (as a neighbor just down Church Street in Skokie) and my allusion to the new pothole repairs as "making the crooked straight and the rough places smooth," with the reminder that Isaiah 40 is not to be confused with earth projects, lest we mess up both street projects and Kingdom clarity. He specifically chastened me that Skokie Jews did not believe that the "Highway up to Zion" had already been built, as we Christians sometimes supposed.

What interfaith does give us was something true (that secular political reasoning could not proffer): that God reigned over historical acts through justice and mercy, effecting blessing and curse on our actions. "The land" and "Jerusalem" are also a divine bequest to humankind and only secondarily a political expediency enacted by a guilt-ridden Europe and America in 1948. A second affirmation arises from this discussion for our Interfaith Manifesto: again the Manifesto affirms that the faith families whose history and destiny involve Israel, Palestine, and Jerusalem, even Antioch, Lebanon, and Sinai, are bound together in a covenantal drama concerning this region, upon that hinges the peace and justice of the entire world. We are obliged to be the *avant garde* of justice here, without which there can be no peace elsewhere. The war on terrorism is a disharmony resulting from our failure to make justice and peace in this region of the earth. The land hallowed by Abraham, Jesus, and Mohammad is meant to be a trust to God's peoples and an inheritance to all the peoples on earth. Playing national and international politics here, suicide bombers, wars on Gaza, crusades, and counter-crusades, are not only "clashes of civilizations," they are actions offending the God of Israel, the Father of the Lord Jesus Christ, and Allah of Mohammad and the

Emmanuel, God with us in the world in all traditions, the Will of that One God to and for His creation.

I have come to believe that the world needs to be viewed interfaith-wise. It must be much more than a knee-jerk reaction to the 9/11 trauma. We are living in an age of global history that can only be addressed by a global theology. In our time, the world is witnessing freedom-justice revolutions, in Africa, now the Middle East. This revolution is best understood in terms of the interfaith movement. Anyone engaged in work today in the Middle East, Jerusalem, Israel and Palestine, realizes that in recent times, the region has become a kind of axis-point in the crises of agony and hope for the whole world. The meeting of Jewish, Christian, and Muslim cultures is a feature of modern history that gives a kind of tropism, a drawing of all peoples to this region of the cradle of civilization. Religion, especially monotheistic faith, is sweeping the world today, in Africa, Asia, Latin America, even in North America and Western Europe. The epicenter of these global movements is the Middle East. The God of Abraham, Isaac, and Jacob is the God of creation and history. This is the One Name.

Monotheism seems to be a vital causal impulse in science, economics, environment, both for blessing and bane. The worldviews of India and China, as well as secular humanism, are also vital in modern history.

I agree that the Israel/Palestine challenge is the greatest "test" to the "cogency" of viewing the theological world through the interfaith lens. Here is where the constitutive events of monotheistic faith take on concrete historical form. Here the God of Israel, Jesus, and Islam touches down into the history of the world.

King Abdullah of Jordan, one of the sages of our contemporary world and sponsor of key interfaith institutions and programs, has stressed the reciprocal validation of the Middle East peace talks and interfaith scriptural study. He was one of the three companion figures, with Egyptian President Mubarak and Envoy Tony Blair of Great Britain, standing beside Presidents Abbas, Netanyahu, and Obama in the recent renewal of talks.

The world is weary of Middle-East strife, just as it is weary of hearing endlessly that the European genocide of Jewry is the only and definitive holocaust of peoples. Nearly a century of agonizing geopolitical turmoil, diverting the resources and energies of the global community from more constructive endeavors and an ignoring of the cleansing of the Palestinian peoples from their homeland, has resulted from this amnesia. Now a new configuration of powers in the world, China, India, Brazil, Indonesia, and countless distressed peoples in Latin America, Africa, and Asia, is pressing the world community to turn its concentration on the Middle East and Israel/Palestine to other pressing global concerns like disease, gnawing poverty, environmental collapse, destructive militarism, and economic inequality.

With the monotheistic trio of peoples, I am required to provide rationale for our placing Israel/Palestine at the epicenter of the holy-history of the world. We argue that human global history in all its redemptive impulses and perplexing vicissitudes, its good and evil, is ultimately related to the One God of history, nature, and the world, the God of Israel, the Jesus phenomenon and movement in global history, and the still-to-be-discerned meaning of the rise of Islam within that universal history. Middle-East tropism and concentration is therefore a requirement of the reality of what we have come to realize is the very nature and purpose of the One God.

I draw my direction from this tricky question of "the land" and the territorial localization of the "work of God in the world," from Martin Buber. Of course the invisible God, ever transcendent and mysterious, does not dwell in buildings of "human hands" and is not confined to particular and parochial cultic rituals or systems of thought. God is the God of all creation, if implicated at all in world nature and history. Buber wrestles with the obvious geo-centrism of biblical faith that rests on creation and incarnation, history, places, and people. Given this disposition of the biblical witness, the drama of the living God must involve both the mystery of place and the invisibility and unknowability of God. God's inscrutability begins with universality and validity within a variety of faiths and proceeds into transcendence, invisibility, and infinity. Buber therefore affirms in numerous studies, such as "On Zion" (Jerusalem Lectures of 1944), that the purpose of Zion, a transcendental and universal belief positioned at a particular time and place, is to "found a just society and to initiate the Kingdom of God." Jews, Christians, and Muslims share something of this belief, though the details may differ.

Zion involves "Hebrew renaissance . . . internal liberation and purification (sanctifying a place for the Name) . . . and redemption for the nation."[10] At the very center of this conception is redress for the injus-

10. Martin Buber, *On Zion: The History of an Idea* (trans. Stanley Godman; London: Horovitz Publishing Co., Ltd.: 1973; repr., Syracuse: Syracuse University Press, 1997), viii.

tice and restitution of a *Hashem/Shema* people in concrete existence in the world. Zion is not achieved by the sword, but is a *Liebeswirkung* (a deed of love).[11] For Buber, there can be no "Zion" without Christians and Muslims.

Will the unfolding will of God for this "land" be two states, a confederation, such as Europe or America, or some "yet-to-be-envisioned" entity or collectivity? To my mind and heart the deepest "identity quality" of such "divine presence" in the world will have something to do with the display of Abrahamic Faith, universally conceived.

Contrary to this geocentric confidence, we can be sure that the globe is not collapsing into an "interfaith cluster" with the rest of humanity and faith-oriented peoples dwindling away at the edge. Perhaps 60 percent of the world's peoples may now belong to these three faith communities. The religions of India, Hinduism, and Buddhism and of China, Taoism, and Confucianism, together with a resurgent humanism and secularism, constitute a formidable third force in the theological composition of world population.

Indeed, part of the enigma of world theological history is the fact that the global monotheisms, despite their present renaissance and fervor, still generate much of the world's atheistic and agnostic humanism and secularism. Wherever Western education, science, economics, philosophy, and democratic politics go, secularism, even materialism, narcissism, and dissociation from the imperatives of justice in the world of the "have-nots," seems to flourish. High religion generates two responses: faith and piety or apostasy and injustice.

I offer an illustration of the connection between public culture, religion, and crisis in history. Congo in Africa is now spoken of as the richest per-capita nation in the world (in potential) and at the same time actually one of the poorest. In this war-torn nation, embattled by Tutsi and Hutu, a near-failed nation, the bones are now being picked bare by the mighty powers of the world and their economies. The petty surrounding powers, like vultures, now circle the carcass.

Valued minerals (cell phones) and metals abide here in the earth underneath peoples tossed to and fro by internal and external threats. What do these crises have to do with Christians (including Catholics and prosperity- Gospel-oriented Pentecostals)? What of Muslim and

---

11. Ibid., viii.

Jewish peoples and interests? We remember that the million-man massacre in neighboring Rwanda occurred largely in churches. Large banks,
investment interests, and corporations, peopled by Jews, Protestants, and
secularist opportunists, seize the day. Muslims hover around and within
the tribal warfare, seeking evangelical opportunity, as do evangelical and
Catholic Christians. At the same time, a great cause for hope in Congo
comes from concerned Jewish and Christian philanthropists (as in South
Africa) and in the phenomenal dedication of masses of interfaith women
(Christian and Muslim), poor and powerless, but determined to "take
back the night" from the "child-soldier" recruiter gangs, the economic
and political exploiters, and the wretched, contrived, lack-of-opportunity
ethos that greedy local leaders have fashioned.

I correctly assess the situation in Congo, religion, especially through
interfaith configurations, although greatly contributing to the problem,
is the greatest hope for justice, reconciliation, and peace. Schools, for
the most part, are under religious sponsorship. Hospitals and clinics, the
same. The sponsors of our institution, Garrett-Evangelical Theological
Seminary at Northwestern University, have just received the announce-
ment that the United Methodist Church, a body that includes the African
church, has become the first parochial sponsor of the United Nations.
With a $70 million contribution, it will focus its cooperative work on the
ground ministries such as children, HIV/AIDS, peace-building efforts,
and the like. World Methodists will cooperate with U.N. agencies and
installations, and the U.N. will be able to use the considerable network of
hands-on-ministry of Methodists in places like Congo.

In the new post-modern world in which we find ourselves, interfaith
interactions and structures will become increasingly vital in establishing
peace and furthering reconciliation and concerted endeavor. Post-modern consciousness at present seems to either hold that public endeavors
must be entirely secular in discourse and execution, a widespread view in
America, Europe, Japan, China, and Israel, or it is held that the world is
irrepressibly a religious environment in that faith voices must have a seat
at the table of public discourse and decision-making. The religious voice
is not privileged, but it has an indispensible gift to offer. This Manifesto
affirms that reason and revelation are inextricably intertwined in effective, ameliorative work in the world, as are secular (public) and religious
groups in the sphere of public decisions.

My own career centered on 30 years in the public sphere in the realm of medical care. Thinkers like John Rawls (*A Theory of Justice*), Jürgen Habermas (*Religion and Rationality*), and Amartya Sen (*Development as Freedom*) expound this latter view: reason and revelation are inextricably intertwined as are secular (public) and religious groups in the sphere of public decisions.

I next proceed to argue that the failure of the "modern project," both intellectual and moral, sets the stage for "interfaith endeavor" to assume and undertake the cultural project of meaning and justice. Where parochialisms fail, interfaith endeavors may work. Just as religious wars brought about the severance of religion from culture, interreligious rapprochement may affect the possibility of recovering the spiritual/ethical-meaning/value dimension into the cultural discourse.

How did the modern project fail? Many belong to that community of revisionists who feel that the Enlightenment was mistaken, especially in its confidence in reason and progress, science and technology repudiating religion and bringing about godless, materialistic, and demonic nation-states that have visited great violence, holocaust, genocide, and ecocide on humanity and the earth.

I take a different view. I feel that we need to carefully delineate the salutary gifts from the unethical harms of the broad period we call Enlightenment and modernity. Karl Barth, for example, finds great wisdom in the Enlightenment philosophy of Kant and Kierkegaard and in the theology of Schleiermacher. We need further to distinguish the secular *Aufklärung* and the religious Awakening. The work of Wesley and Wilberforce, Jonathan Edwards and Cotton Mather, Jewish philosophy and neo-Thomism, the New England Transcendentalists and the revolution of Walter Rauschenbusch, all brought about great humanistic blessing to the world, grounded in cogent theology.

The Enlightenment, secular and sacred, was not only about the pretensions of human autonomy, becoming laws unto ourselves, as it was about a noble insight into the dignity of human beings, the reassertion of the sublime natural law of the Greeks, Romans, Aquinas, Renaissance artists and scientists, and Calvin. It concerned the receiving of the benediction of our human interdependence and God-dependence.

The overarching premise of postmodernism is that the Enlightenment is a dangerous age, both it its presuppositions and programs. The assumptions of human autonomy and totality, no longer subject to higher law or transcendent sanctions or to the common-law of community, gives rise to programmatic aggressions against and subjugations of others (colonialism), objectification and ruination of the natural world (desanctification), and arrogant assertion of unbridled power over against a rapidly retiring, deity-voiding divine presence from the workings and affairs of the world (idolatry). Spokespersons of the Enlightenment are not so much the gentle Kant and Wesley, Adam Smith and Hegel, but now Hobbes, Nietzsche, Clausewitz, Marx, consummating in Stalin, Hitler, and totalitarianisms of left and right and totalisms, liberal and conservative.

The Enlightenment has run its course in Western history, and it has chastened the three monotheistic faiths through internal socio-cultural higher criticism, in the medieval period in Islam, in the Renaissance and European Enlightenment in Christianity, and in modernity in Judaism. Today, these two philosophical-theological deconstructions (culture and faith) can pave the way for a renewed interfaith wisdom that can again establish legitimate discourse on truth, meaning, and justice, public and personal, drawing on a myriad wisdom grounded in reason and revelation.

Our scripture reader in church declaimed it with great eloquence in her pastoral prayer yesterday. "We pollute and hoard, others sicken and starve." The theme of worship was to unclutter and simplify our lives in response to the "Simplicity of God" (Psa 24:1-12). We recalled the lyrics, "it's a gift to be simple, it's a gift to be free, it's a gift to come round where we ought to be" (Elder Joseph Brackett, "Simple Gifts, 1848). I recalled in my class following worship: "Sing God a simple song . . . God loves all simple things . . . For God is the simplest of all" (Stephen Schwartz, "Sing God a Simple Song," 1971). The simplicity of God, a cardinal doctrine in Anselm and Aquinas, claims that God transcends the plentiful designations of his attributes and is simply the One over and in all. God is not divisible into parts. God's being is God's action, and God's action is the inspiration and substance of our reaction.

This means that the simple service of our lives finds its energy and efficacy in the Spirit of God. There is, therefore, no discontinuity between God's works and "the work of our hands" (Psa 90:17). To negate God's lordship in the world by virtue of our emancipation and autonomy is to negate our own competence and capabilities. To withhold our gifts is to rob God of God's resplendent virtuosity. Enlightenment and post-Enlightenment synergy is possible and indispensible in renewing the forgotten humanity and divinity of our post-modern world.

Our arguments call for such restitution under the cool shadows of Abraham's tent. Here, faith-siblings join hands and hearts over the repast of grace (the cry of a mother camel searching to recall her children lost in the wasteland and desert of perceived abandonment). Here, the Three Cups of reconciling Tea send us on our way refreshed.

Peter Ochs, the eminent Jewish theologian goes to the very heartland of scriptural exegesis and hermeneutics (then followed this by carrying his *Koine* Greek New Testament and Qur'an in his satchel), founded the Scriptural Reasoning movement in the world, along with David Ford and Aref Nayed. Together, they have prepared the fertile ground, along with many of us who have been convening underground interfaith-discussion groups for almost 50 years. Ochs specifically struggles with searching for the antidote for modernity's failed agenda. The world finds itself *Gerissenheit* (" torn asunder"/ Simone Weil), suffering, Holocaust, relentless enmity, which only God- bestowed healing and repair, *Tikkun Olam*, can remedy.

I was among the company at the funeral for Dan Hardy, the true pioneer of interfaith studies (while he was at Birmingham with my Princeton teacher, John Hick and his son-in law-to-be, David Ford). He was the first person to encourage me toward interfaith studies decades ago. The requiem/eulogy was held at old St. Benet's (10th-century) church in Cambridge. Peter Ochs offered the homily on the Christian scripture, John 17, a *midrash* (in my view) on the *Shema* ("Hear o Israel, the Lord our God is One"/ "so that they may be one, as we are one" (John 17:22b). Peter went on to say, "I will not leave you comfortless, but will send the Comforter, the Spirit, to be with you."

One by one, he spoke to Dan's daughter, to David, to the grandchildren and to all of us seeking peace and recommissioning into the ominous night and glorious dawn of Jesus betrayal, last supper, and high-priestly prayer. Afterwards, I shared with Peter two passages that were running through my mind during the service: "Israel is redeemed out of Egypt so that it may live before God, as God's people on earth" and "Israel will restore the wholeness of human nature through the work of its people in the natural world of the countryside."[12] Peter resonated with these texts from Dietrich Bonhoeffer and Martin Buber.

12. Dietrich Bonhoeffer, *Letters and Papers from Prison*, Dietrich Bonhoeffer Works,

Today, interfaith awareness tells us that we are in the "flesh-pots of Egypt" and, like the proverbial frog in the pot of boiling water, we don't know how to decipher our situation, cry for help, or jump. Modernity has seduced us to think we are in the Promised Land, when we are slowly being consumed by the plagues meant for Pharaoh.

Interfaith discourse—where particular parochial orientations such as those of the Abrahamic faiths—is unlayered and unpacked, until we can see the interstitial lineaments between traditional texts and interpretive hermeneutics of each other's traditions. Then we can see the *midrashic* chains of golden illumination and intuit the bearings of revelation into our structures of reason and public discourse. Then we can address concrete matters of life in the world in terms of "concrete maxims" of action.

Och's pastoral and prophetic approach is ultimately rooted in the One redemptive God who is mending the world through collaborators discovering their own particular narratives of redemption and renewal enriched and deepened in the others. The common experience we all have in Scriptural Reasoning or interfaith engagements is that we are sent back home in retrieval missions to our particular traditions, then dispatched together in reconnaissance missions at the new frontiers of our common life in this rapidly shrinking, interwired, and intertwined world. God is reconciling, remaking, and renewing the world as we join minds and hands with the God-Redeemer. Scriptural Reasoning begins public discourse that, in turn, undergirds public action, necessary concentric ripples in a radiating renewal of the God-given and God-to- be-redeemed world.[13]

Interfaith activity ultimately then moves to Scriptural Reasoning together and the requisite hermeneutical transformation. Here we lay the foundations of a new kind of community ethics and public philosophy, completing his important proposal for "responsibility" in our time.

Reading scripture together begins with examination of the question of whether the three monotheistic faiths are really fraternal and, in any etiological or substantive sense, complementary. I have argued throughout my interfaith work that we find in Judaism, Christianity, and Islam not only a continuous *midrashic* (internal scriptural exegesis) tradition,

---

Volume 8 (London: SCM Press, 1953/1967/1971; repr., Minneapolis: Augsburg Fortress, 2010), 447; Buber, *On Zion*, 156.

13. See David F. Ford and C.C. Pecknold, eds., *The Promise of Scriptural Reasoning* (Oxford: Blackwell Publishing, 2006).

but three sibling faiths that can offer each other affirmation, admonition, correction, and enlargement.

Jon Levenson disputes my expansive thesis, claiming that what we have is not corroboration and continuity in the three faiths, but rather distinct and unique traditions. Finding at least three "Abrahamisms" (Mosaic, Messianic, and Islamic), Levenson counsels extreme caution in establishing some grand syncretistic theory starting with the critical-historical truth that, although the figure of Abraham is in some sense the pioneer of biblical history, he is still a shadowy figure, part invention and innovation, especially in the exile experience and literature, and, in part, a concrete historical personage laying down a dawning of biblical realism out of the period of mythic profundity (Garden, Adam, Eve, Temptation and Fall, Cain, Abel, and Noah) into an era where the God of Abraham, Israel, and Moses becomes *Yahweh-Adonai* of the history of the world as well as of holy history.

Levenson argues that Jews and Muslims may call the same figure to mind when they invoke the name Abraham. But "it is not at all clear that Jews and Christians are talking about the same figure . . ."[14] While Abraham, for Jews, is the servant of God who receives the blessing, "I will make you a great nation . . . blessing those who bless you, cursing those who curse you" (some kind of proto-Zionist), at the same time, "Christianity has long seen in the election of Abraham the beginning of a movement that reaches fruition only with the incorporation of all the nations of the world into the Abrahamic promise"[15] (a real sweet, ecumenical guy). Levenson does tip the hat to Rashi, "the best medieval Jewish commentator," suggesting that Rashi gets it right and the text means "all nations shall bless themselves through you" rather than the Mikado-like blesser-smiter we have in other textual traditions.

I argue somewhat with Levenson, that we find a conjunction of divinity and humanity in the figure of Abraham, the rich and the poor, whose eternal destiny is portrayed in what is called "the bosom of Abraham" (cf., the Dives-Lazarus parable of Luke 16); the expansion and elaboration of the "faith-family of God" as numerable as the stars of the skies and the sands of the seas (Gen 15:5);the worthy and efficacious trust offering of humanity to the righteousness of God (*Akedah*, the Abraham/

14. Jon D. Levenson, "The Idea of Abrahamic Religions: A Qualified Dissent" in *Jewish Review of Books*: 1 (Spring 2010), p. 40.

15. Ibid., 40.

Isaac, Abraham-Hagar-Ishmael complex of Gen 21, 22); and the complex three-fold divine covenants of life (God, Abraham, Israel, Moses; God , Jesus, and the Gentiles; and God, Hagar, Ishmael, and the Semitic goyim).

This notion of trinity of covenant defies understanding, unless viewed with the interfaith lens via interfaith Scriptural Reasoning. These biblical parables of faith-humanity translate into the workable metaphors to decipher issues of meaning and value in universal humanity. On this basis, we can see that a human and responsible future hinges upon the viability and vitality of interfaith discourse.

In sum we have three variants of the Abrahamic legacy, Mosaic, Messianic, and Islamic, within the broader scriptural heritage, Buber also opens the door to projected futures of continuing strife or eventual reconciliation depending on what occurs in the realm of reciprocal redemption. We may be approaching Buber's vision of Zion, where each parochial fulfillment depends on the justice, mercy, and sacrificial readiness for redemption by the other faith communities. This would accord with the thesis of my comprehensive work, where secular concord in the Middle East depends on theological bodies getting their act together to end strife and venture peace. In *Jew, Christian, Muslim, Ethics and the Gulf War, Ethics and the War on Terrorism, America in God's World*, and *Journey into an Interfaith World*, I argue that internal and intramural tensions in the three Abrahamic faith communities strive toward a composite and complementary redemption.

History tells the sad tale of our fratricidal past. Historic Christian anti-Semitisms including Islamophobia generate the Muslim conquests that, in turn, generate the Crusades, which, in turn, generate Muslim consolidation that, in turn, after the signature event of Christian anti-Semitism (*Shoah*), precipitates Christian and Jewish Zionism and the violent Islamophobia (including (*Nakbar*) of contemporary history, especially in America and Israel. This cascade of misunderstanding and estrangement, culminating in the Holocaust of global Jewry, the establishment of the State of Israel, and the grievous expulsion and cleansing of the Palestinian peoples, now invites the rapprochement of various secular initiatives that will gain inspiration from interreligious endeavors, resulting in a synergic justice and resultant peace. Those who have cautiously whispered "*shalom*," "peace," and "*asalamu alaikum*" for millennia will wake one day as a new Jerusalem rises from the earth as if it is descending from heaven.

The little girl cried for joy as her dad was lifted by the capsule-cage after two months trapped under the earth in the San Jose gold and copper mine. Buried in darkness, desolation, and death now risen into light, community, and life, the world gasps in resurrection hope. And from her outstretched arms we take hope and seek to begin again.

This manifesto is a conviction of faith and a confession of sin. We members of the blessed, God guided faiths of Abraham have been infidels against our election. We have been the harbingers of injustice. We have forsaken the One God and have failed to be obedient to the sacred scriptures, treating them as our play-toys, instruments, and whips to denigrate and hurt the other. We have denied that we are the one children of one *Shema*, one *Hashem*, one Logos-Messiah, one submission, *ulama*, and people in the world. Now God's *ex nihilo* creation hovers at the precipice. Our thoughtless domination has threatened this "good earth," human community is torn asunder, without hope and without God in the world.

V

Into Spring

February 14, 2011 (Valentine's Day)

THE IMMEDIATE EVENT OF combined thrill and terror has subsided and the remaining visitors to Tahrir Square are proud parents with their children coming to remember and take photographs.

The event will be remembered with something of the fervor of the American or French revolution or, dare I say, the day of the founding of the State of Israel. Like each of these analogous events, much hard work, including setbacks and contradictions, awaits for years to come.

The New York Times today carries a fascinating report on what we have observed as the "domino effect."

> . . . put vinegar or onion under your scarf for tear gas . . .
>
> Young Egyptian and Tunisian activists brainstormed on the use of technology to evade surveillance, commiserated about torture and traded practical tips on how to stand up to rubber bullets and organize barricades.
>
> They (Tunisians and Egyptians) fused their secular expertise in social networks with a discipline culled from religious movements and combined the energy of soccer fans with the sophistication of surgeons and psychiatrists . . . they relied on the tactics of nonviolent resistance channeled through an American scholar through a Serbian youth brigade, but also on marketing tactics borrowed from Silicon valley.
>
> . . . Tunis pushed Egypt . . . Egypt will push the world.[1]

1. David D. Kirkpatrick and David E. Sanger. "A Tunisian-Egyptian Link that Shook

February 20, 2011 (Libya and Bahrain)

The cascade continues. Today my pastor speaks of prayer and worship. I tell him, and anyone whose ear I can bend, that the world has witnessed such profound prayer and worship as the world has ever witnessed in Bahrain, Friday, last and in Cairo, the preceding Friday. It was the day of prayers. Those who gathered in Cairo, we know, include not only *Sunni*, but *Shia* and *Sufi*, Copt and Evangelical, humanist and secularist; it was surely a gathering of the whole family of the One God of heaven and earth. As the Christian community stood encircled behind and around the Muslim community on their knees, we witnessed a solidarity that is the true meaning of the glorious event.

The gatherings in Bahrain and Libya were not as multiform and diverse, but were profoundly sacred events. In the face of death, persons bared their soul to death to serve God or Good or Truth, perhaps disparate entities, certainly cognate in the being of ultimacy. Some simply laid down their lives for their fellows or their motherlands, "greater love has no one that this." Hundreds were killed by live fire in the face and chest until the Prince said to the goons, "NO MORE!" Libya, the homeland of Aref Ali Nayed, still lay in more cruel hands, as the world has long known. Sacraments, what Teilhard de Chardin called the "Mass upon the earth," I believe, but it will take years or decades to bear fruit.

February 22, 2011 (Rahm Emanuel Elected Mayor of Chicago)

We are in a critical threshold in Libya. In Green Square, Tripoli "Mad Dog" (Reagan) Qaddafi is threatened. East in Benghazi and Tobruk, old tribal rivalries contend for the upper hand. Chad and Niger mercenaries and other rag-tags ride the streets in pick-up trucks with guns and machetes, AK 47's and shotguns, killing at will. Of course he is threatened. One CNN reporter, the first into Libya, comments, "What we see is the behavior of a cornered animal." Dictator kings have fallen on both sides, Tunisia and Egypt. Qaddafi's life-long revolutionary fiefdom may be unraveling, 42 years since he overthrew King Idris.

The kleptocratic colonel, stealing the commonwealth of the people, has prevented the tremendous oil wealth from trickling down to the

Arab History," *The New York Times*, February 14, 2011.

common people who are plagued by low wages and other depredations. Viewing himself as a reforming ruler, he pledges to defend himself to the "last bullet" and "last drop of blood," "I will die as a martyr." On the side of the liberated, when the journalists arrived today in Benghazi, they were celebrated as in WWII France, with pure ecstasy. Meanwhile Qaddafi taunts his people in an evening speech by asking, "Do you want to be occupied by the U.S., as with Iraq and Afghanistan?"

The deep philosophical and political question arising in the arc of 10 to 12 nations experiencing the "liberty revolution" is expressed by Secretary of State Hilary Clinton and President Obama's dictum: These governments must desist from doing violence to their own people and "respect their universal human rights, especially assembly and speech and the right to determine their own future." The U.N. met today to condemn the violence and murder of peoples. It has not taken firmer actions open to it, no-fly-zone over Tripoli (U.S. and European?), sanctions, and military interventions, charges of crimes against humanity, because of the insistence of Russia and China that these are internal matters. The U.N., we must remember, created the state of Libya in the 1950's.

February 24, 2011

Tomorrow is Friday, the Day of Prayers. The Colonel seems to be losing ground.

In America and Western Europe the panic button has been pushed. The stock market has crashed. Gas prices are going through the roof. Here is how Tom Friedman sees it:

> It is about time. For the last 50 years, America has treated the Middle East as if it were just a collection of big gas stations: Saudi station, Iran station, Kuwait station, Bahrain station, *Egypt* station, Libya station, Iraq station, *United Arab Emirates* station, etc. Our message to the region has been very consistent: "Guys, here's the deal. Keep your pumps open, your oil prices low, don't bother the Israelis too much and, as far as we're concerned, you can do whatever you want out back. You can deprive your people of whatever civil rights you like. You can engage in however much corruption you like. You can preach whatever intolerance from your mosques that you like. You can print whatever conspiracy theories about us in your newspapers that you like. You can keep your women

as illiterate as you like. You can create whatever vast welfare-state
economies, without any innovative capacity, that you like. You
can under-educate your youth as much as you like. Just keep your
pumps open, your oil prices low, don't hassle the Jews too much,
and you can do whatever you want out back.[2]

Though we may wonder where Friedman gets the notion that the
problem in the Middle East is "welfare-state economies," his point of
ethical duplicity is accurate. Do we support the arousal of freedom and
democracy, a breakthrough of our finest values? Qaddafi is now blaming
al-Qaeda (along with Osama Bin Laden and drinking Nescafe) for the
uprising. After all, the North-African branch of *al-Qaeda* has condemned
Qaddafi and supported the uprising of the reformers. Or are we se-
cretly committed to middle East autocracies, militaristic, security-states,
"strong-men" with antipathies to terrorism, devotees of our mischievous
values like surveillance, resort to torture, bring in the oil at any cost, etc.?
One way to further analyze this discrepancy of values and value-conflicts
is to sketch the Jekyll/Hyde profile of Qaddafi?

Some years ago I was asked to offer counsel in a decision at Princeton
University over accepting an endowed chair in Interfaith Studies and Ethics from the Libyan leader. University leaders decided to decline the offer.
What are the positive attributes of the leader and his deficiencies? His
flaws now rise as a terrible specter before the watching world population.

He and his forces and thugs have opened lethal fire with live ammo
on his own citizens, bombings of his own cities, and thousands have been
and will be killed, just in the recent events. He has generated terrorist
acts, Lockerbie and other plane bombings; kleptomaniac stealing of the
people's petro-dollars for his own enrichment and the establishment of a
spying and internally-violent state. He was especially vindictive and vicious to those who had crossed him, torture, imprisonment, Javert-like
hunting down, assassination, squads across the world, and all the rest. In
light of this profile he deserves the justice of banishment and disgrace.

Yet, I believe that the process should be that proffered Hosni
Mubarak, respect for the aged father in the house, truth and reconciliation, a protected retirement, should be offered to him , not for any goodness on his part but for reason of a meaningful new state to rise in the
years ahead. Because of the reforms he has already enacted, based on

2. Thomas L. Friedman, "If Not Now, When?" *The New York Times*, February 23,
2011.

his original intent that was revolutionary and an appropriate response to Italian colonialism and genocide, wise arbiters, like Aref Ali Nayed, should be dispatched by Interfaith Central, to negotiate this transition. Libyans, like Tunisians, Egyptians and all the uprising peoples are historic and great peoples who alone can put together a new, peaceful, just, and faith-filled future for the region. So let it be.

Some strengths(virtues) can be offered in the support of this proposal:

Tribal hospitality is an ancient value that Qaddafi affirms. When a besieged reporter sought refuge in a home near Green Square he was welcomed. "The Libyan people believe in One God, therefore we are all brothers," he was told. In the same light one Mullah preached at Friday prayers (February 25) on Qur'an ". . . if you dislike your ruler, do not raise your sword." This accords with the Christian teaching (" Obey your rulers, they rule by God," Rom 12).

Colonel Qaddafi is also instructed by "Islamic Egalitarianism," where "in the eyes of God all are equal."

After nearly 50 percent of the eastern Province of Libya was killed between 1911 and 1943 by the colonial occupiers (Italians), Colonel Qaddafi committed himself to "be a bulwark against the predations of the West." At the originating heart of his revolution was a salutary idea, opposition to colonialism and imperialism.

In recent years Qaddafi had renounced "WMD's" and had proposed a unitary Israeli/Palestinian State, Israel, in his ill-conceived words, despite his daughter being killed by American bombings.

What will be the end scenario? As many have said, once one fires to kill his own people he has signed his own death sentence. Qaddafi probably will not go easily, a close associate may kill him as July 20 officers sought with Hitler or he may commit suicide as the Fuhrer did ultimately in the bunker.

Revolution is a complex phenomenon. The English and American revolutions were influential in world history but none, not even the Russian or Chinese, was as salient as the French. *Liberté, égalité,* and *fraternité* are enshrined values, deeply embedded in the religious heritage, their power and ever-fresh currency is unimaginable apart from Judaism, Christianity and an heir of these two faiths, Islam. Even Buddhism bears a profound sense of spiritual and political freedom and power.

These are the cache of universal values for that now countless citizens of Middle East nations have sacrificed their lives, yet they are espoused by Q. These are the values spoken of by President Obama and U.N. Secretary Ban Ki-moon, the universal rights of speech and assembly, of travel and press, of being free from tyranny and persecution, free to choose and make one's life. Life, liberty and the pursuit of happiness is the Enlightenment-Jeffersonian twist. And as many recent studies of the American Enlightenment (Great Awakening) show, even Jefferson is working from a theological agenda.

March 1, 2011

Off to London, Heathrow this evening. It will be exciting to be around Cambridge, King's College with Evensong and good colleagues from many fields arranged by our linguist son, Bert. The Divinity Faculty provides my main circle of associates, interfaith studies, Islamic and Jewish colleagues, outstanding historical and biblical colleagues, especially in first century and Jewish-Christianity studies. In these three weeks, I plan to hone in on two areas, Van Gogh studies, which looks at Vincent's ministry in England and further in-depth consideration of the version of British evangelicalism, Bishop Usher, the Scofield Bible, dispensationalism, John Darby and the deeper impulses of East Anglia theology, Puritanism, Wesleyanism, etc., all of which shaped Vincent's faith and world-view. Secondly, I will be working on my project on the interfaith dimension of the freedom uprisings in the Middle East. I'm also interested in pondering, on a deeper level, exported American-based Evangelicalism and Zionism, as it rises in the political and economic milieu in movements such as the American Tea party, the Methodist circuit-riders (I'd like to see those fat guys on a horse) and the Ten-Commandments, murder movement in Uganda.

My hunch is that Islam is a formidable contributor within both the arousal of and certain challenges to the issues raised from Tunis to Tripoli and beyond. Christianity is also a formidable force in Africa and in the modern Western world. Judaism, of course, is an indispensible player both in her originating influence on faith and value formation and the enigmatic mystery of her history, especially in the modern world. I am also testing the triangular hypothesis that interfaith perspectives, however nascent and difficult to grasp in this age of fundamentalisms and parochial passions, have attended the inspirations and the ongoing formulations of the revolution and the reconstruction.

March 4, 2011

Safely ensconced in Cambridge. The cornered Libyan "bull dog" is growling and attacking rebel outposts with mercenaries and obsolete but deadly MIG fighters. Defense Secretary Gates threatens a "no-fly zone" imposed by NATO, which means the U.S. The fervent movement called *Dar al-Islam* by Islamophiles and *al-Qaeda* by Islamaphobes is back in the picture by activation or insinuation. In Yemen, for example, small in comparison to the other reforming players but big because of the ripple effect into Saudi Arabia, and Tom Friedman's warning about our "spigot diplomacy," Abdul Majeed al-Zindani appears in the capital's square along with ten men with AK-47's to declare that an "Islamic state is coming." For much of *Maison Blanc* and the CIA this "funder of terrorism" and friend more of Osama than Obama, is public enemy number one and not a pastor of the people. Yet, ironically, he is on the same side as the Western patriots calling for regime change as he chants that Sahan Chieftain Saleh "came to power by force and not by the will of the people." The beat—and the still-obscure *denouement*—goes on.

In Cambridge we did our Friday prayers at Christ College (with the haunts of Darwin and Milton supervening from the hallowed halls of all saints). The Rev. Dr. Sarah Coakley, of the Divinity Faculty, gave the meditation on "bread," where she sought us to attend all the famished peoples in the world who now hunger for the bread of justice as well as food, in keeping with the biblical truth. "Give us today tomorrow's bread." Earlier that morning, I was in Sarah's class as she pondered the meaning of "soul" in metaphysics, which we both agree and teach has much to do with the substance of theological and natural truth. If "soul" is rendered ethereal, it is not fully human and if it is rendered material, it is not fully divine. So the prayers, once again, around the world, for Libya, Egypt, Somalia and Congo, France and China, and all others, are for "bread for the world," in all its satisfying and sustaining substance.

March 6, 2011

Sunday Matins or Eucharist and Evensong at close of week-days are the central anchor of my being while in Cambridge. As any reader of my books (especially the diary-type narratives) can see, many of my centering thoughts arise at these great worship centers in Oxford and Cambridge.

Today after Matins at Kings, I visit with some fellows and students. My ruminations focus on the seminar I will give at Kings next week, on the "Uprising in the Middle East/Interfaith Perspectives."

My reflections on this day are largely beyond the vicissitudes of this world. As one of my editors at the *The New York Times* chided, "Vaux, you watch too much CNN" (now *Al Jazeera*). But now I'm meditating, as at Christ College on Friday, on the beginning of Lent this week, on the mysteries of grace and judgment, of this world and that to come, of forgiveness, suffering and resurrection. All of this is mightily biographical after meeting our son Bert's new girlfriend last night, a Scot lassie from Ayershire, her parents having met in Edinburgh about the same time I met my bonnie lassie, Sara on Auld Reekie, now 50 years ago. In defense of my persistent worldliness, remember my mentors, Barth and Levinas, with Bible in one hand and the newspaper in the other.

Arriving back at the flat, I'm inspired to quickly recover course. Prime Minister Cameron has just seen *The King's Speech* and sees himself as the good World War II King, or perhaps Winston. He may have even have dispatched the "special forces" embarrassingly captured and given safe passage out by rebel forces. U.S. Defense Secretary Gates asks Cameron to chill out for the moment.

I ask myself whether using the military against one's own people is a war crime. Today the elite Khamis brigade, named for the Qaddafi who commands it, surrounds the small town of Zawiyah, and indiscriminately opens fire on the citizens with mortars, machine guns and other heavy weapons. It's a martyr's witness, like Gandhi's Salt March right into the teeth of death. I ask whether there is not a better way or must blood, "always be the seed . . .?" Colonel Qaddafi may not be as amenable to moral suasion as was the British Raj. He may see himself as the defender and savior of his people. I'm not sure either whether his wife hears divine voices that Muammar is destined to save the people and her palaces.

"They have used gas," one said," when you leave they will shoot us with machine guns." Can Qaddafi not see that he will never be at home again in his own country, so many killed? And what of his son? "The way he punishes and kills his own people," said another, "only Mussolini and Hitler have done that."

Rashid Khalidi of Columbia is one of our best political experts on the Middle East. The Palestinian scholar conveys wisdom to be compared with his deceased compatriot, Edward Said. He writes in *The Nation* of March 21, 2011:

> Today Turkey does provide a model of how to reconcile a powerful military establishment with democracy, and a secular system with a religious orientation among much of the populace. It also serves as a model of economic success, of a workable cultural synthesis between East and West, and of how to exert influence on the world stage. In all these respects, it is perceived as a more attractive model than what is widely seen in the Arab world as a failed alternative: the thirty-two-year-old Iranian theocratic system.[3]

I agree with Khalidi that a new kind of state needs to emerge in the world starting with the peoples at earth's spiritual epicenter in the Middle East. If the present uprising can yield a community of holistic, right-minded states, each unique, of course, but having the common denominators of popular reciprocity and support, economic vitalities and vibrant cultures, democratic, pluralistic and religious (within the ethos of each particular heritage), then the blood will not have been shed in vain.

That the West installed these dictatorial states as it dismantled the Ottoman Empire was a political blunder that has come back to haunt us. In place of what I have offered as states with faith and interfaith sensibilities, Khalidi offers secular states with a kind of Habermasian public-square ethos with religious systems having a voice at the table but not special privilege. A long-time colleague in Chicago, Khalidi and I agree that at this moment of history that Israeli and Christian Zionism must be buffered, along with militant Islam, into a more secular and pluralistic religio-political ethos.

Combating the terribly distorted media depiction of the Middle East, Khalidi reminds us of the great wisdom hospitality and generosity of those peoples and of the historical blossoming of democracy in the Ottoman Empire of the 1870's (before Western machinations). To this I would add the historical recollection of Amartya Sen, son of both Cambridge

3. Rashid Khalidi, "The Arab Spring," *The Nation*, March 21, 2011.

Universities, now chairing the Harvard center of Economics and Ethics, that town meetings and participatory forms of government begin as much in Western Asia, Indo-Europe, and the Middle East as they do in Greece, Europe, Britain, and the U.S. A careful theologian, Khalidi offers a cautionary note.

> Nothing has yet been resolved in any Arab country, not even in Tunisia or Egypt, where the despots are gone but a real transformation has barely begun . . . All of it could turn sour, whether through civil war in Libya or Yemen, paralysis in Tunisia and Egypt, or endless fruitless contestation with those in power in Bahrain, Jordan, Morocco, Oman, Iraq and elsewhere.[4]

This may be the Hobbesian scenario. I hope for the Augustinian, where *Civitas Dei* continues in creative but non-utopian tension, with *Civitas Terrena.*

March 8, 2011(Shrove Tuesday)

Simon Shama is back at his old haunts tonight. From his home in Amsterdam, he came to read history at Cambridge. Now teaching history at Columbia, I am moved by his documentary on the great artists, Van Gogh included. I also hear that his History of England is outstanding. He spoke this evening at St. Edmunds on the new project, Jews among the Nations, a history of toleration and persecution. As the Middle East continues to unfold, the issue of Israel among the nations is critical. I keep hoping that Israel will join a confederacy of Middle East Nations to foster economic and cultural development and supply the cornerstone for interfaith interchange and practical cooperation.

Appeals are out today for a "no-fly zone" to check on Colonel Qaddafi and his continuing violence against his own people. He is now blocking the supply of aid, wheat, and foodstuffs from the Red Cross and Red Crescent to millions of people. Requests are being received by the U.S., England, and NATO and by Turkey and Egypt. The latter response might carry far more credibility. Qaddafi seems quite content to starve his people into submission even if direct machine-gun fire fails.

In America, President Obama distances himself from advisors such as Hilary Clinton and Bob Gates by saying that Qaddafi must step down

4. Ibid.

now and that American assets must be put in place now so that the U.S. and world have full "capacity to act if we have a humanitarian crisis on our hands." This coincides with my concerns that we are already dealing with "humanitarian crisis" and "war crimes" that now require international intervention.

March 9, 2011 (Ash Wednesday)

Today, in Britain, gasoline is six pounds ($10) a gallon. In America, when I started driving, it was 20 cents. Europe relies on Libyan oil, especially Italy. Colonel Qaddafi continues to fire on his own people with weapons supplied by a U.S. contract through General Dynamics for $165 million. The "Golden Rule"—those who have the gold make the rules. I can only wonder whether this domino effect of freedom will end in Libya. If oil rules the world, won't it wind down to France, Britain, Italy, and the U.S. sending advisors who are actually "oil futures venture capitalists?" C'est la vie.

Muammar al Qaddafi, once an anti-imperialist, is imperialist in his shrinking empire in a most imperious way. Beginning as a tyrannical reformer and a cooperative head of state (weapons of mass destruction), currying the favor of the West, he has gone the way of a megalomaniac Robert Mugabe and now terrorizes Israel, America, and Europe, along with his own people.

Professor Hamid Dabashi, who holds the major Chair in Middle-Eastern studies at Columbia University, whose roots and expertise are in Iran, feels that, as in his homeland, freedom and democracy will only come as there is some building of human-rights-type institutions, labor unions, women's and students organizations and (various religious and interfaith associations, my extrapolation). The three regional types of this character, Mugabe, Ahmadinejad and Qaddafi, all duplicitous and dangerous, pose similar issues for peace and justice in the world.

Dabashi's reflection shows how deeply ingrained are the scars of Western colonialism and the stigmata of post-Ottoman manipulations. These wounds may portend even greater healing possible after the surgery is complete in these exceptional lands and peoples.

The greatest grounds for hope right now in Libya is today's report in *The Wall Street Journal* that Qaddafi's inner council of leaders has offered to meet with opposition and tribal leaders to discuss an orderly step-down and transition. I've learned from friends in East Libya that legal scholars, presumably with the learned theological (e.g., Nayed) and philosophical experts, have been preparing constitutional documents, both in terms of human rights and governmental processes. Perhaps as the acute–and so dangerous–phase of this uprising recedes, such careful preparations can prove useful. In Brussels tomorrow, the EU ponders "no fly." Sarkozy and France have declared their own, as is fitting with their so advanced doctrines of *liberté, égalité,* and *fraternité.*

March 11, 2011

I met with my old acquaintance and admired teacher, Eamon Duffy, before his class on Theology and the History of Art. In his office before class, I told him that his work in past years was a factor in my pursuit of the present project on Van Gogh. He was especially intrigued with the Rubens connection and the coming work in Antwerp Cathedral and environs. Like most of the Divinity Professors , Janet Soskice, Ian Winter, Philip Ford, Sarah Coakley, Catherine Pickstock (giving a lecture tonight on theology and politics), and others, he challenges the paradigms. With his stripping the altars he showed that our concepts of "Catholic" and "Reformation" were terribly simplistic. He changed the course of Church history.

Libya seems to be thrashing out like a wild boar. Perhaps he is seeking to establish his chips at the poker bargaining-table that inevitably must come.

As with Egypt, one must be filled with admiration and hope for this nation and people because of its history and heritage as well as her promise for the future. Libya resides at the crossroads of nations and history. She is a rich store of Greek and Roman cities. Christians will remember the Cyrene pilgrims at Pentecost and one, named Simon, would to God that there was still the vibrant Jewish Diaspora around the Mediterranean and up into Europe, who would literally "take up the cross and follow," like the other insurgent or thief, who was "crucified with Christ."

Sabratha, Leptis Magna (Lepdah), Tripoli and Benghazi are rich centers of classical, Islamic (643), Byzantine, Ottoman (1551) and modern history, a chain of Phoenician (Punic) ports stretching like pearls from the Levant around to Spain. The sea of sand called the Sahara flows into this artifact of ancient and modern states constituting 90 percent of the Libyan land mass. Oases and caravan towns such as Ghadames and Ghat are rich in legend, lore and the concrete history of the Silk Road (southern branch) that ties East to West through the middle, the Middle East or Western Asia, axis site to the ancient epicenter of secular and sacred history.

Modern history has not been kind to this ancient seat of culture and commerce. In 1911, the Italians invaded the nation, killed one fourth of the inhabitants in the Western region and set up three decades of occupation culminating in the conflicted events of world wars and more recent political intrigues. A desperately poor nation discovered oil in 1959 following independence in 1951. Colonel Qaddafi and the Revolutionary Command Council seized power from the king in 1969. Now Libyan leaders abroad are seeking international recognition for a National Transition Council. States are born and die like the sparks from a campfire, before the One before whom all nations will bow and all tongues confess, the One God of history.

The U.S. declared Libya a "terrorist state" during the Reagan years after Pan Am Flight 103 from Lockerbie, Scotland exploded in December 1988, and other bombings, bombing Tripoli and killing Qaddafi's daughter. Recent rapprochement with the U.S. and the West, after eschewing terrorism, calling for a dual or unified Israeli State (with the Palestinians) and giving up "WMD's" is now strained by the regime's attempt to crush the reform sweeping the region, flushed with petrodollars, armed to the teeth with arms shipments, now boycotted by Russia and the West, though heartily supplied in due capitalist season, she has become the lynch-pin for the freedom revolution of 2010-2011.

As Libya enters the 21st century, she will be a dynamic player in the unfolding drama of the nations on the stage of world history. With a resident, predominantly Muslim population, she will be a place of faith and hopefully interfaith toleration and cooperation, one who welcomes churches and houses of worship for other faiths As a player on the world stage, political and economic, African and Arab, she will continue to find herself at the crossroads of Orthodoxy (Greece, Russia, Balkans), Christianity, the U.S., Africa, and Judaism in the U.S. and Israel.

Democratic and pluralistic constitutions will rise to the surface now, or in the coming decades, unless dark forces intercede. A vital secular state undergirded by vital faith is my hope, the hope of her martyr-patriots, secular, Muslim, Christian, and the hope of the world.

March 12, 2011

Last evening at McCrumm Hall in the Eagle Pub Close, which says something about the great wisdom of Cambridge academic life, Catherine Pickstock, a Van Gogh starry night light in the Divinity firmament, delivered the Bullinger Lecture, first given by T.S. Eliot, in philosophy of religion. Her subject was theology and world order. Her argument and conclusion are close to mine, or rather mine are to hers, except for a few flourishes. In the realm of public philosophy, which we also call public theology, modernity, which we presently struggle through, inherits two moods, ways of life, and convictions from the Medieval period.

First there is the Duns Scotus view, something like Occam's razor, which involves measuring, counting, designating, dividing, delineating, a violent mood that cuts into discreet entities, affirms nationism and sovereign separation of peoples, in sum the quiddity, the thingness of things, Descartes' extension, a mood that fears that we can only know and manipulate particulars, while universals are ineffable and elusive even if they are real.

Invoking an image of Blaise Pascal, one who struggled with the mathematical and the mystical, deciding for the *Coeur et sa raison*. We see a town, a dot on a map, a pin-point that we can bomb devastation unaffected with Dr. Strangelove from our high soaring Hiroshima distance in our epistemological B-29, releasing, in J. Robert Oppenheimer's words, the radiant terror of the Vedas, 1000 suns. We can either do it in person or with the weaponry we supply Colonel Qaddafi.

Pascal and Pickstock invite us to walk into town, to see the leaves and the trees, smell the scents and the cooking-fires, even the grain of wheat we know of old and new whirls a splendorous cosmos, mingling the mitochondrial substance from the dawn of the cosmos and the creative beyond. Here we see the faces, each unique and quintessential to the whole. Here we feel the pulse of humanity, yea divinity, within the common life.

This is the second medieval posture toward reality that Pickstock offers for today's global issues and international relations. We now need to set our sights on the infinite beyond impinging on the finite. If the earth in Japan can move on its axis, plates move three meters overnight, Japans coastline recedes two meters and tsunami tides sweep 10 miles inland, then we know that even the material world is a moving feast rather than fixed in place by our confining reason. A thousand people here today and gone tomorrow, in Japan or Libya, is also evidence that life is transient as is death. As Leonard Bernstein reminded us in *Candide (1953)* and his version of Romeo and Juliet, *West Side Story (1961),* with life under the conditions of time and eternity, ethics and bewilderment, love and death, "there's a place for us, a time and place for us . . . somehow, some day, *somewhere*"(Stephen Sondheim, "Somewhere," 1956/57).

Drawing on Suarez, and his laws of nations, Pickstock contends that we could well anchor our pitiful human negotiations, Egypt, Tunisia, Morocco, Libya, in *jus naturalis and jus divinitatis.* Only order fully human and fully divine will be able to reconstitute peace with justice. We need to rediscover from our constrictive categories of thought covenants of mutuality and transcendence, only thus can we move beyond our vicious mentality to a kind of generosity and universal human awareness. Such mentality, which she finds in Aquinas as well as in Avicenna's study of Augustine, can offer hope in the world in place of meanness and self-serving. Then spontaneity and surprise, right ordering and redemption, can accompany our international orderings and *Hashem*, the One Name above every name, the infinity of human namings, can make all things new.

Augustine, with whom we began, proposes a frustrating paradox; we must struggle with all our might to live in justice and peace in this world, even though true justice and peace will always elude us here, in fact our utopias will always turn on us to our terror and horror. Here is where we need the counsel of our more secular, more down-to-earth Semitic bookends in the rainbow of world faith. As you consult both Ibn Sina and Ben Maimon on Augustine, you first see that they gravitate from Plato to Aristotle for a more naturalistic vision. Then they both say this, if you want real justice and peace, seek that from above, in the concrete commands of *Hashem* Allah, to borrow a bit of Maimonides' Judao-arabic, in the Common Word of the love of God and, equally important if you seek here and now the peace with justice of *Civitas Dei*, do it now, put down your swords and money boxes and seek the love of others and let righteousness right now, roll down like rivers.

That, my colleagues, is the challenge of this present hour.

March 15, 2011

The talk given at Kings College went well. Some 20 people, students and professors, townspeople and members of various interfaith associations, gathered to hear and discuss the preceding section of this diary. One Jewish woman from Cairo lamented the proselytizing activities, Christians of Jews, in past years in Egypt. She had been coerced to become a Christian as a youth, she said. Now she had been forced to the very sad task of rejecting Christ for the sake of the integrity of her Jewish faith. She would find it very hard to forgive these well-meaning but misguided Christians for manipulating her in that way.

I told her that many of my colleagues are Christians while remaining observant Jews. She would have none of it. I told her of the numerous professors at Cambridge whose specialty is the first century before "the parting of the ways," when there was a phenomenon we might call "Jewish Christianity." I assured her that most Christian bodies had formally accepted the permanence and lasting validity of God's covenant with Israel and God's continuing purpose with this people in the world. I asked if she was aware of and what she thought of the disavowal by Catholicism, Orthodoxy and most Protestantism of supercessionism (the idea that the Jewish faith has been superseded by the Christian), and asked for forgiveness of the violence Christians have done to Jews from the earliest Christian centuries. She was too offended and wounded to consider any of these points.

The news today from the Middle East is not good. Colonel Q is advancing with the full force of American and British armaments against the reformers, even approaching Benghazi. Secretary of State Clinton has met with European leaders in Brussels, where I head in a few days, then on to Tunisia and Egypt, to shore up the fragile new situations there. The G-8 has opposed a no-fly zone, led by Germany that wishes not to get involved in anything protracted in Africa or the Middle East, so terrifying has been the U.S. occupations of Iraq and Afghanistan, and the endorsed and funded Israeli occupation of Palestine territories. Meanwhile Britain and France are prepared to do it on their own (frightening thought). President Obama meanwhile vacillates, while outright brutality and war-crimes ensue across Libya. I wrote to the president this morning, signing the petition to immediately extend a no-fly-zone as requested by the Arab League and almost everyone here in Europe and in the Middle East.

While I Have Being

David Ford, head of the Cambridge Interfaith Center and my mentoring colleague here at the Divinity Faculty, handed me today the critical document from the religious leadership of Libya entitled Network of Free Ulema. It reads:

> In the Name of God, the Merciful, the Compassionate, Blessings upon our Prophet Mohammad, his kin, and his companions.
> We are a network of some of Libya's most senior and most respected Muslim religious scholars with various specializations and tribal backgrounds from across our beloved Libya. Out network also includes some of the most respected Sufi teachers in our country. Some top judges, lawyers, doctors, engineers, university professors and intellectuals, as well as writers and poets, are also members. Our network includes both men and women, old and young, locally educated and educated-abroad. We are not a political party, and our only agenda is that of upholding the highest religious, spiritual, moral, and human values and the service of our beloved Libya. We are diverse groups of different schools and outlooks, and we believe in the richness of plurality, and the wisdom of dialogue and communication with all other faiths and cultures. Our network is only one dimension of Libya's very rich and sophisticated civil society, which has always been there, but has had to go clandestine for many years because of the regime's repressive policies. In the new Libya, all these seeds will sprout into a rich and vibrant culture, unified, and mutually respectful. For the time being, security conditions do not allow us to publish a list of members. We will publish such a list as soon as we can.[5]

How I wish our good, free, democratic, generous and faithful land could renew its reputation as a haven for the oppressed, the world's "huddled masses yearning to breathe free" and rid ourselves of the reputation of the harbinger of violence in the world, the bad cop, even to our own poor and oppressed, say the millions of blacks in our jails. People all over the world know that our roots are in liberty, justice, and peace and that we are just on a temporary stint of forsaking those cardinal virtues and values.

5. "An Introduction to the Network of Free Ulema," Network of Free Ulema website, http://freeulema.org/.

March 17, 2011

A lovely Lenten Concert at Trinity presented by their mixed voice Chapel Choir. Somber-death, but hopeful-life texts. "The Worldes Joie," by an anonymous poet, was set to a sublime music by Arnold Bax:

> 'Winter wakeneth al my care,
> Nou this leves waxeth bare;
> Ofte I sike ant moume sare
> When hit cometh in my thot
> Of this worlds joie,
> Hou hit goth al to noht.
> I added my own with the help of a Prudentius text (348 c.e.):
> Take him earth for cherishing, to thy tender breast receive him.
> Desert and sea enfold and engulf him
> Libya and Japan now hold him
> Lenten souvenirs.
> Take him to sand and sea for cherishing,
> to thy tender breast receive him.

(Anonymous, "The Worldes Joie," c. 1300)

In Libya today, the word is ominous. The resigned Ambassador to the U.N. says that genocide and cleansing will begin in 10 hours. The only help would come from a no-fly-zone, but the U.N. "fiddles while Rome burns," and Obama waffles. Colonel Qaddafi has given orders, the Ambassador says, to destroy everything and kill whoever you find in the Eastern city of Ajdabiya. James Claxton has again invited Bo and myself me to High Table at Jesus—always a joy.

March 19, 2011

Arrived safely in Antwerp. Yesterday, in Cambridge, I conferred with my good friend and interfaith mentor, David Ford, who had written an opinion essay in last weekend's *London Times* on Libya. He suggested I send the talk I gave at King's College last week to the editor.

Today is a crucial day. The coalition, which we used to refer jokingly as America, the United States, England, Great Britain, and the United Kingdom, has given an ultimatum to Libya to cease fire or it is prepared to take action, "no fly" or whatever is necessary to stop Qaddafi's "war crimes" of killing his own people. Qaddafi says he has ordered cease fire but assaulting continues unabated in several cities, Benghazi, Misrata, Ajdabiya and Zawiya and apparently he has the goons bombarding Tripoli. Are Qaddafi and Qaddafi, Jr. really there, we may ask.

Qaddafi asks for observers from China, Russia, Germany, Malta and Turkey to verify the cease-fire and today the foreign ministers meet in Paris to plan "the political strategy" that will go into effect in the next 48 hours if Qaddafi has not withdrawn from the coastal cities. The new coalition, which includes much of NATO and some Arab nations, is already amassing ships and air power to counter the air, sea, and land forces, which we have provided Qaddafi in the recent years of *rapprochement*.

At six p.m. in Antwerp, it seems that it may be over in Libya. Rumor has it that Qaddafi has decided to take a holiday in Venezuela. Thank God for Chavez. Stay tuned.

March 20, 2011

False alarm. He's still here. Supporters are building a human shield around his house as they did when Ronald Reagan bombed him in 1986 and America did when his daughter was killed earlier. Last night the formidable "air armada" swung into action in response to the U.N. resolution that held that grave humanitarian issues were at stake when the government and army (mercenaries) launched attacks against civilians, those citizens now taking up defense of their homes and towns. The U.N. has the right and duty to protect persons when they appeal to the world. This action the U.S., Britain and France made clear, was a prelude to imposing a no-fly-zone.

Another grave concern has been Qaddafi's masochistic readiness concerning his people, towns, and self. "Even if I go up in flames . . . to the last drop of blood . . . if the world goes crazy . . . we will turn their lives into hell. The Mediterranean will be ravaged. No air or sea traffic will be safe."[6] Obviously the leader's sanity and veracity have pretty well been self invalidated.

By contrast truth, justice, and faith claims have been made on this weekend:

> *Prime Minister David Cameron*: "This course is good and just and right. There is a moral cause for action, the duty to stop a humani-

---

6. "'Hell' Awaits Anyone Who Attacks Libya," *The Daily Star*, March 19, 2011.

tarian crisis from unfolding. But the case for action is also rooted in our hard-headed national interest."[7]

President Obama: "Our goal is focused, our cause is just, and our coalition is strong."[8]

Rabbi Jonathan Sacks: "From the Hebrews we get human rights, freedom, and right to life . . ." From the Greeks, Democracy, free from tyranny . . .

Tony Blair: "moral outrage" and strategic interests must be combined. Democracy, the rule of law and human rights are universal not just Western values, the universal values of the human spirit, includes free speech, assembly, freedom of religion and free markets. Such comprehensive scheme of values, personal and political, may entail not only immediate protection against the abrogation of those rights but something like a Marshall Plan of Development with at least some of these values: Spread of democracy and universal values, modernization plus reasonable pace of change, sensitivity to the special needs of particular peoples, capital development and regional economic opportunity and growth, resolution of the Israel-Palestinian crisis that threatens the region and world. And finally resolve the persisting concern with Iran (WMD's)."[9]

March 21, 2011

In London, at St. Ethelburga's Church, a victim of WWII bombing, in the midst of the financial district, the Cambridge Interfaith program has helped put up a "Tent of Abraham" where various programs of interfaith activity take place. Dialogues with people from around the world, Asia and Africa, America and Europe, the Middle East and Russia, considering issues of world conflict, justice and peace, of poverty, sharing and relief of starvation, all within the purview of interfaith wisdom.

Tonight we witness another Bedouin tent in Tripoli, Libya. Shrapnel from last night's saturation bombing can be seen scattered. Colonel

7. *Daily Mail U.K.*, February 15, 2011.

8. President Barack Obama, Address on America's response to the situation in Libya, March 18, 2011, Washington, D.C. The full address can be accessed at http://www.whitehouse.gov/blog/2011/03/18/president-libya-our-goal-focused-our-cause-just-and-our-coalition-strong.

9. Roland Watson and Jill Sherman, "Cameron Abandons Softy-Softly Approach to Whitehall," *The Times of London*, March 19, 2011.

Qaddafi, the "great Father of the revolution," as he calls himself, says that many innocents were killed—the U.S. said that Qaddafi had the corpses removed from the city morgue to plant at the tent for international media to observe. The old game again. The U.S. might as well admit that there will be numerous collateral casualties from our answer to the call of the rebels, Arab League and pretty much the world community, and we know that Qaddafi is a liar, which is the rule of the game in war, politics and business, at the very least.

Tents of Abraham—these are places in theological history of profound enmity and surprise visitation and hospitality, places of showdown as well as truth, even revelation. In the tents of Abraham, like the bosom of Abraham, "all is made plain." It is like the temple of God for God dwells in those divine and human places. They are places for the lost and the stranger, even the enemy is here given refuge. *Civitas Dei* and *Civitas Terrena*, will the anguish of world history ever be transfigured into justice, hospitality and concord? God only knows.

For now we must seek cease-fire, cessation of violence and an end to the old ways of dealing with one's own people and others. The tents of Marmre and Abraham, like the tents of the "next one," *nachsten*, neighbor, are residence to the other whom we are to serve with our food and drink, our clothes and shelter, our attention and love, even the laying down of our lives for our friends.

March 25, 2011

Day two in Amsterdam, day three tomorrow and back to Antwerp. This was a very successful research time. The Reich's Museum, Van Gogh Museum and the Van Gogh research center and library have all been useful. Seeing again the basic Rembrandts and Vermeers and perhaps 40 key Van Goghs whet the appetite and the scholars and librarians at the Research *Bibliothek* were most helpful. Telo Meedendrop and Louis Van Tilburgh are both exceptional scholars. Louis has written hundreds of the most important works on Van Gogh, for example most of the interpretive essays in the important Paris conference on Millet and Van Gogh. They have asked to see the manuscript I'm polishing up now with the view of perhaps publishing it through the Van Gogh Foundation.

Meanwhile, on the world front, 15,000 are dead in Japan and 15,000 missing. Rockets fly from Gaza into Israel and back following a suicide bomber yesterday. In Libya, President Obama is trying to hand over the bombing and no-fly responsibility to NATO. In Tripoli, many areas are ablaze from coalition bombing that seeks to protect citizens from being attacked. The strife between Qaddafi forces and rebels seems at a stand-off. In South Syria, government forces kill many and President Bashar al-Assad has guaranteed higher wages and more democratic rights. The exuberance of the first wave of martyrdom for freedom and opportunity seems to have receded while the hard work to consolidate gains is just beginning.

March 27, 2011

Fiona's birthday party. What a blast! Sara senior arrived safely but tore her knee again getting out of Kris's car or lugging those four bags.

I spent the day at Sunday service at the cathedral, the most inhospitable cathedral in the world. Peter Paul Rubens must be ashamed that the place is always under lock-down and with exorbitant entrance fees. An interesting collection of cognate works there for an exposition beyond the treasures of the house. The three I focused on this morning were "The Elevation of the Cross" and "The Descent from the Cross"—both triptychs, and the little "Last Supper," which makes me wonder whether Van Gogh got his idea for "The Potato Eaters" (his last supper) from this Rubens or Rembrandt's supper at Emmaus.

In the afternoon, a wonderful presentation of Bach's *St. Matthew Passion* was held at St Paul's Church, one of my favorites, at the end of tram line number 7. This *Passion* was the best we have heard since we joined Peter Schrier at Utrecht, some 20 years ago. Two choirs –the children were from Leuven and the adults from Antwerp, as was the orchestra. Good Bach in Catholic (Protestant) Antwerp.

While devastating carnage continued and destruction still simmered in Libya, Bach's *Passion*, prototypic and phenotypic of all world passion, seemed to be a narrative of everything going on in the world, of all terror and transfiguration of life and society, nature and history, existential and historical. I'm continually impressed how scripture is always about these two dimensions as if itself belonged to another *dimension.*

Take Isaiah 6, does it belong to the Syro-Ephraimite political crisis or on some plane in the mind of God for all times and places? Or take Matthew. Is it about the Roman occupation of Palestine and the end of historic land and temple-based Judaism as we know it, or is it a sublimely spiritual message for all time and space? For Calvin, these texts reference the sixteenth century of King Francis for Barth and Bonheoffer these scriptures pertain to Nazi time, as if they were meant for that moment. Now they seem meant for Libya, I wonder whether the *Qur'an* and *Hadith* have the same sense of historical-political currency.

The penultimate "Word" in the "St. Matthew Passion" is from a Libyan, Simon of Cyrene, who, as a black guy, was conscripted to carry the cross. He offers this aria:

> *Komm, süßes Kreuz, so will ich sagen, Mein Jesu, gib es immer her! Wird mir mein Leiden einst zu schwer, So hilfst du mir es selber tragen.*

> Come, sweet cross, I will say then: My Jesus, give it always to me. Should my pain become too heavy, Then help me to carry it myself.

(Guiseppe Verdi, "Libera Me," Messa de Requieum, 1868)

The hermeneutic and exposition are complicated, but the meaning is clear. Here on earth, we bear crosses as specimens of the One overarching and undergirding Cross. These are not the little aches and pains so much as they are "taking up our cross to follow . . ." Scripture claims that Christ is crucified from the foundations of the earth. Scripture also implies that the work of the crucifixion continues as the sufferings of Christ are being filled up in the world. *Peccata Mundi* is the enfolding environment of the particular sins, say of Qaddafi, Italy, the U.S., and all other players and parcels of complicit guilt in Libya, Egypt, Tunisia, etc., and of the generic and endemic wrong that informs all activity, even that thought to be noble.

The "St. Matthew Passion" also pertains to the young couple in front of me in the cheap seats at St. Paul. Obviously unacquainted with the subtleties of Christian literature, they stumbled in off the streets to see what was going on with the perhaps 1000 people gathered. It spoke to them, their demeanor showed, I dare say. It reminded me of the afternoon we heard Alec McCowen recite the Gospel of Mark in its entirety in a London theatre. Some women of the street came in and were transfixed, perhaps by hearing these moving words for the first time. Will some Philip mount their chariot to explain the strange words to their lives and situation? I had the thought, but hurried on my way on the other side.

April 3, 2011

This Sunday moves us one week closer to Easter when, *Inshallah*, we will be settled in Paris and be present at Notre Dame. Last night, the Verdi "Requiem Mass," the mother of all requiems, was performed in St. Michelli's in Antwerp. Though I studied the text, I didn't make it as we watched over grand-daughter Fiona while her parents were in England for a house warming.

The juxtaposition of texts strikes me, as the Middle East crisis seems doomed to a stalemate and America makes ready for a massive celebration celebrating working people, this in the wake of the Wisconsin demonstration of public workers, teachers in particular, called by one tea party candidate, "thugs," (like Libyan mercenaries?). What does Verdi's "Requiem Mass" offer to our *Politisches Nachtgebet*?

Take just one portion of the Mass—"Libera me"—always aware that the meditation is profoundly existential, personal, spiritual, and universal:

> Deliver me, o Lord from everlasting death
> on that dreadful day,
> when the heavens and the earth shall be moved.
> When thou shalt come to judge the world
> by fire.
> I quake with fear and I tremble,
> awaiting the day of account and
> the wrath to come
> when the heavens and the earth shall be moved.
> That day, the day of anger, of calamity, of misery,
> that great day and most bitter.
> When thou shalt come to judge the world
> by fire.
> Eternal rest grant them, o Lord,
> and let perpetual light shine upon them.
>
> (Guiseppe Verdi, "Libera Me," Messa de Requieum, 1868)

On Monday, April 4, we will join with friends and colleagues in Europe in a sympathy strike with "the working people of America." It is a day of terror and trial because we are not sure that the majority of American people really want the "Common Good" any more. A growing majority, 53 percent, say no public funding and public programs (at least federal and state) for education, health, retirement, out of work support, public radio, and the likes of these. Police, fire, homeland and national defense and international security, that's pretty much it. The other things should be taken care of privately (tax breaks for the "well-to-do" should cover all needs through the philanthropic mechanism). I guess a 72 year-old man should realize that this "epitome" of "capitalist states" (Max Weber) has always been like this, especially in economic "hard times."

Something, surely, is coming "with fire," even Thomas Jefferson said, "I tremble for my country when I reflect that God is just: that his justice cannot sleep forever."[10] May it have to do with the poor and working people of this land, and the world; the present crisis in the Middle East?

So, what of the immigrant laborers, yard men, food workers, hotel workers, child-care givers, etc. and the broad swath of other "working people," postal workers, garbage workers, health care and education staff, secretaries, teachers, day laborers, construction workers, street workers, assistants in the business world, clerks in stores and shops, single moms, the unemployed and under-employed, what of all of these hard working, heavy lifting, tax- paying folk?

Vincent Van Gogh, the missionary-prophet, as I show in my present research, *The Ministry of Vincent Van Gogh in Religion and Art*, drew at least 500 works on poor laborers: miners, diggers, weavers, sowers, coal and peat carriers; they were his stock in trade, and they are ours. Studs Terkel, look down from heaven on our God-forsaken world, that "good earth" that He created and keeps on creating, with us his co-workers, *Tikkun Olam*. Amen.

April 11, 2011

We're in Paris, beautifully accommodated at Rue de St. Placid, number 48, right in the heart of all the action. On Passion Sunday, we visited our old haunts at the American Church, reconnected with Fred Grahamm, the superb music director and organist. He promised to send me some of the "not-to-be-missed music events" and, when I told him of my project,

10. Thomas Jefferson, "A Denunciation of Slavery," 1785.

he said not to miss *Auvers-sur-Oise*, Vincent's last living and resting place. Will do pretty soon, maybe when our first guests appear. For now we're getting settled in at *Institut Catholique*, just around the corner, getting various passwords, IT connections, etc.

The Middle East awakening seems to have passed and slumber has returned. This strange lack of divine vindication and human verification of the right and the just always shows up on the stage of history. Even the dawning of Christian faith in the world is accompanied by infanticide and genocide. Now things seem to be in stalemate abroad and at home, setting up for a Palm Sunday and Easter, blissfully existential, spiritual, Jungian, as people crave. No transformation of history bringing prophetic command and no transfiguration of nature bringing requirement of change. How did Bonhoeffer put it? "Cheap grace is grace without discipleship, grace without the cross, grace without Jesus Christ. . . ."[11]

My only pacifying pause is taken from yesterday's pastor at American, Bedford Transou, a Methodist from Charleston. He preached on Dry Bones in Ezekiel and John 10, for his message on "Human Fulfillment." Most memorable was his story of an antithesis to the point, Blanche Du-Bois, in *"Streetcar Named Desire"* (1947) by Tennessee Williams, the first American play performed at *Comedie Francaise* in Paris. Take *Streetcar Named Desire* to Cemetery Street and get off at Elysian Fields. Bedford's closing was even better.

In Desmond Tutu's biography, he tells of God in heaven crying profuse tears when he looks on the world, by reason of the suffering we humans inflict on each other, not, as Vincent Van Gogh would say, for his own blunder with the canvas. The tears flow down like rivers. Suddenly, he breaks into a great smile, when, in a Kierkegaardian moment, he finds one person on earth who gets it right, who has a heart for justice and kindness, and his smile becomes a hearty laugh. "By holding others in honor, you vindicate me," laughs God. "You verify the resurrection of my dear Son."[12]

Palm Sunday comes this week, then Easter. In some ways Paris defines Easter, at least in the realm of Organ music, at least in the triumphalist mood of celebration, as I develop in an essay called *Prophètes Parisienne* that I will incorporate into this Diary. Prophets seeks to define

11. Dietrich Bonhoeffer, *The Cost of Discipleship* (New York: Simon & Schuster, 1959), 45.

12. This is my extrapolation from Kierkegaard.

the particular religio-ethical ethos of Paris across the two Christian millennia.

Holy Week, 2011

My reflection at this culmination of Lent/Easter season runs along two paths: 1) vicarious or representational suffering, death and resurrection (in this case Jesus, the Man for Others enacts in His own Flesh and Blood the historical/objective atonement; and 2) the secular rendition of this same scriptural redemptive drama, i.e.—pain, mortality and transfiguration of human beings acting heroically effect moral transformation. I'll focus on a mingled sacred-secular enactment focused on what the French call *resuscitation*. The banner is emblazoned on the catacombs here in Paris, Christ *est ressucité*.

The natural, organic meaning is suggested by the great Easter symbol, the egg, epitomized by the glorious intricacy and color of the Byzantine, Franco-Russian-Faberge egg and the Franco-Russian metaphor of the Swan song (the use of Tchaikovsky as the Eucharistic hymn in the film *Des Hommes et des Dieux, 2010*, Xavier Beauvois, Director). This quasi-religious context is celebrated today through secular analogues and interfaith co-celebration in myriad non-parochial settings. The burden of my ruminations is on the latter theme.

My reading of the Passion narrative is textually focused in sacred and secular renditions of the raising of Lazarus, expressed in my case by Vincent Van Gogh depicting himself, red hair and blue eyes, as Lazarus, in his painting (after Rembrandt) in St. Remy in 1888 and closing with Sören Kierkegaard's gospel midrash on the same parable in "Sickness unto Death" (1849). As I develop thoughts on my thesis, I will also allude incidentally, as I prepare to view the Jesus works of Rembrandt at the Louvre, to the paradigmatic post-resurrection *Word-meal event of the Emmaus incident*.

Between these bookends, I will consider a rich interfaith tapestry of the paschal mystery by three theologians at two periods, the medieval and modern, considering what Avicenna, Aquinas and Maimonides and then Emmanuel Levinas, Paul Ricoeur and Aref Ali Nayed do with death and resurrection in scriptural purview and worldly application.

In *Totality and Infinity*, Emmanuel Levinas argues that "Resurrection constitutes the principal event of time."[13] What is unique to human beings is the confrontation they have with infinity in the suffering and death to that our existence is subject. Even Lazarus cannot disguise the fact that it is Vincent who is "sick unto death." Still we have awareness of infinity from the fact that crucifixion and resurrection occurs within our being and within "being itself." After Heidegger, philosophy must deal with the ultimate conjunction of the Divine and humanity in the phenomenon of death itself in "The Ground of Being."

So we start with Vincent. As I write on the theology and ministry of Van Gogh, I have studied his Arles self-portrait or Alfred Hitchcock-like appearance of himself as Lazarus coming out of the tomb ("Self-Portrait," 1887). The *textus classicus* is John 11 (KJV):

> When Jesus heard that, he said, "This sickness is not unto death" (11:4).

> "Our friend Lazarus sleepeth, but I go to awake him out of sleep . . . Lazarus is dead" (11:11b–14b).

> Jesus saith unto her, "Thy brother shall rise again" (11:23).

> Martha said, "I know that he shall rise again in the resurrection at the last day" (11:24).

> Jesus said, "I am the resurrection and the life: He that believeth in me, though he were dead, yet shall he live and whosoever liveth and believeth in me shall never die" (11:25–26).

> When Jesus therefore saw (Mary) weeping . . . and said, "Where have ye laid him?" Jesus wept (11:33–35).

> He cried with a loud voice, "Lazarus come forth" (11:43b).

13. Emmanuel Levinas, *Totality and Infinity: An Essay on Exteriority* (Pittsburgh:Duquesne University Press, 1969), 284.

VI

Vincent Van Gogh

PARALLEL MEDITATIONS ON RESURRECTION

THIS SCRIPTURE WAS DEEPLY inscribed in Vincent's being. For years before the last two years of his life, at Arles then Paris, Vincent has been sinking into the tomb with sickness unto death, real bodily and spiritual pain and suffering. He bears in his body the stigmata of a brain disorder, perhaps epilepsy. He suffers from the diseases of acute poverty. Psychosocially, he is a "wounded healer." His lifestyles, from smoking to absinthe to sexual promiscuity, compromise his well being, though a tremendous creative energy surges for the 10 years of productive work, in one sense he is already Sein zum Todt as he creatively lives on.

Several times in the correspondence he alludes to tomb-time and chides the post-resurrection admonition, "Why do you seek the living among the dead? He is not here, he is risen." This resonates with the other Johannine bit that witnesses that "Abraham is the God of the Living" (Matt 22:32), and "before Abraham was, I am" (John 8:58). Therefore Abraham and "righteous humanity" is alive in him, now. The dismissal that the rejecters of the Messiah offer now that "we are children of Abraham" becomes absurd.

Vincent embodies the crucifixion/resurrection ethos in his very being and work. I call his corpus and legacy, an accession into resurrection. Vincent saw works or fruits as of no merit in the drama of salvation, but also of all surpassing merit. Our works are to shine before humanity (*anthropon*) that glory may redound to the Father, the "giver of all good and perfect gifts" (Jas 1:17). He also was rooted in the Pauline, Augustinian, Luther/Calvin ethos that emphasized *tout est grâce* and the all sufficiency of the atonement effected by the crucifixion/resurrection of the" Beloved Son" (John 3:16).

He was the epitome of *l'homme Protestante* (even though the Dutch Church denied his ministry), according to Max Weber and Paul Tillich (The Protestant Ethic and the Protestant Principle) because he is one who is totally dependent on divine grace for any merit, but at the same time works very hard to "work out his salvation with fear and trembling" (Phil 2).

MAIMONIDES

The master and in some ways the creator/compiler of Hebraic Moral teaching would be expected to root human salvation and justification in divine expectation and such human action, i.e., *Torah*. The great empiricist/physician/philosopher of course adheres to the pure divine essence of *parole Dei*, "the Word of God," but the human bearing and quality of justice within human deliberation and intention in the life-world is very "here and now."

As Martin Buber said famously, "God made Israel to dwell with him on earth forever." Ben Maimon, writing in Judeo-Arabic, in Muslim *Al-Andalus*, weds human conduct to faithfulness before God. He therefore would likely agree with the Law-Man, William Stringfellow, who meditated throughout his work on private and public faith that the reality of the resurrection brought to life was verified when strife against the demonic thrived. The point of suffering, into persecution, toward righteousness, into resurrection, is the vindication of God's goodness and power, the honoring, even in death of the *Shemah/Hashem*. From the biblical origins of the faith, therefore, we are dealing with ontological and axiological meaning.

THOMAS AQUINAS

Thomas Aquinas is steeped in this same ethos. Born in lands of Muslim settlement in Sicily, he naturally finds affinity with both Maimonides and Avicenna, whom he variously calls the "Doctor," "Philosopher," and

"Sage." Research into Aquinas in recent decades has stressed these Semitic-interfaith roots of every writing and teaching of the "Angelic Doctor." In his various treatises and sermons on the resurrection he strains to contend for the reality and physical verity of God's power over death and for the logical coherence and consistency of the doctrinal (creedal) formulation.

The vitality, consciousness, even dexterity and movement (Avicenna) of the resurrection body intrigues him. He also adheres to the Pauline logic, in its divine /human necessity. "And if Christ has not been raised, your faith is futile, you are still in your sins (1 Cor 15, NIV) and "if only for this life we have hope n Christ, we are of all people most to be pitied." (1 Cor 15:17). "But Christ has indeed been raised form the dead, the first fruits of those who have fallen asleep" (1 Cor 15:20 NIV). Lazarus text seems to express this incontrovertible reasoning, "Do you believe this?" Our faith/works vindicate God as God vindicates our belief and "good works."

AVICENNA

The "Father of Modern Medicine" rounds out the medieval interfaith triad and offers further corroboration to our composite assertion of resurrection truth and wisdom. In my hermeneutical approach, triangular scriptural attestation offers strongest evidence of solidity of doctrine. Years ago Jaroslav Pelikan showed that textual material begun in Hebrew scripture, with *midrashic* continuation in Christian then Islamic scripture, offered solid tradition basis of, for example, the Mary through the Ages tradition.

Ibn Sina was a genius of a generation of imaginative scholars, Jewish, Early Christian (especially Abyssinian) and proto-Islamic, who translated Greek and Latin texts, medicine, science, philosophy, logic and theology, to the edification of the rather unenlightened peoples farther west and north, eventually inspiring awesome renaissance in monasteries, cathedral schools and eventually universities like Salerno, Sorbonne, Oxford and Cambridge. He added Persian and Indian to the mix bringing about one of the brilliant awakenings of history. Knowledge was combined with skills in treating the sick, teaching the young and comforting the ageing, forever chastening knowledge into healing, a new meaning for "profession."

For the Muslim physician, the biblical realm is woven into the fabric of the reason of the great Hellenic, as well as Persian and Indian mind. He is pursuing *Fikh*, the doctrine of Justice, a fruit of philosophy and *Kalam*, a theological wisdom. He had memorized the Qur'an when he was 7 years of age and, as a teen-ager, was performing medical wonders. A very young person in a very early moment of spiritual and natural history, he saw the inextricable intertwining fabric of receiving and furthering knowledge, healing the sick and teaching the young, the three-fold composition of wisdom. Bewildered by the complexities of metaphysics, *Betrachten* (Kepler) was his epistemological break-through, praying all night, until insight arose, then offer alms to the poor as thanks to God, the fount of all knowledge.

Upon receipt of this epiphany, he settled near Tehran to practice his art and belief. Existence was now understood to be the domain of the contingent and accidental, a fully Platonic, even Pythagorean (Indian?) notion except for this irascible thread in Semitic faith (Judaism and Islam that what is, the existent, is for real, is good, not to be denigrated, divine creation. Essence (*Mahiat*) is where the money is, not existence (*Wujud*). This is the cardinal doctrine of all philosophy and theology, which asserts, above all, under and within all, before and after all, is God. Ultimately, we collapse back upon some subsumption or synergy of essence and existence, we groan primordially and eschatologically, God is! Being itself, what God Is, is what always exists, it exists to itself and is beyond definition, comprehension and certainly manipulation. There is no God but God, *Shemah, Hashem*, I and the Father are One, over against that all else is nothing. But God is known to and through reason. The three monotheisms concur that a concomitant philosophy is all we have by that to know (comprehend), believe (*credere*) and do (conscience/ethics). Within this metaphysics, philosophy and ethics, resurrection is an event in the soul, in the corporate body (family, society and communion) and in the nature and history of the world. The "Night Journey", the pilgrimage, faithful observance, is "realized eschatology", "Eternal Present" Kingdom of God. All monotheism follows Paul's logic in I Corinthians: if Christ is not risen, then the dead do not rise, and if the dead do not rise, then neither did Christ.

CRUCIFIXION/RESURRECTION IN LEVINAS

"Infinite being is produced (apperceived) at times" within the mystery of existence and not, as is supposed, in the "experience of finitude of being." The fact of being alive in time yet being aware of the eternal, grants us, according to Levinas, to the grace of seeing that time is continuous and in that "continuation the instant meets death and resurrection," so that death and resurrection constitute both time and the glimpse of the eternal *l'autre*.

Levinas here finds death and resurrection embedded in the experience of life. Existential freedom from the heritage of the Greeks on to Husserl and Heidegger in philosophy and hope grounded in the celebration of the gift of life in Hebraic futurity where God's very being is directional leading into the grace of "living" *per se* in the opportunities for liberation and justice.

Resurrection is a critical doctrine for all Abrahamic Faith. Jon Levenson, who leads the company of American Jewish scriptural theologians from his post at Harvard (as Levinas did for French Jewry from the Sorbonne), has composed three works on resurrection in Judaism-beginning with *The Death and Resurrection of the Beloved Son*.[1] Though Christianity and to some extent Islam, conceive resurrection as a future and ineffable phenomenon, Judaism insists on the historicity and "down-to-earthness" of the doctrine.

For Christian belief and life, the mystery of time and eternity, of God and humanity is the mystery of the Triune God. This mystery seeks to decipher the reality that God is present beyond and within. This reality is addressed by the symbols, Emmaus or Emmanuel. For Levinas, this is the critical scriptural premise where "the Other" and "others" constitute the essence of the sublime presence within the reciprocity of calling one another into recognition of being and into the Divine One who is All and "in all." For Christians, this is life in the One who is the resurrection and the Life (John). Crucifixion that is like "creation" (giving over and laying down) is the precondition of resurrection. As we will see in Ricoeur, fullness or overflow is the bestowal of the superabundant God, *pleroma* for the Greeks, *shalom* for the Hebrews, now, in Martha Nussbaum's words,

---

1. Jon D. Levenson, *The Death and Resurrection of the Beloved Son: The Transformation of Child Sacrifice in Judaism and Christianity* (New Haven: Yale University Press, 1995).

"capability" supersedes "contemptibility" so that those who have given up all now receive all and to those who from that all has been taken, even more is given. Job, the ultimate parable of suffering and deprivation in order to restoration and resurrection, is like the "Sign of Jonah," where death is swallowed up in victory. Those who hope in Christ, wrote Jürgen Moltmann, (an interlocutor with Paul Ricoeur) now live in prophetic justice, "for the promise of the coming future stabs inexorably into every unfulfilled present."

"Messianic time is the triumph over evil," wrote Levinas. The "son" and the "creator," in Christianity is the mystery of the Church (or the "yet being redeemed community') that no longer lives for itself but for Him who loved her and gave Himself for her. In Kierkegaard's image in sacred suspension, here death is swallowed up in victory and time is transfigured into eternal life so that the *"Ganz Andere Gott,"* comes across eternity to be near us in time, swallowing up death and darkness and bringing life and immortality to Light through the Gospel. Now light is precisely as Vincent defined it: the good works that so shine that people at last see, and give glory to our Father in heaven. This is the Word-event of crucifixion/Easter.

RICOEUR

Since I will be working in the Ricoeur Library at the Protestant Faculty after Easter, I will only briefly state his position here and elaborate his deeper legacy further in the diary, which will then take its place as the capstone of this sabbatical essay. For Ricoeur, resurrection means freedom and hope. As we noted in Levinas, the philosophical heritage that is the chosen handmaiden of all three Abrahamic theologies is Hellenistic. It is a metaphysic grounded in ethics and eschatology, with the ontological premise being the liberty and dignity of the person, family, and societies especially in their reciprocal interactions, and the axiological premise that actively pursues justice and opportunity as the stigmata of God's delivered future that is the basis of human hope. Graeco-Latin ontology, anthropology, and axiology thus becomes the vehicle for conveying the theological elements of Jewish, Christian and Muslim Faith and Ethics. There is no version of faith and theology, evangelical or liberal, fundamentalist or progressive, which does not have its own concomitant and interpretive (hermeneutical) philosophical handmaiden.

Like his near contemporary, Emmanuel Levinas, Ricoeur stands in the modern linguistic, phenomenological, and existential heritage of de Saussure, Husserl, and Heidegger. This gives a certain coloration to the freedom and hope as envisioned. Metaphysics is construed as realism, epistemology is immediate and personally mediated, and transcendence is projected from the eternal to the temporal plane. To existentialist phenomenology, Ricoeur has added biblically-grounded hermeneutics to fashion his philosophical posture.

He has honored the Protestant Faculty here in Paris by gifting them with his remarkable library that should become one of the important sites for philosophical and theological research in the world. As I work here, I begin to see his importance. Though trained in philosophy, he is also considered one of the most important theological and biblical minds of the 20th century.

Let me first illustrate his wisdom on our calendric theme of crucifixion and resurrection. In *The Book and the Text: Bible and Literary Theory2,* my colleague at Northwestern, Regina Schwartz, offers an essay by Ricoeur on "Interpretive Narrative." In this essay, he offers a *via dolorosa* through the narratives of Passion Week: betrayal, arrest, crucifixion, and empty tomb. With deft textual and normative analysis, he shows how the irony in the inner meaning of the narratives themselves conveys their truth. Now the disavower (Peter) is the one invited to offer "the great confession," "who do you say that I am?" Now the betrayer (Judas) himself becomes the vehicle by that the great destiny of the Christ, the Lamb of God, is carried through.

In the crucifixion, "He saved others and can't save himself" is eerily true, the only way the Son of Man/Son of God mystery can be realized is the apparent failure of that plan. In the empty tomb narrative, Ricoeur asserts, the redemptive logic of his namesake, the Apostle Paul in I Corinthians, "If Jesus lives and lives elsewhere, here there has to be an empty tomb and the only tracer of Christ alive is a missing body."[3] Indeed it is only as body diminishes that "Word can flourish." Here Lazarus, Emmaus, and empty tomb coalesce into one compelling kerygma. The apos-

2. Regina M. Schwartz, ed., *The Book and the Text: The Bible and Literary Theory* (Cambridge, MA: Blackwell Publishing, 1990).

3. Ibid.

tle Thomas carries kerygma far and wide in his repentant rigor for his literal demands. The apostle Paul carries kerygma far and wide by virtue of a pure *en Christou* theophany and his touch and feel for literal body now become literary Word. Calvin, then Barth and Ricoeur, would bet the bank on the continuity binding living, Written then preached Word, *Logos*-Messiah. Philosophy in this transfiguration has become phenomenology, then hermeneutics. Paul Ricoeur has become for the 21st century what Plotinus was for the early church and for nascent Judaism and Islam, the triad of monotheisms in world history.

As we view Mark's ever-troubling passion narrative with its lack of a triumphalist ending, Paul Ricoeur saves the day with his blended phenomenological-hermeneutical theology. For Mark (Peter) Christ's suffering must not in any way be subsumed into an easy theology of glory, nor must the crucifixion be allowed to diminish the accomplishment of the risen Son within the world. In the first case atonement is threatened and in the latter creation/incarnation. In this exaggeration hope and freedom gives way to the stigmata of the passion. Docetism and patripassionism are the Chyrus and Charibdis shoals threatening the safe passage of the Gospel ship and the integrity of kerygmatic Doctrine.

Ricoeur's systematic approach combines philosophy and religion, reason and revelation, phenomenology and ideology (explaining tangibles and intangibles), anthropology and theology (examining the human and divine). In light of this his main theme is theological anthropology, i.e, the search for "capability" of human action under God, he has not overlooked his colleague Martha Nussbaum's seeing the "contemptibility" in human action, for example, his study of "fallible man." If I, as a theologian, were to identify Ricoeur's contribution it is to liberate and motivate the natural and supernal power (virtue) that is ours at hand in a world produced by and "purchased back" by God. "He opens His Hand and fulfills the desire of every living thing" (Psa 145:16), God gives primordial and natural piety to every being in the world. Wesley rightly called this, after Augustine and Calvin, prevenient grace.

Ricoeur's focal reflections on resurrection concern freedom and hope as is made clear in a collection of essays assembled by Lewis S. Mudge in *Essays in Biblical Interpretation.*4 Ricoeur's presumptive premise is pure philosophy, "the truth will make you free "(John 8:32). That phrase, of

4. Lewis S. Mudge, ed. *Paul Ricoeur, Essays in Biblical Interpretation* (Philadelphia: Fortress Press1980).

course, probably does not mean what the Galilean rabbi meant, but what critical philosophy means. Ricoeur believes that there is a primordial precursor to thought and belief in natural human perception, language, emotionality and reason, Truth or truth, goodness and beauty, are fundamental impulses of humanity in our natural state.

Jürgen Moltmann has resonated with Ricoeur on another side of his mind: that represented by the conversion in an evangelical church between 20th-century mathematician Edmund Husserl, philosopher Martin Heidegger as a seminarian, political theorist Hannah Arendt, Sören Kierkegaard and Karl Barth as deculturated kerygmatic exponents. The two have also shared an eschatological horizon found in both *The Theology of Hope* and *The Crucified God*.

As kerygmatic thinkers they are centered on the preaching and Didache (*Didascalia*) of the primitive church. Here the "Kingdom of God" in its full Hebraic, Messianic, and Islamic tenor is the tutor of all thought, belief, and ethics. As Kingdom ruptures into time, space and existence, all "falsehood" (sin) is displaced by the Truth that Christ is and all "past" is transfigured by the "New" that is Yahweh Israel, the God and Father of the Lord Jesus Christ, the *Ruach Elohim* and Holy Spirit in all creation and the God over all Gods in the Abraham/Hagar covenant of Islam in that all "peoples of the Book" are conjoined. In Paul Ricoeur's language, the hermeneutics of the biblical witness, including that of the passion narratives, especially death and resurrection, is about the faith that new eternal being, Kierkegaard's *Autrement*, has become present in the midst of our *Sein zum Todt*. In the midst of the death of the world, and all therein as well as the new creation that that *thanatos tou cosmou* portends, the Eternal life of God has begun to appear.

For Moltmann, resurrection is biblical. It is the hope of the history of Israel, the promise and fulfillment of biblical covenant, which is of all creation. In Ricoeur's words, it is a promise of "surplus," a "not yet" but secure and trustworthy, "yes." It is phenomenon, a coming to be being carved out of "non-being" by being becoming being for Others as the messianic power of Passover and Emmaus present themselves to faith, justice and peace in our being and doing. When justice interrupts prevalent violence, when forgiveness interrupts prevalent revenge, when love wins out, even for the moment, God hears the "right note" of praise and sings for joy.

RECAPITULATION OF THE PASSION

"Touch me and believe" is the watchword to Thomas and the entire Clementine and post-Clementine tradition of the primitive Christian community, such as the *Mar Thoma* tradition in Africa and India. Then there is the "one better" way, which may be a Johannine accession, "blessed are those who have not seen but still believe" (John 20:29). In the empty tomb texts in John, Mary is cautioned not to touch the Lord as He has not yet ascended.

In Sartre's memorial essay in honor of French philosopher Maurice Merleau-Ponty, he attributes to the phenomenological revolution the fact that what is apparent and obvious needs no further proof. Green was precisely the green leaf and the glare of the sun was light. Rembrandt believed it and Van Gogh lived it.

At the same time, the phenomenon or epiphenomenon of a thing is connotes something ephemeral. For this reason the human mind shirks the dialectical demanding either subjectivity or objectivity, pure realism or idealism. But these positivisms avoid depth.

Ricoeur is a biblical empirical realist, given his proclivity to the phenomenological approach and to the biblical commitment to creation and incarnation as decisive qualities of the nature of God. Hermeneutics is the matrix mediating humanity and divinity. Here in the realm of linguistics and narrative Ricoeur anchors his epistemology. Husserl weighed in at the objective side of epistemological certainty as opposed to the subjectivity emphasis of Kant and Hume, further enhancing the Judao-centric and Christo-centric propensity of their protégée. Ricoeur also remembers that Heidegger was an inveterate Seminarian (like Van Gogh and Gauguin) as well as a theologian.

An example: What is the objectivity of the chestnut tree? we might ask. Is it Yeats in his poem, "Among School Children" (1928), the tree as the symbol of mystical unity? Is it Van Gogh's tree ablaze with blooms or my poor copy of his from the park at *Asnieres Sur Siene*? Here the phenomenon is aesthetic, a picture, or a song, "April in Paris, chestnuts in blossom . . ." (E. Y. Harburg, "April in Paris," 1932).

After Heidegger, Ricoeur is seeking *altheia* (truth), that is, not a photograph or a frozen specimen section as it is that that is revealed out of the bank of the concealed, or what becomes unconcealed as it presents itself. Truth for Ricoeur, like resurrection, is that disclosed, to those ready to seek and believe.

We have just finished the Lenten Season and Easter Week in particular. The last three evenings we were graced by the Tennebrae rituals from the Responsorium of Tomas Luis de Victoria (1548-1611)—performed in the *avant garde* Saint Martin (Saint Merry) Church near the Pompidou Center in Paris. The Thursday, Friday, and Saturday evenings of Holy Week are dynamic moments when the texts move through the elements of the sacred drama of Dark Friday, Holy Saturday, and Resurrection Day, here masterfully presented by the famous *Academie Vocale de Paris*.

These events are profoundly palpable and engaging, yet elusive and gripping. Last evening, for example, we followed the living Jesus and Rubens' moving body, going up on, then coming down from the Cross, the Ascent and Descent, now the presence is gone and an eerie silence lingers. The words involve the infernal and diabolical, as if somehow the principalities and powers of the world are enraptured in a final and cosmic confrontation.

Adversus Dominum et adversus Christum, the full fury of the world is marshaled against the One who came out, who appeared, who became present and vulnerable to the fallen cosmos, who was subjected to a spectacle of torture, and was rewarded by a victory spectacle in that He who was subject, subjected the world to Himself in offering Himself for her redemption. Now the defeated powers were led captive in Himself after his descent into and ascent from the bowels of hell.

AREF NAYED

Meanwhile the business leader and trained theologian has taken leave from his home in Tripoli and sought refuge in Saudi Arabia. The idea man, with David Ford and Peter Ochs, of "A Common Word," an assertion to Christian and Jewish leaders from the leaders of the Muslim world, remains their best thinker. Common Word is anchored in the double imperative "to love God and the neighbor," finding our best hope for cessation of violence and achievement of peace in the great mingled transcendental/virtue "love," with all that means in terms of philosophy and theology, of descriptive and normative knowledge.

These recent weeks and months we have seen how deeply and fervently the Muslim world waits to find justice and freedom, hope and peace. But to alone God remains the judgments and the outcomes. This is the univocal witness of Moses and Psalms, Jesus and Paul, Augustine and Hugo. The destructive powers in the world rain bombs from missiles and air-craft. Powerful brokers strut their might and vultures soar around awaiting the spoils. The impulses of the season remain clear in that message.

In the night before the death of his close friend, Emmanuel Levinas, Christmas Eve, 1995, Paul Ricoeur listened to the Midnight Mass from Manger Square in Bethlehem. PLO president, Yassir Arafat, was in attendance. Fifteen years later, we still struggle to bring *Fatah* and *Hamas* together, and Israel, and evangelical, dispensational America.

A few hours later, Ricoeur received the news of the death of this Emmanuel. He quickly looked through his books for his *Dieu, La Mort et le Temps* (1995). Their common teacher, Heidegger, had written *Sein zum Todt*.

Levinas liked to think of death as starting with time, time not as *chronos* and obliteration, but as procession and accession. Ricoeur called this Levinas' greatest book. Both Ricoeur and Levinas used the Heideggarian subtitle phrase, "Otherwise than Being or Beyond Essence." These words evoke crucifixion and resurrection, not only of the Galilean rabbi but of the countless millions of his fellow Jews and Christians and Muslims, perhaps half of the Jews who have ever been born, and our own witness as we face "that day." Death, as Levinas discovered and Ricoeur would in a decade, is the face of another and the Other.

Here at the end of this Holy Week, I add the hymn that framed the liturgy in San Sulpice, Paris. The old text attributed to Bernard of Clairvaux is now a beloved universal hymn of the season set to music by two Protestant hymnologists, J.S. Bach and Paul Gehrhardt:

> O sacred head now wounded, with grief and shame weighed down,
> Now scornfully surrounded with thorns, Thine only crown;
> O sacred Head, what glory, what bliss till now was Thine!
> Yet, though despised and gory, I joy to call Thee mine.
> What Thou, my Lord, hast suffered, was all for sinners" gain;
> Mine, mine was the transgression, but Thine the deadly pain.
> Lo, here I fall, my Savior! "Tis I deserve Thy place;
> Look on me with Thy favor, vouchsafe to me Thy grace.

While I Have Being

Men mock and taunt and jeer Thee, Thou noble countenance,
Though mighty worlds shall fear Thee and flee before Thy glance.
How art thou pale with anguish, with sore abuse and scorn!
How doth Thy visage languish that once was bright as morn!
Now from Thy cheeks has vanished their color once so fair;
From Thy red lips is banished the splendor that was there.
Grim death, with cruel rigor, hath robbed Thee of Thy life;
Thus Thou hast lost Thy vigor, Thy strength in this sad strife.
My burden in Thy Passion, Lord, Thou hast borne for me,
For it was my transgression that brought this woe on Thee.
I cast me down before Thee, wrath were my rightful lot;
Have mercy, I implore Thee; Redeemer, spurn me not!
What language shall I borrow to thank Thee, dearest friend,
For this Thy dying sorrow, Thy pity without end?
O make me Thine forever, and should I fainting be,
Lord, let me never, never outlive my love to Thee.
My Shepherd, now receive me; my Guardian, own me Thine.
Great blessings Thou didst give me, O source of gifts divine.
Thy lips have often fed me with words of truth and love;
Thy Spirit oft hath led me to heavenly joys above.
Here I will stand beside Thee, from Thee I will not part;
O Savior, do not chide me! When breaks Thy loving heart,
When soul and body languish in death's cold, cruel grasp,
Then, in Thy deepest anguish, Thee in mine arms I'll clasp.
The joy can never be spoken, above all joys beside,
When in Thy body broken I thus with safety hide.
O Lord of Life, desiring Thy glory now to see,
Beside Thy cross expiring, I'd breathe my soul to Thee.
My Savior, be Thou near me when death is at my door;
Then let Thy presence cheer me, forsake me nevermore!
When soul and body languish, oh, leave me not alone,
But take away mine anguish by virtue of Thine own!
Be Thou my consolation, my shield when I must die;
Remind me of Thy passion when my last hour draws nigh.
Mine eyes shall then behold Thee, upon Thy cross shall dwell,
My heart by faith enfolds Thee. Who dieth thus dies well.

(Paul Gehrhardt/James W. Alexander,
"O Sacred Head Now Wounded," 1656, translation 1830)

Note the morphology and bodily concentration from each part of the body that was the theme of Tennebrae and has been the focus of the meditation since Bernard of Clairvaux. This accords with my theme of resurrection and phenomenological theology.

KIERKEGAARD ON SICKNESS UNTO DEATH

We began this Holy Week meditation on the Lazarus narrative as seen through the eyes of the painter/poet/pastor, Vincent Van Gogh. An aesthetic existentialist before Kierkegaard's works were known in the "non-Danish" world, Vincent saw clearly the same Gospel dialectic. Kierkegaard expresses it in the masterpiece story of Lazarus, *Sickness Unto Death*. We conclude this meditation with those theological tracings.

Vincent was often on the train to portentous destinations. It was often like Last Train to Marienbad or perhaps we remember the film, *The Train*, chugging along in an endless circle with priceless art work, to avoid Hitler's feckless and artless maneuvers. Vincent arrives at Paris (*Ansieres sur Siene*) then at the Station near the infamous yellow house in Arles. He arrives at *Gare de l'Orleans* for his final few weeks at Paris (*Auvers-sur-Oise*). Kierkegaard begins his exposition of the Lazarus story with the train-stop analogy. The death that awaits us is not death, it is merely a train stop before the rest of the journey toward eternity. "This sickness is not unto death" (John 11:4) is his verdict on Lazarus. The sickness unto death is the sickness of soul and spirit, the sickness of sin. This death is not physical it is spiritual. It is "despair" that is not good news but bad news. Sin, sickness, despair is misalignment with God, which is also to be out of relation with self and others.

The sickness unto death is not our original condition. It is a break and aberration. It is a loss of self, disorientation, a confusion of the infinite and finite, eternal and temporal. The sickness afflicts us when we deny the self, the Self, the *autre* and the *Autri*. There are three kinds of sickness unto death: 1) being unconscious of being a self; 2) not wanting to be oneself; and 3) wanting in despair to be a substitute self. Real courage is to fear the still more dreadful than the most dreadful. Despair is not the cure, as much existentialism has held, it is the disease. Sin (despair) is indifference, "ignorance' (Socratic definition), and isolation. The false antidote of sin is *cogito* (presumed self-knowledge) and self-assertion, Hegel, Descartes and cultural "Christianity."

Resurrection is relief from apostasy and injustice, estrangement and failure to love, so that a human being becomes Spirit (Self). And what is spirit? It is life. For this reason our three philosophers, Levinas, Ricoeur and Nayed, start with Kierkegaard as the true heir of Plato and Aristotle and of Scripture.

May 1, 2011 (May Day)

Sara is off to England for a week of work on fellowship matters. On Friday, at Pompidou Library I watched the wedding at Westminster. The Anglican Church still amazes me, an artifact of cultural Protestantism in our world now so passionately evangelical and secular and interfaith and warring and money-mad and desperately poor, and what else. The throng of perhaps three million around London and three billion on the coverage around the world, sang lustily *Jerusalem* by William Blake and *God save the Queen*. I could only think of *The King's Speech* as we scanned Elizabeth, with whom I once enjoyed a short walk through Balmoral, her Scotland residence. Like the 102-year-old Mum with the young queen with her corgis commended me, "for bringing a little good news."

Our friend and fellow theologian, Rowan Williams officiated, the first Presbyterian Archbishop of Canterbury, he once told me, formerly clergy from Wales and Canon at Christ Church. In 1991, he and I and the other Regius Professor, Oliver O'Donovan, did some "circuit-riding" debating the Gulf War. His bearded and crinkled presence seemed much too yuppie and professorial and "I'm going to chain myself to this fence to protest the war culture is waging against Muslims or gays or women ordinands," or whatever, downright blasphemous. All decked out in gold queries this fellow Puritan, a blessed man of God. Something like that old bishop of Hippo, named Augustine or the 23rd John in Rome.

At American Church in Paris, Scott Herr preached on the Thomas, "unless I see and touch" matter and a composition of Fred Gramman added to splendid organ work by Charles Tompkins from Furman, who will be playing at Notre Dame this week. Today he offered Bach's *Prelude in C Major* and Saint Saen's *Prelude in E flat Major*. Fred's composition, *Blest are the Eyes*, picks up on the Thomas incident, "Blest are they who have not seen, yet believe." In a moving text he broadens the faith issue into a broad spectrum of the sensorium. Kierkegaard takes this tough theological point to its inner anguish, only when in ultimate disgust with life, with complete loss of prosperity and any sort of provision or providence, only when one offers a song of praise from that crucible of doubt or better, agnosticism, does God say "yes, that's the right note."

Sentimental phony epiphany after epiphany, theopany after theophany, revelation after revelation, blessing after blessing, conversion after conversion, "Now, at last, I see," is not God's way or desire. We demand coddling. He seeks justice. It is as Scott shared this morning what God offers in the tedium of "ordinary time" that really counts. God's wish of us is our faith to his prior faith, our love to his prior love, our interhuman justice to his yearning to blast through our recalcitrance to do justice and love mercy, and effect His justice that is salvation, which is the efficacy he chooses when we become coworkers.

The deep down theological matter in this Thomas incident is a paradox and promise, how can we see the invisible God, touch and be touched by the untouchable God and know the unknowable God? It is only when we do it for its own sake, not for sake of our deserving or the proffered goodies. "When two or three gather in my name (Commandment 3), in my power, justice, righteousness, then I am in the midst." Albert Schweitzer (1875–1965) writes of that promise in that memorable passage . . . when we are there with him as the inexorable wheel of the world's wrong turns on and crushes Him—the only good person the world has ever seen, only when by the lake we hear His voice as of old, "follow me," and we follow, then we will know Him in "the hum drum comings, goings and doings of every-day life and we will know who He is" (my paraphrase of *The Quest for the Historical Jesus*). This is crucifixion and resurrection, Emmanuel and Emmaus, passion and *parousia*.

May 2, 2011 (Osama Bin Laden is Dead)

If I am surrounded with books and articles from fellow theologians from the Jewish and Muslim traditions, even more are my daily contacts frequently from the Eurabian Muslim communities, European Jews and especially, here in France, with folk from North and Central Africa, Algeria, Tunisia, Morocco, Senegal, Ivory Coast. I begin each Saturday morning with the Algerian street market, which is the life-teeming, bargain basement of *Le Pus* (the great Paris "flea market").

Today as I clean up my diary and prepare for two talks, one on my work on Van Gogh and the other on recent interfaith aspects of Eastertide in Paris, I learn of the assassination and killing of Osama Bin Laden. I suddenly realize how my life and work have been shaped by his infamous refugee status for the last decade, if not two.

It is likely that intelligence forces from around the world knew where he was, U.S., Britain, Russia and Israel, at least. Though he kept moving like Saddam Hussein, everyone in the area of Abbott Abad seemed to know where he was. Something made the close-in and wipe-out allowable and appropriate at this moment, we'll never know. U.S. Special Forces, Navy SEALs came in last night from two helicopters. There was certainly collateral damage, which means women and children. Our strikes across the years in Pakistan, Yemen, and elsewhere take their toll.

The theme and tenor of my work changed 20 years ago, when again I was travelling in England and France during the Gulf War. We remember that all the bed and breakfasts were empty and reasonable and we had easy travelling even on a poor man's salary.

The civil engineer was a trainee and friend of the U.S., as the close relationship with the Bush family, which allowed easy departure from the country after 9/11, attests. He was fighting the Russians and communists in Afghanistan. Only then did he turn to theological studies as he became fascinated with fundamentalist Islam. This strenuous school of thought he came to believe was the only bulwark against Western and American decadence, theological apostasy and idolatry, ethical injustice and promiscuity, materialistic and sexual, and political violence especially from the epicenter in Palestine, through our client Israel. Such action was deemed righteous and obligatory, and thought to be the instrument of Christ's victory on earth for militant evangelical Christianity.

During the Gulf War, when America had 300,000 troops on Saudi soil, Bin Laden felt the blasphemy of unbeliever presence on *Terra Sancta*, having been wrongly taught by teachers ignorant of *Qur'an* and *Hadith*, that Jews and Christians are not "Peoples of the Book." In massive abrogation of his own Holy Word, he went on the rampage killing thousands of innocents and turning *Dar al-Islam*, the world of Peace, into a world of violence, *Dar al-Harb*, this not of God or of Jesus or Mohammad's *Allah*, but of his own making and the result of our own commensurable provocative and revengeful sing-along.

Speaking of the Hallelujah chorus, how now ought we now speak, sing, believe and act? What ought to be the Psalm of all God's people in the world? My original proposal after the events of September 11 still holds "send out the prince of peace corps, the sons of the prophet, an upgraded and pacified Mujajadin, forget retaliation, a life or 10 for each one lost, send a global red cross, crescent and star of David together to heal the sick, educate the children, feed the hungry and raise the dead and dying."[5]

5. Kenneth L. Vaux, *Ethics and the War on Terrorism* (Eugene, OR: Wipf and Stock,

Specifically, now we need to: 1) come out of Afghanistan and Iraq and not search and destroy in every small village, to invert the Easter message ("He, Osama is not here. Why do you search for the dead among the living?" A new Mahdi, Messiah is among us, he is risen indeed!); 2) support with Marshall-Plan-like rejuvenations the social fabric of all the strife torn residual, failed, artifact- nations (after Western colonialism and its continuing rape of their fruitful and well-endowed lands) and; 3) not create new festering safe-havens for terroristic frustration, like Pakistan, Yemen, Sudan, Somalia, and most of Africa.

Amid the paeans of praise let us listen carefully to the words of caution from *Hamas* in Gaza that have drowned out the truths of the Goldstone Report. "We condemn the assassination and killing of an Arab "Holy Warrior," a continuation of American policy of shedding Arab and Muslim blood." Bin Laden's hands are as bloody as the American bombers who rocketed and killed Qaddafi's daughter in Tripoli or the 100,000 Japanese and Germans who met fiery or genetic deaths in Hiroshima and Hamburg.

With this mingled, mea culpa and "here am I send me," we can slightly alter President Obama's wise words, "We are not now and never will be at war with Muslims." God bless America, (and all the peoples of the earth). Amen!

May 12, 2011

I have met the news of Bin Laden's assassination with "fear and trembling" (Phil 2) afraid that our nation in celebration and dancing did not show reverence in this moment of Kaddish . . . that a nation's moral and spiritual character is disclosed in such a moment that we seem ethically debased in the eyes of the world, of God? that Chomsky is right that we violated all canons of international law that American revenge grounded anti-terrorism with its underlying Islamicide is as much a menace to the world as militant homicidal Islam.

Afterword: On Tuesday, January 24, 2012, Gabby Giffords appears in her seat at the president's State of the Union Address. She has resigned her office (for the moment) to attend to her rehabilitation. She is doing well; what a hope and inspiration!

2002) and *Ethics and the Gulf War: Religion, Rhetoric, and Righteousness* (Eugene, OR: Wipf and Stock, 1992).

VII

A Theological/Political Heritage

PROPHÈTES PARISIENNE

THROUGHOUT MY PUBLICATION CAREER, I have tried to trace what might be called an Anglo-centric theory of evangelical theological history. Christianity, I ventured (at least my own tradition of evangelical Protestantism, Puritan, Reformed, Presbyterian), proceeded along a course that began and ended in England, leaping midway to America, in that fateful moment when English became the official language of the United States, then the colonies.

The thread I saw running through the western "spiritual robe of many colors" ran from Wycliffe to Wesley, through Hus, Luther, Calvin and the English and American puritans. Over five centuries, dare we say a demi-millennium, 1350–1850, a clear theological and cultural movement of belief and action became evident in the flow of history, both religious and secular. Today, together with Islam, this movement dominates the spiritual impulse in the world. Some say that Christianity is moribund. I rather offer that while many movements and denominations are quiescent, three movements are enjoying dynamic growth: Roman Catholicism, Christian Evangelicalism, and Pentecostalism. These three movements may soon reach 3 billion of the world's 7-billion population. My home church in Evanston, Illinois (First Presbyterian) is now a blend of the last two traditions with our new ministry team: some Pentecostalism, holiness folk, some evangelical-fundamentalist folk, some mainline Presbyterians, and one liberal-Catholic (Benedictine), my wife Sara.

The spirit and ethos of this "Christian-Evangelical way of life" involved a mixed bag of values: freedom of conscience, economic freedom and markets, assent to biblical authority, the sovereignty of God over all life and all nations, baptism and born-again (evangelism) fervor in Christ, and the penchant for democracy and political liberalism. As a protégé of Max Weber, I believe that spiritual transformation can give rise to economic and political systems and that the social movements can prove causal in forming a religious ethos.

Charles Wesley's hymn, suggested by the frosty morning bells at St. Johns College, Oxford, captures the Christmastide endowment:

> Hark! The herald angels sing,
> glory to the newborn king,
> peace on earth and mercy mild . . .
> risen with healing in his wings,
> mild, he lays his glory by,
> born that man no more may die,
> born to raise the son's of earth,
> born to give them second birth.

(Charles Wesley, "Hark the Heralds Angels Sing," 1739)

These qualities became intensely exemplified in my own American homeland, given that we were about to become the first post-colonial and immigrant people who chose also to pursue "empire." My book, which articulates this thesis most explicitly, carries the revealing title, *Ethics and the War on Terrorism.*[1]

Many historians now argue that the constitutive religiosity of America is not religious pluralism or separation of church and state, but evangelical Christianity. A new PBS documentary, "God in America," suggests in six hours of programming that frontier Methodist and Baptist faith has always been, and is now, the new dominant religion in America—even finding resonance in Thomas Jefferson, Ben Franklin, John Adams, Abraham Lincoln, and the misnamed "deists" among the founders.[2]

Now a close second in loyalty, founded in a somewhat deeper heritage, one cognate that might be called Anglo-French leads me to make a Franco-centric trace. The French revolution, along with the British

1. See Vaux, *Ethics and the War on Terrorism.*
2. "God in America," co-production of American Experienceâ and FRONTLINEâ, http://www.pbs.org/godinamerica/.

(Puritan) and American revolutions, have gifted modernity with *liberté and égalité*, if not always *fraternité*. The colors of the French Flag, red, white, and blue, are borrowed from the Christian Flag, depicting the Trinity and therefore are steeped in a more biblical Triad: freedom, equality, and community. What I define as the contemporary quality of "evangelical" is as French as it is Japanese, elusive, yet ubiquitous.

Gaul Nord (France and Belgium) founds an ancient tradition of freedom and faith. *Laïcité* arguments today about whether Muslim women may wear the head scarf to school and work occur in Antwerp and Paris. Labor unions strike for rights and benefits in both Amsterdam and Provence. Here Faith and justice are perennial issues of culture, and they hinge on underlying cultural beliefs and values derived from faith.

Beyond Anglophilia and Francophilia, in this essay I am also re-hearsing my own history, geographical and religious. When I first began travelling to Europe 50 years ago, I felt I was among my own people in England, Scotland, and Ireland. Then I came to France, and I was really at home, not only in name.

The French tradition retains its fierce Roman Catholic loyalty, an intellectual/spiritual candor in life and death, and of a "Protestant principle" (which almost was nationally embodied under Henry IV), as well as a strenuous anti-clericalism and a commitment to the transformation of culture. That culture has been shaped by Calvin and Ignatius just as England has been shaped by Tyndale and Newman.

A parade of notables from Genevieve and Clovis, Abelard and Aquinas, Calvin and Pascal, Hugo and Ricoeur, Levinas and Derrida, have contributed to an ethos that has resisted the compromise to freedom threatened by the Indo-Europeans and Huns, Celts and Muslims, Protestants and Fascists, secularists and communists, skin-heads and anti-immigrants—for two thousand years, all along the way incorporating into the national character certain virtues (and vices) from each of those movements. Across recent years, I have seen on the streets (or strike-barricades) of Paris the likes of Camus and Sartre, Derrida and Levinas, de Beauvoir, Irigaray and others who carry this Olympic Trinitarian torch as both Pierce and Wittgenstein have defined it.

One reservation, but it is monumental. I'm French in name only. I have never taken the time to learn the language, although I love its song. Actually, if the truth be known, I'm as closely related to Daniel De Foe, the archi-techtonic novelist of the English language, as I am to Roland De

Vaux, the reluctant publicist to the world of the Dead Sea Scrolls. Note: they both were proclaimers like this scribe.

SAINT GENEVIEVE

The Christian history of Northern France first involves a person from whom our dear Paris friend, Genevieve des Champs, is named. Born in her elegant home on the Rue de Franqueville in the 16th arrondissement on the day France was liberated by GIs from the Third Reich (and thus named for this proto-liberator of France), she provides a good point to enter the story of someone named Vaux in the spiritual trace-way we now seek in France.

At age 7, Genevieve was specially blessed by St. Germanus of Auxerre (d. 437, 438) who, like the later St. Germanus (496–576) who would became Bishop of Paris, made a home here. Here also, a later figure in our story, Jacques Lefèvre d'Étaples, would teach.

Genevieve had a peculiar destiny for Paris.

St. Germanus had befriended the Frankish conquerors of Paris who, in those early centuries, before and during the beginnings of Christianity began to strive toward the recognition of the "One God" of Abraham, Israel, and Jesus Christ.

France was an early Christian outpost of faith and witness. Bishop Irenaeus of Lyon was a missionary leader from Smyrna in Asia Minor (A student of Polycarp), who presided over a strong church in central France where the Rhône and Saône rivers flow together. His «*Adversus omnes haereses*," a sophisticated and detailed critique of Gnosticism, shows how highly developed theology and church life was in 170 c.e. in Gaul, where we have some hints in Christian Scripture that even Paul the Apostle was hoping to reach.

When violent persecution broke out, his witness was decisive. His recently discovered "Demonstration of the Apostolic Preaching" found this century in an Armenian translation, shows the rigorous biblical orientation with a theology based in Hebrew Scripture that was held by the early church in Roman Gaul.

Roman Gaul, however, was a martyr church, the purity and the honor she accorded the divine name was brutally achieved, especially in the killing of 1 million and the enslavement of another million. The experience of freedom-of-faith-fighters had exerted a civilizing and organizing order on the region where we locate the origin of *famille* Vaux.

A SERMON ON IRENAEUS' "ON APOSTOLIC PREACHING"

The original, like all of Irenaeus' originals do not exist. This was found in 1904 in Armenian and is thus translated into English. This passage below is clearly an economic view of the Deity. Here, there is but one God-Father who is the first principle, the Creator. God is reason, logic, *Logos*, therefore, through His very Word, He created all of creation. *Logos* is the channel of creation (John 1.2–3). God is spirit, as again we find in John. Irenaeus united these to the Word and Wisdom, Son and Spirit.

In the great French theological tradition we are tracing, the following statement is one on which monotheistic believers and Trinitarians can both agree.

5. Thus then there is shown forth[a] One God, the Father, not made, invisible, creator of all things; above whom there is no other God, and after whom there is no other God.[b] And, since God is rational, therefore by (the) Word He created the things that were made;[c] and God is Spirit, and by (the) Spirit He adorned all things: as also the prophet says: *By the word of the Lord were the heavens established, and by his spirit all their power.*[d] Since then the Word establishes, that is to say, gives body[e] and grants the reality of being, and the Spirit gives order and form to the diversity of the powers; rightly and fittingly is the Word called the Son, and the Spirit the Wisdom of God. Well also does Paul His apostle say: *One God, the Father, who is over all and through all and in us all.*[f] For *over all* is the Father; and *through all* is the Son, for through Him all things were made by the Father; and *in us all* is the Spirit, who cries *Abba Father*,[g] and fashions man into the likeness of God. Now the Spirit shows forth the Word, and therefore the prophets announced the Son of God; and the Word utters the Spirit, and therefore is Himself the announcer of the prophets, and leads and draws man to the Father.

a. Or "shown to be": cf. V, xviii. 1: "*Et sic unus Deus Pater ostenditur* (= *dei/ knutai)."*

b. Cf. Isa. xliii. 10.

c. God is *logikoⅇj*, therefore by *loⅇgoj.* He created the world. The play on the words is given by the Armenian, but cannot be given by the English translation.

d. Ps. xxxiii. 6.

e. "Gives body:" apparently representing *swmatopoiei=*: cf. I. i. 9, of the Demiurge of Valentinus.

f. Eph. iv. 6.

g. Cf. Gal. iv. 6.

The sermon captures a very unique spirit of divine greatness and magnanimity. Seizing on the spirit of the One God of all creation, peoples and faiths, one known to believers in Western Asia, the Middle East, including Armenia, Chaldea, Egypt, India, even, as we now know, formulations of the Christian kerygma from those in close proximity with Jews and Muslims, the sample text expresses appropriately an irenic mood in a period prior to Constantine triumphalism, Muslim conquests, Christian Crusades, and Jewish ghettoization and extermination. This was the age of faith that we know existed but that we have great difficulty describing, an age of Jewish Christianity, Islam nascent in pre-Islamic Arabic poetry, an age of profound inter-determination and inter-penetration of the three monotheistic faith families of Abraham.

This age of exemplary magnanimity would crescendo into the golden age of Avicenna and Rumi, Averroës and Maimonides, Al-Farabi and Aquinas before the horror of crusades, pogroms, Muslim conquests, and Conquistadoran containments and counter-assertions would distort the three movements of Abraham into bellic, defensive, and exclusive faith-formulation and even worse punitive action. Such "circling of the wagons," "convert-or-die" evangelism would distort the very substance of the monotheistic faiths.

The world had to be cleansed each from the others, believing erroneously that God did not have enough generosity to embrace all. This world, which is conceived as not big enough for both of us accelerates today into the disgrace mutual accusations of apostasy, of Muslims torching out the last Christians in northern Iraq, militant Zionism expelling or killing remnant Christians and Muslims from Terra Sancta, Israel, Muslims eradicating the last Jews in Cairo, and Zionist Christians in America and fundamentalist Muslims in Europe turning the world into a dangerous bipolarity organism of two faith cultures: Americo-Israel and Euro-Arabia.

In the France of Irenaeus, the surrender of indigenous political and linguistic (but not religious) freedom seems to have been worth the price of Roman protection against the Germans. Nevertheless, the Arian tribes would cross the Rhine and they would be followed by violent visitors from even farther East, communities of virulent paganism and idolatries of human power—the Huns.

Despite this historical crisis the magnanimity of Roman culture and the even more spiritual Celtic culture prevailed and the three parts of France: *Gallia Belgica, Gallia Iberica and Gallia Celtica flourished under the Pax Romana. Beginn*ing in the Christian era, the Celtic tribe was transformed into the Gallo-Roman city state (*civitas*), and Latin replaced Celtic as the lingua Franca. The Vaux family finds its roots here in the Celtic peoples resisting the Romans or perhaps in some intermarriage with the ancient invaders.

St. Genevieve's miraculous story takes place in this Christianized Roman Gaul still threatened by pagan and barbarian elements. Here, historians' counsel must be heeded to show that the external invaders were not nearly as "uncivilized" and "unreligious" as we have been taught to think. Similarly, the indigenous people were not nearly as "pacific" and "pious."

The caricature of apologetic historians is as grievous as Gibbon's description of Attila the Hun in his *The Decline and Fall of the Roman Empire*. He may have been a square block of a man with small receded eyes and a flat nose. He certainly was a bow-legged, fleet-footed horseman but whether he was such a Fred-Flintstone-cartoon character must be doubted. In the year 451, at the battle of Chalon, after he had devastated Gaul, he was not doubted, but intensely feared.

By this time, the early Christian outposts were bishop cities, following the pattern in the Christianization of the Western Roman Empire under Constantine's Edict of Milan in 313 c.e. Attila, who had been a hostage in Italy for many years, had come to despise the decadent and excessive life-styles of the Romans (another exaggeration). The Hun Empire, centered on the Hungarian Plain, also despised the tribes.

By 440, Attila had destroyed the Ostrogoths and was now in pursuit of the Visigoths. These vast migrations of "Barbarian" tribes had occurred starting roughly when the Eastern and Western Roman Empire began to split in 395 c.e. In less than 100 years (476), the Western Empire would fall. But in 406, swarms of tribes crossed the frozen Rhine River scarcely noticing the ancient "Reingold" glitter from the river's bottom.

The Franks moved into Gaul, *Allemagne and Alsaces* and the Vandals and Angles entered into Spain and Africa. The Burgundians located in North Gaul and the Visigoths occupied Toulouse (via Italy) and then moved into Provence (472), Auvergne (474), and Spain (475).

Amid this vast movement of peoples, Attila and the Huns burned churches and monasteries and, in 440, demanded from Theodosius, the Eastern Roman Emperor, double tribute. In 442, he conquered the Balkans and, by 447, he had conquered all of Illyria from the Black Sea to the Mediterranean. He then set his sights on Gaul.

With the infamous ruse of a ring from Valentinian's (Eastern Emperor) sister Honoria, Attila rationalized that he needed to "liberate" the Western Empire. After demanding half of the Western Empire as a dowry, he crossed the Rhine, sacked and burned Strasbourg, Mainz, Cologne, Reims, Trier and other cities. But *Lutetia* (Paris) was spared.

Attila had heard of the reputation of the ministry of Genevieve and believing in omens and soothsayers, he avoided Paris. He headed south to Orleans and eventually was defeated in 451 at the battle of Chalons. Retreating back across the Alps that winter, Attila drowned in his own drunken nose bleed and was buried in a case of lead and gold at the bottom of the Theiss river in Hungary, fostering another glittering Reingold myth to forever intrigue other voyagers.

On a 1500-year-old monastery wall in Pavia, Italy we read the words: "*Flagellum Dei,* The Scourge of God (Attila, the Hun)."

But our story has meandered like the river Theiss or Rhine, or more accurately like a Charlton Heston movie. As we search for the unique zeitgeist of which Genevieve was a part and to which she contributed, we need initially to note her commitment to solidarity between faith and politics and the themes of her life and faith. We know she swayed influence over the early Frankish rulers. She exerted an awesome history-changing influence over Attila, the Hun. She is credited with averting another crisis, the Plague of 1129. It is no mistake that, with St. Denis, she becomes the Patroness of Paris.

What was the secret of her witness? She lived a life of mortification—dying to the flesh in this city of great bodily and worldly pleasures. Recent studies have focused on her influence, however indirect, on the baptism of Clovis, perhaps this came about through her influence on Remi, the Bishop of Reims.[3]

Our friend, Genevieve des Champs, finds her namesake's genius in her ability to inspire the solidarity of the French people, a remarkable feat for a fifth century woman, one perhaps equal to Deborah, Cleopatra and Hildegard in the annals of history.

Much like her *Nachfolger* up the Rhine, Hildegard of Bingen, Genevieve seemed to have had a keen political sense. Aware of the insecurities of the people in the face of surrounding threats, of the need for rulers to pacify, placate, and yet lead the people in ways of peace, piety and justice. She sensed what rulers needed in that early age of "divine right." Indeed, it is her influence that inexorably works its way out in the baptism of Clovis. Here a synthesis, subordination, or at least synergy of religion and politics, church and state is affected and achieved. The English and French option in political theology and the Vaux clan will ultimately choose a secularizing and separatizing path, thoroughgoing non-conformists all.

Careful definition of the synthetic church-state attribute must be offered here, given the travesties that would follow in theocratic politics in this realm. What Genevieve achieved in a world where power and terror ruled—was a sense of the divine realm that ruled over and through local governments and that to whom all earthly rulers were accountable for their mandate, their validity and credibility. The reason she enjoys the legacy of veneration of a martyr and saint is that she demanded and ascetically authorized such fealty and reverence before God, this enhancing human responsibility.

Yes, she demands acceptance of the church's authority but, we must remember, that the church is still quite frail, vulnerable, and fallible, witness the easy collapse of most of Europe before the Huns. Like Calvin, a millennium later, rather than religio-political consolidation and compromise, she sought the truth and peace of God.

---

3. Joseph-Claude Poulin, "*Geneviève, Clovis et Remi: entre politque et religion*" in *Clovis: histoire et mémoire [actes du colloque international d'histoire de Reims]* (Paris: Presses de l'Université de Paris-Sorbonne, 1997), 331–48.

Our best knowledge of Genevieve comes from Gregory of Tours (538–594). In his *Historia Francorum,* with "Eusebius-like" apologetic history, he extols the faith and witness of Genevieve.

Yet even critical historical study seems to claim that:

- She certainly endorses the language of Rome which has become the linguistic authority of the church. As we will see later in Paul Ricoeur, language becomes the symbol-world and story-world of a people.

- In moving into a Latin world at this time of flux, she solidifies her influence in church and state.

- She seems to have established a reputation as defender and protector of the people.

- She traveled widely—especially to imperiled areas—e.g. her "defensor" visits to Meaux.

- She saw a synergy between "defending the faith" and "securing the people." No Qaddafi, nestled in Tripoli, ignoring the other coastal cities with their different tribes here.

Pelagianism had become a strong disorientation to faith, along with the Arianism of the various tribes. Trinitarian doctrine was only then being formulated in the Christological councils (4th-6th centuries) and would not become a full-blown, fully-defined articulation until it became critical in defense against the Muslims under Charlemagne (800). A delicate equipoise of monotheism and Trinitarianism was here being tested "*in nuss.*" Again, it is not so much that Genevieve is a defender of "orthodoxy" as she is a preserver of the integrity of faith when all external and internal forces were ready to discard or discredit it.

CLOVIS

- The amazement of the baptism of Clovis, a perplexingly controversial event, is that it affirmed the message of the Apocalypse of John—written in the moment of the full-terror of the Pagan Roman Empire as the "New Babylon"—wherein the process will begin of "the kingdoms of this world becoming the kingdoms of our God and His Christ" (Rev 11:15). Humans are no longer subject to the principalities and powers of this world" (Colossians), to the fears and superstitions, to the enemies of God, to the prevalence of injustice and terror, to the neglect and contempt of the poor and weak. The earthly ruler is now subject to God and responsible to the people.

- Clovis became legendary with the French people, a *"novus constantinarius"* or in Augustine's sense a holy ruler like Theodisius. Though brutal centuries of crusade, inquisition and suppression of sister faiths would follow (especially Judaism, Islam and Reformation faiths) a sense of accountability.

- Before the Divine had become paramount for rulers, even more important than the prevalent expediency principle of *consensus populorum.*

- Genevieve's preparatory work had built on the precedents and precursors of vital faith in Paris and environs. She operated out of the Basilica of St. Denis and was active in healings, miracles, and ministries in this ancient holy site.

- Certainly there are elements of "opportunism" in Genevieve's work just as there are in Clovis' baptism and the vision of Constantine. Historical moments come and go with that kind of *kairos* moment or opportunity.

But this is not cynical exploitation like Stalin calling on the Russian Orthodox or Sadaam Hussein calling out the Islamic prayer rug. It is more of the order of George Bush or Tony Blair who, out of sincere religious impulse call on God's blessing and vindication being co-opted by cynical "handlers" who have no gods but expediency. With ominous forces abroad in the land (and around the world) perhaps one can forgive such cooptation and "civil religion," but truth and justice are better. A long range view of salutary religio-political ethics proves this especially if it leads to divine accountability, democratic sensibility, piety, justice, and peace.[4]

4.. See M. Heinzelmann and J.C. Poulin, *Les Vies ancienne des de Sainte Genevieve de Paris* (Paris: Librairie Honoré, 1986).

THOMAS AQUINAS

Some of the *famille* Vaux may have crossed to England with *Guillieme*, William the Conqueror, or they may have remained in France until later centuries, even as late as the Huguenot exodus before the faith genocide in France in the sixteenth century (St. Bartholomew's Day, 1557).

French theological history now follows Thomas Aquinas (1225–1274), the first "interfaith theologian" and his compatriots—Eloise, Abelard and Cure Jean de Vaux as the drama of the Merovingian and Carolingian rulers perpetuate the legacy and the spirit of Genevieve and Clovis. Through difficult centuries, the challenge Islam is confronted. The result is a military stand-off where while European soil is protected much of the Middle East, Near Orient and Africa becomes Muslim, even as Aquinas from Sicilian Italy, is influenced by *Ibn Sina*, the Muslim, and *Ben Maimon*, the Jew. Even worse was the inference of this holy war/crusade/jihad that Jewish and Muslim sister faiths were somehow incompatible with Christian life and needed to be purged from the world.

It is in this world of high medieval culture, the topside brilliance of Chartres, Mont St. Michele and *Al-Andalus* and the *Summa Theologica*—along with the dark underside of Crusades and Inquisition—that we meet a set of Parisians, great and legendary, Thomas, Abelard, Eloise, and a simple parish priest Curé Jean de Vaux of St. Eustache, the parish where the Kenneth Vaux, perhaps-related, family, came to live in the winter of 2004.

Being the father of the *lectio divina,* Thomas' thought about God and the world (the leitmotif of Francocentric theology) is captured in his commentary on Psalm 8 and Romans 8.

The general tenor of his thought is Aristotelian, Pauline, and Augustinian—with a strong tinge of biblical monotheism and what I have labeled elsewhere as Abrahamism (cf: Avicenna and Maimonides). From the panoply of his work, we focus on his views about the natural world and history. Under the salient influence of Albertus Magnus, an important naturalist (1248), he pondered Aristotle's ethics and the *Sentences* (*Libri Quattuor Sententiarum*) of Peter Lombard, and he wrote a treatise on the "Principles of Nature" (*De Principiis Naturae).*

In this treatise, he celebrates the "light of reason" that opens to human awareness the structures and processes of nature and humanity. The human world, accessible to reason, known in the investigations of science and history, is a gift of God. Philosophical reasoning is therefore essential to being human—to the pursuit of truth. The created reality is the procession (*procedes*) of the infinite love of God.

From this primacy of being, God becomes the original and final cause (determination) of the creation as well as the sustaining vitality which is the *animus* (spirit) of the world. Creativity is of the essence of the divine being and therefore of the creation—including humanity. Timing (*kairos*) is the form and substance of creativity in the very being of God. *Kairos* is the "outgoing" and the "outgiving" of God into the world as Creator, Redeemer, and Sustainer.

Thomas' theological starting point for this perspective on nature and history begins with Anselm's *Cur Deus Homo*—influenced by the works of Peter Abelard, which conceive of the mystery of the world in terms of the Word made flesh—"God become man." Why must God have come out to the world—and to man? Why the bloody death?

This Paschal mystery is the mystery of the world's constitution and continuation. It is also of moral significance as the Cross becomes the key to the enigma of history. The laws of nature and of God are woven into the redemptive mystery of Christ.

In the words of Luke Timothy Johnson "Jesus is the teacher of *Torah*, the fulfillment of *Torah* and the very personification of *Torah*."[5] This develops in Aquinas,[6] as he holds to a view of history akin to his masters, Maimonides and Avicenna, within which the human drama is an enactment either of righteousness in God's "way" or rupture and retraction from that way.

Just as David Noel Freedman[7] sees *Torah* as a chronicle of successive breaching of *Torah* until paradise is finally spoiled, covenant forsaken and exile assured, Thomas also sees history as the theatre either of acceptance or abandonment of God's ways.

---

5. Luke Timothy Johnson, *Living Jesus: Learning the Heart of the Gospel* (New York: Harper, 1999), 154.

6. See Matthew Levering, *Christ's Fulfillment of Torah and Temple: Salvation According to Thomas Aquinas* (Notre Dame, IN: University of Notre Dame Press, 2002).

7. See David Noel Freedman, *The Nine Commandments: Uncovering the Hidden Pattern of Crime and Punishment in the Hebrew Bible* (New York: Doubleday, 2000).

Now the church and world reenact either Israel's advocacy or apostasy, as all theology affirms God as known in nature and Scripture. Jesus was this embodied wisdom, word, and way of God. "Jesus is enacting" writes N.T. Wright "in the great healing, the great restoration, of Israel,"[8] the manifestation of divine intimations. The (Franco-centric) passion is this very synthesis of sacramentality in Israel.

History is therefore the enactment of divine meanings within humanity, just as nature is the vehicle of divine purpose within the cosmos.

So in verse 4–6 of Psalm 8, Aquinas asks the question of nature and end of man. "When I consider the heavens . . . you have made—what is man that you visit him?"

As in Cicero and Aristotle, the world is the construction of a palace of wonder, orchestrated in magnificent splendor, setting, and story. Then amid the wondrous panorama, God has placed humanity—not only as spectator and receptor of this glory but as a partner in the creation, a resident representative and partner in the unfolding drama. To the work of God's hands and fingers are added the collaborating (*stellvertreter*) human hands and feet (vs. 6).

Humanity's God-exultation ("close to the angels") is the signal purpose of the creation.

In Rom 8, Thomas sees again the magnificence and mystery of the cosmos now defined Christologically as Christ's new reality (manifesting the old). The spirit of life is transmitted through the *Torah* and the "law of nature" (Rom 8:2). In the suffering love of God for humanity and His world, the architecture and *raison d'etre* of the glorious "outcoming" (Psa 8) is made clear. Christ's body is broken for humanity and for the World—in order to renovate the innovated creation.

To keep alive and keep going what had gone away and gone astray, Christ continues and renews the fallen world (*tikkun olam*). "No condemnation" endures now for those "*en Christou*," the *Akedic* Son (John 3:16), the dearly beloved, "only begotten" son (*monogenos, agapetos*) has reassured God's outgoing love for humanity and the world.

The present suffering (18–22) of the creation is prelude to the glorious consummation that is now underway as the God-given,

---

8. Nicholas Thomas Wright, *Jesus and the Victory of God* (Minneapolis: Fortress, 1996), 130.

"being-redeemed" world is transfigured by the reality of a sacrificing and saving God.

The world, in other words is not confounded by the problem of evil, the vicissitudes of history or the frailty of nature. Rather, these seeming imperfections are enraptured in the same cosmic purpose of Genesis and the Psalms.

Creation and history are the depiction and invitation of the reality of God.[9] Thomas furthers the Abrahamic strand (freedom, venture, goodness, "way," (faith and reason) and the worldly connection between piety and politics.

This reporter finds continuity with Thomas, the Huguenots, and the Jansenists of the last millennium, affirming their witness into the present world. Next to this, we must place beside Thomas the story of Eloise and Abelard and that of an unknown parish curate, perhaps as incognito and insignificant as my own Vaux ancestors, who made their way along the intellectual, spiritual, and cultural pathway we trace.

The reader will have noted by this point that a biographical thread is weaving its way into this tapestry. Three significant events of my own biography carry theological import. The first is this very old French influence by which I trace ancestry in early Christian France as well as in the Calvin, Huguenot, and revolutionary *sequelae* in France of recent centuries.

Another ancestor enters from Switzerland or the Pfalz (Palatinate) region of Germany, his name Rosenberg and the disgrace of previous generations of ancestors, has become my pride. When I struggle today to recover the Jewish basis of Christianity I know I honor this persecuted forebear. I even go so far as to affirm my roots in Hebrew history even as I pursue a calling of reconciliation among the Abrahamic and world faiths. The third root source of who I am by faith is the English heritage I mention in the outset of this essay, again Calvin, via the Puritans, Churches of England, Scotland and North Ireland and the Methodists and other non-conformists. I also feel a part of the contemporary French Jesuits such as Teilhard de Chardin, Henri de Lubac, Jews such as Emmanuel Levinas and Jacques Derrida, Muslims like Souleyman

---

9. See Thomas d'Aquin, *Commentaire Sur Les Psaumes* (Paris: Les Éditions du Cerf, 1996); *Commentaire de l'Épître aux Romains* (Paris: Les Éditions du Cerf, 1999).

Bachir Diagne and Nasrin Qadar, and other architects of Vatican II and post-Vatican II humanism and the critical French tradition.

PETER ABELARD

Peter Abelard (1079–1142), a brilliant theological scholar, student of Anselm of Laon— that beautiful mountain city near Paris—was critic of another teacher, William of Champeaux, whose "realism" threatened to breach the dialectic of the heritage we follow, the dialectic and oscillation of realism and theism, nominalism and realism, freedom and faith, which we claim as a normative heritage.

This heritage is extended into recent days through the work of Paul Ricoeur. Abelard, Like Ricoeur, lectured to throngs at Paris, Sorbonne, until his love-affair with Eloise forced him to retire to the monastery of St. Denis. He then had also to resist the denunciation of his life's work by Bernard of Clairvaux and the church. Eloise suffered the curse of notoriety being the niece of Fulbert, canon of Notre Dame as she became abbess of the Nunnery at Troyes, a significant theologian in her own right.

Abelard was condemned in several councils and about to be condemned by Bernard of Clairvaux, when he was defended by Peter the Venerable and was reconciled to Bernard. His *scito te ipsum* (ethics) and *sic et non* (contradictions in the Bible) join his hymnbook written for Eloise for the nuns of the Paraclete as classics of early medieval devotion.

His realism (vs. nominalism/"name only") was based on his belief on the nature of human language and reason and "the mind of God." His delineation between "universals" and "particulars," resonating with the English thought of Duns Scotus, Roger Bacon, and others remains a crucial philosophical distinction clarifying, as it does, the distinction between "language-notions" that are significant in truth value and moral substance and those that are mere social conventions. Modern analytic (Anglo-American) linguistic philosophy is built on these foundations.

Jean de Vaux, curate at Eglise de St. Eustache (1305–1330)

The great circular, octagonal structure now holds the cruciform transepts deep in the center similar to the great mosque in Cordoba or the recast cathedral/mosque in Seville. On an inner wall of St. Eustache, we find the roster of curates from the 1200s until the turbulent days of the Revolution and the Napoleonic reconstitution of the state of France.

In the fourteenth century, the parish lay at the long passage on the north side, (*rive droite*) of the Siene coming off the *Pont Neuf. Le septieme quartier* was in ancient Paris called *quartier St. Eustache.* Here the ancient north wall of the city and the moat was marked by the Rue de la tonnellerie. To the northwest slanted the ancient pre-Christian Rue de Montmartre. Several great cathedrals and abbeys dotted the landscape.

The ancient Cistercian Cluny St. Sulpice and St. Germain de Pres to the south, Notre Dame on the east in Ile de la Cité, and to the north St. Eustache and Sacre Coeur in Montmartre.

Pere de Vaux conducted all of the duties of the parish priest. Officiating at regular *messe* at various times during the week, making parish rounds to the sick and dying, conducting catechism, keeping the parish records, recording marriages and funerals. His fellowship would have been the workers who congregated here: fishmongers and salt scrapers, fruitier and second-hand clothiers—the rich menagerie of the *Les Halles Grand Marche.*

The plague was a regular visitor to the city and the filth of Paris, the sewers and rats, which Victor Hugo would portray, was already pronounced. Life expectancy was short and very few children survived, even into infancy. Radical thought was everywhere in the air.

The Catholic orders, Dominicans, Franciscans, and women's orders like Eloise Nuns of the Paraclete offered fresh thought. Scholars in the university like Peter Abelard and Thomas Aquinas were seeking to formulate the faith, and science in general, all in accord with the knowledge of the time.

All across Europe original and creative thinkers were arising: Wyclif, Hus, Cathari, Albigenses, Lollards. In the local parish, the faithful were confused but also thrilled by the ferment. By the time the Vaux ancestors appear in the parish records of England in the sixteenth century, they already have ventured heretical tendencies for centuries—Baptists, Puritans, Lollards, non-conformists all, eventually, even Methodists.

In the late 1700s, the parish priest in our hometown, South Petherton (near Taunton, in 1441, a Lollard stronghold) is dismissed for "Wesleyan tendencies." Thomas Coke accompanies John Wesley to America and becomes his first bishop.

We may assume Vaux ancestors and relatives were among the free-thinkers of the day, still in France. Jean de Vaux may have been among them. Today St. Eustache serves breakfast to the homeless *clochards* and jobless *chômeurs* in the crypt of the great cathedral where it faces on Rue de Montogril, a remaining great market street.

Here in the solemn halls of St. Eustache is where Bizet first performed the *Te Deum*, where Liszt auditioned *Le Grand Messe,* and where Moliere and Richelieu were baptized.

Saturday night recently, a small band was holding forth in the same lower room, leading a community sing-a-long. On a recent Sunday afternoon, the great organ played by Jean Guillou, a student of Marcel Dupré, performed several Bach organ cantatas.

One never noticed any dissonance of the genius of Lutheran and Protestant church and his Catholic antagonists. Glorious music filled the great Roman Catholic cathedral, and on occasion one might hear *Ein Feste Burg ist unser Gott.*

JEAN CALVIN

Frère de Vaux studied in the Parisian universities where Thomas taught. His study would often begin with Aquinas after the required foundations in Scripture and the early fathers, including Augustine. Though it would be hard to tell if Ignatius or Erasmus or Lefèvre d'Étaples or John Calvin were Catholics or Protestants, lines would be drawn by lesser lights, and Calvin would be censured by the Sorbonne.

The nascent inquisition and the «heresy hunters» were alive and well. Yet Calvin sustains that same French ethos in its several crucial dimensions: 1) *Lectio divina*, a Scripture as divine Word as the starting point for knowledge; 2) a stubborn insistence on the synthesis of God and world, reason and revelation; and 3) a worldly theology totally woven into secular life (science, politics, economics, classical learning and the like).

He received a church beneficence to study theology from the Cathedral in Noyon, his birthplace, where he was born to devout parents. He studied first at College de la Marche then Montagu in Paris. He then moved to study law in Orleans where his interest in the *devotio moderna* (critical study of texts) flourished under scholars like Cordier. After his father's death, he returned to the newly founded College Royal in Paris which, under the humanistic influence of Erasmus (and opposed to the scholasticism of the Sorbonne), allowed him to concentrate on biblical and classical languages.

At 23 years old, he published *de Clementia* on Seneca's tractate, seeking to persuade King Francis I to accept religious toleration and to call him to biblical orthodoxy and the "true faith" (he was part of a French circle of Reformers centered around Bishop Briçonnet of Meaux).

When his friend, Basel physician Nicholas Cop, became rector at the University of Paris, and gave his inaugural lecture on «The Beatitudes of Jesus and justification by faith without the works of the law"—he surely understood the reaction he would stir.

The Inquisition (based in the theology faculty at the Sorbonne) rose up and chased him to Basel, where Calvin, also accused of guilt by association, had also fled.

This effectively ended his Paris career, his work finding more fruitful ground in Basel, Strasbourg, and ultimately Geneva. His *Institutio christianae religionis*, a compendium of the faith, and one of the most influential texts in Christian history, was published in Basel in 1536 (Latin), then Strasbourg (French) in1539. It was during those years that William Tyndale of Cambridge, translating the Hebrew and Greek Scriptures into the first English Bible, was apprehended in Antwerp and burned at the stake outside Brussels.

While his faith was to waken and deepen under the influence of Martin Bucer and Phillip Melanchthon it was Parisian influences that had decisively shaped his thought. The influence of Mathurin Cordier (1479–1564) and Jacques Lefèvre d'Étaples (1455–1536) stand out. Cordier (a student of Lefèvre) helped Calvin find the love of Latin (and classical linguistics) and implanted his critical textual mind.

The commitment to pedagogical vigor and bringing theological influence to bear on public officials was also instilled by Cordier. Both devoted detailed attention to biblical training and petitioning King Francis for sympathy toward the evangelical movement.

Calvin also sought to secure religious recognition for the Reformers. The influence of the school in Strasbourg (Sturm), where Calvin's ministry was as much biblical and theological exposition as preaching and pastoring, is a clear influence of Cordier.

Jacques Lefèvre d'Étaples, whom Calvin likely knew in the Bishop Briçonnet circle of Meaux, was an even more salient influence. A biblical exegete in the tradition of John Chrysostom or Augustine of Hippo, he was librarian at the great monastic complex at St. Germain de Pres in Paris (c. 1510 ff).

A pervasive influence on Erasmus and translator and liturgist of the Psalms, he was a disciplined biblical exegete and commentator. Calvin›s shelf of New and Old Testament commentaries remind one of Lefèvre's shelf, a generation earlier. With a focus on the Psalms, Genesis, and the Pauline letters, a whole world of theological and humanist renewal is opened before us that will find deepened and persuasive influence on Calvin.

Paris would provide a harsh environment for Reformers in Calvin›s later years. St. Bartholomew›s Day / *La nuit de la St. Barthélémy* (23 or 24 August 1572) will forever be a *Kristallnacht* darkness on the brightness of the soul of France. Although the nights will eventuate in the end of the religious wars, the French Revolution and the founding of the secular state, the grievous loss of the Protestant population continues to plague the French people to this day. The intrigues and vacillations of Henri de Navarre (to be King Henry IV) and his sister Marguerite de Valois unfolded in the drama where, on those nights, perhaps 50,000 Protestant Christians were killed.

The Huguenots, A Gallican movement, based on Calvin's theology, first met in Paris in 1559. A movement of urban Christianity, bibliocentric and opposed to imperial absolutism included some influential families (Navarre, Coliguy) would be engaged in religious wars in France for the entire second half of the sixteenth century. Their movement concentrated in Southeast and Southwest France, where it still enjoys vitality along with a pocket in the Northeast and in the environs of Paris, e.g. Meaux. Eventually Henry IV's Edict of Nantes in 1598 would grant toleration to the Protestants. Only the counter-edict of Fontainebleau in 1685 when 200,000 Huguenots fled France would seal the stigma of St. Bartholomew's massacre. Only the Napoleonic Code of 1804 would finally secure the rights of *l'Eglise Réformée*.

On his recall to Geneva in 1541, Calvin imported a concept learned with Bucer in Strasbourg, which would resonate with and eventually transform the French ethos. Priests and pastors together with laity (elders) would administer the church. The Geneva Consistory would eventually become the model for town meetings, electoral government, and democratic process in the West. Though a subliminal "tyrannicide" lies within this radical spirit (doing away with tyrants and tyranny), an impulse that will emerge in Cromwell's violence and eventually in the French guillotine, at heart like Calvin there is a more irenic clemency—even conservative spirit! This is the Judean exiles in Babylon who are admonished to pray for and build the city where they are exile guest-workers (Jer 29).

As with Luther's reformation, when radicals and rabble took the reforming ideas—they became iconoclasts, subversives, even terrorists. It is no accident that King George feared that "Presbyterian" commonwealth in North America and that the Puritans would spill the tea and ride from Lexington to Concord. Yet Calvin's spirit of a church (and society) advocating for the oppressed, seeking justice for the poor, and advocating a conservative ethos was overly law-abiding and obsessed with order, and if anything, comfortable in affluence.

The early reservation on whether the French ethos sustains the spirit of *fraternité* comes back at this point. In the modern world, the Catholic and Muslim faiths portray with far greater fidelity the divine concern for the poor than does Protestantism, which, as Max Weber has clearly documented, has gravitated to capitalism, even *capitalism sauvage,* and the Protestant ethic.

Like Aquinas and Augustine, Calvin poured great energy into exegeting and expounding the Psalms and Paul. For Calvin the world is the theatre of the divine glory. Building on Aquinas and Irenaeus of Lyon, he fathomed the rich resources of the Bible in light of creation theology. On Psa 8, the resplendent creation, much like the ineffable glory of God, renders miniscule, by contrast, the puny glory and capacity of man.

Yet as he first develops in the Institutes, "humans are the glory of God." The chief purpose of humans on the earth is to "glorify God." Humans therefore are the "Glory of God." The dialectic here is the most important. It is in the mind and heart, the soul and body of people that God is manifest to the world. The incarnation epitomizes this reflection. Still the sublime creation, the imago has been marred and distorted. Only God, therefore, can be the glory of man. "The order of the heavens" was a bastion of beatitude certainly in contrast to the "dreadful confusion on earth."

Calvin's rendition of Rom 8 is similarly complex. On the one hand, as Karl Marx would quote Calvin, the sigh of the "oppressed creature" was the impulse to a falsely projected religion of the masses, "the opiate of the people."

Rather than following Calvin's teaching on the manna in the wilderness, where "none must have too much and none too little" and where justice and sharing would prevail in the distribution mechanisms in this world, Marx here sees the apocalyptic tenor of Romans as a prediction (prolepsis) of revolution that would one day "topple" the powers of government, wealth and management as "workers of the world arose."

For Calvin, it is not human upheaval and revolution that ennobles but divine service and justice. Human pretense, audacity, and violence always lead to destruction. In the Romans commentary, he speaks of the "filthy and torn garment which disgraces man," which should be put off and exchanged for the "clean and decorous one that brings him much favor." The topsy-turvy world that Romans elucidates is a seismic change, not from human rebellion, but from the cosmic transformation of God.

How does the Vaux story trace alongside that of Calvin? It is likely that my ancestors were Huguenot Puritans, Presbyterian, German and Swiss Reformed—all the children of John Calvin. The French connection is difficult to trace. The name, of course, portrays a distant connection although it must be remembered that Vaux appears early in England. It is also a geographical designation—"de Vaux is (of the valley). Thus Daniel De Foe, Robert De Valle, even Guy Fawkes are flowers from the same bulb. My guess is that there are Anglo-puritan pastors, Swiss Reformed ministers, even members of

l'Eglise Réformée in France and observant Jews in whose family tradition we stand. If not, we take a standpoint with these folk; in any case we have become their spiritual heirs.

BLAISE PASCAL

Another French radical constitutes and conveys the noblest heritage of France. In the great amphitheatre at the Sorbonne the figures honored are Pascal (1623–1662), Voltaire, Rousseau, and Louis Pasteur.

Born at Clermont where Pope Urban launched the first crusade, he enjoyed the finest education anyone can receive by sisters: Gilberte and Jacqueline. A precocious mathematician, he had a conversion experience under the Jansenists at Rouen in 1646, beginning a theological pilgrimage that eventually led him to associate with the Port-Royale community (Augustinian) in Paris, where Jacqueline was in the convent.

A vigorous confrontation with the Jesuits both on theology (molinism) and ethics (probabalism) ensued. His faith was radical and pure "The God of Abraham, Isaac, and Jacob is not the God of the philosophers and the men of science." The *Pensées* and his cleansing diatribe against the Jesuits (*Lettres serites a un provincial*, 1656) have woven themselves into the pious, freethinking, anti-clerical and humanistic ethos of Paris and France.

The concern for the "little man," the "worker," the poor and simple that is found in Victor Hugo, Camus, Bresson, Levinas and Ricoeur imparts through the spirit of Pascal. Humans are situated, he claims in the Augustinian spirit, between greatness and wretchedness. Only faith can liberate the person from this dungeon to live in the pure air and light of freedom. Risk in life (wager) is necessary and is founded in this faith.

Religion is as much a matter of the heart as of reason (a sentiment fully in accord with Thomas Aquinas). Indeed an ironic (paradoxical) spirit is founded by Pascal with a sublime blending of passion and precision. Catholic and Protestant, traditional and post-modern, classical and contemporary—much of the ethos of France is embodied in Blaise Pascal.

His dual interest and competence in theology and science mirrors that of his contemporary Robert Boyle in Oxford. In the 1640's, the turbulent years of revolution in England—he published his work on the "Equilibirum of Liquids" (Hydrostatics). Pure mathematics enticed his mind and his work on probability theory is foundation to that science. Like ancient Pythagoras, his genius followed the abstract, theoretical beauty that the mind could fathom: Infinity, cubic surfaces, parabola, Pascal's mystic Hexagon and calculator (the Pascaline), the infinitesimal calculus (from which Leibniz developed the calculus), the simple mystery of the triangle (two angles = 90°), the theory of probability.

After his first religious stirrings when visiting Mercenne and the religious order of Minims, he presented his "mystic Hexagon." His early essays on conic sections (1640) [includes Pascal's theorem] and, after a visit by Descartes, the paper on the existence of vacuums seemed related to these mystic experiences.

The Jansenist side of his consciousness ascended and he retired to Port Royal des Champs (18 miles southwest of Paris) to an extreme ascetic existence focused on theology. When Robert Bresson, following Georges Bernanos has the dying and forsaken priest in *Journal d'un curé de campagne* write serenely *tout est grâce,* he reflects Pascal's spirit. After a near death experience in October of 1654 when the horses bolted and left his carriage hanging over the Seine, he again pondered the synergy of themes like suffering, chance, risk, God. He then posited the famous wager: If God does not exist one will lose nothing by believing in Him, while if He does exist one will lose everything by not believing. So "we are compelled to gamble"—"*voila!*"

On his father's death, he wrote his sister Jacqueline on "the meaning of suffering and death in the grace of God." These thoughts would mature into *Pensées*. Concentration on the theme of grace as that arose in Augustinian and Jansenist circles, captivated Pascal, now a sick man.

A planned book, *Truth of the Christian Religion* (*Vérité de la religion Chrétienne*), was not completed as he turned to *Pensées*. One might imagine it to have been something like C.S. Lewis' *Mere Christianity*. As his health deteriorated, he wrote "*Priere pour demander a Dieu le bon usage des maladies*" (Prayer for good to come from sickness). At age 39, his death from an agonizing stomach tumor metastasizing to the brain symbolized his short intense life of suffering, yet joy.

The mystical-mathematical wisdom echoes the work of Nicholas of Cusa, John of the Cross, and Teresa of Avila. It sings the strains of Julian of Norwich and Hildegard of Bingen. To this day, his vibrant strings and stirrings are found in the French soul.

Pensées is Pascal's Psalms and Romans. Plying the full strains of the elements of life and thought: radical biblical faith, grace in existence and the science of mind, heart, and spirit, Pascal's *Pensées* are one long meditation on the "Gospel of God"—the title the Apostle Paul gave to the pronunciation of the One he called the God of Abraham, Isaac, and Jacob. Here, he sought to contemplate the greatness and the misery of man. His is an ecstatic joy, joy, joy—in the presence of suffering. Apologetic as Thomas' *Summa*, as severe, yet earnest as a Calvin soliloquy, a philosophical treatise as convincing as Ricoeur, *Pensées* rehearses the genius of the French soul, the sacred touching the secular. The themes follow the long tracing we have outlined:

- The whole mind embraces mathematical and intuitive reason-differing principles and premises belong to each.

- To make light of philosophy is true philosophy. You would have others think well of you—remain silent.

- No amusement is as dangerous and to be feared as the theatre. It deceives us to think that passions are natural; its violence excites our self love.

- We come to live as if theatre were truth and real life.

- Words arranged differently have different meanings: Britney Spears unscrambled spells Presbyterians.

- Rivers are roads that move.

In Pascal, knowledge is perceived at a new synthetic level (after Descartes) where a complementarity and clarity exists among spiritual ethical and scientific technical thought and language. He also finds a way to connect virtue with the vicissitudes of life and privilege with the poor. He thus reconciles sacred and secular truth and furthers *l'esprit* of French wisdom and deservedly stands in the first position on the makers of French thought in the Amphitheatre of the Sorbonne.

VICTOR HUGO

A modern Parisienne prophet, who has had the influence of Goethe on the German soul and Shakespeare or Dickens on the English spirit, is Victor Hugo (1802–1885). Hugo emulated la Chapelle and Notre Dame, St. Eustache and St. Germain de Pres, but abhorred the authoritarian obscurantism and oppression of the established church and clergy. An energetic royalist he admired Huss and Cromwell (to Napoleon's amazement) and, with them, felt a spiritual affinity with the joy of the least common man. A leader in French neo-gothic revival of the Notre Dame Cathedral and a devotee of the beauty and sanctuary of stone, he yearned more for a blessed cathedral in the heart of cruel humanity.

Despite estrangement of his parents and an unsettled youth, in his late teens (back from Spain to Paris) Victor was an aspiring poet, artist and theologian. In an early notebook, he confided his highest ambition "I will be Chateaubriand or nothing." We think of Chateubrand's masterwork on the *Génie* du *christianisme*. His earliest odes (winning prizes at age 17) reveal a religious and historical interest flowing already as the Rhine River into his art and writing such as "Les Vierges de Verdun" and "Le Reta blissement de la statue." When the statue of "Henry IV" was being placed, moved by pity seeing the oxen who could not drag the statue up the steep slope of the Pont Neuf, Victor joined the throng of people in pulling it up themselves.

He was already a precursor of Rodin's "Les Bourgeois de Calais." This "ode" won the coveted golden lily and eventually graced a room in his Paris salon/house.

On the death of his mother Sophie when he was 20, he was cast into deep poverty. This experience surely inspired his description of Marius in *Les Misérables*: ". . . a terrible thing it is, containing days without bread, nights without sleep, evenings without a candle, a hearth without a fire, weeks without work, a future without hope, a coat out at the elbows . . . a door which one finds locked on one at night because one's rent is not paid. . . ."[10]

His work was finally recognized by King Louis XVIII who provided a small annuity (1200 ff) which allowed him to marry his Adele Adorle in St.-Sulpice on October 12, 1822. In his "Preface to Cromwell," Hugo takes top position in the Romantic literary movement. In reviewing the work of a Shakespeare troupe who had performed Othello, Hamlet and Romeo and Juliet in English, he finds in the Bard of Stratford the genius of enunciating the true Christian spirit—"the dual nature of man"—the grotesque alongside the sublime, the suffering alongside the contented, love alongside the pity; in this very contradictory and paradox (Pascal) is found the depth of the human soul. Human care in the face of

10. Victor Hugo, *Les Misérables*, Volume 2 (New York: Thomas Y. Crowell & Company, 1933), 651.

suffering as the benedictum of God becomes the secret mystery of life. Eventually he can sing in *Les Misérables*, "To love another person is to see the face of God."[11]

Now discord is part of cosmic concord, the "hunchback" is a person of beauty. Art for Hugo becomes a science of the divine-mingling of these contradictions into a sublime aesthetic, ethic, and episteme. Like his near contemporaries Henri de Toulouse-Lautrec, Edgar Degas, and Vincent Van Gogh the dancers, the poor and the workers bring elegance and hope to life transfiguring life's sadness, as Vincent said, into joy.

In the third act of the interminably long play, Hugo has John Milton chide Cromwell for his aggression and violent ambition. Hugo is playing out the ambivalence he also felt for the sequel to the English Revolution in the French Revolutions I (1787) and III (1880). Humanity, he pleads, needs to yield to gentleness, justice, and purity—lest greater upheaval and evil ensue.

With success, Hugo's home at 11 rue Notre Dame des Champs became the salon for the literary and artistic *avant-garde* (Cenacle). In 1882, he begins to write about Greece and the Muslim Mediterranean world. "The Orientales" celebrates both the Greek war of Independence and the beauty of Moorish Spain (e.g. "Grenada").

This period of classical fascination is also a phase in his episodic career as an artist as his designs flourish. Moved again by compassion he spoke out against the death penalty in "*Dernier jour d'un condamne*." The insensitivity and harshness of the early industrial revolution pains his heart and soul not only with the Romantic lake poets of England, but also with those who will protest injustice, greed, and the loss of kindness of that age: Dickens, Engels, and Marx.

Necessity channeled the excellent foundations and brilliant creativity of the now-28-year-old writer. He completed the manuscript for Notre Dame de Paris ("Hunchback") in months. Not only is the book memorable for its intricate description of fifteenth-century Paris with the vast network of the city ringing at the base of the cathedral, but also of the left bank the *université* with its «thousand angular roofs» and in *La Rive Droite*, the ville with the commerce of St.-Denis and St. Martin—but he saw the cathedral as a peon to the middle-ages—splendidly

11. Alain Boublil, "Finale," Original Soundtrack Recording of *Les Misérables*, Decca U.S., 1990.

drawn as the human drama that ever wafted praise heavenward like incense.

The moment of glory is followed by crisis that will further hone the soul of this modern poet and prophet. An aged king had been sent into exile, and Hugo endorsed the revolution that sent him there. Now his dear friend Charles Augustin Sainte-Beure was in love with Adele. After a turbulent season, Hugo himself took as a mistress the actress Juliette Drouet—with whom he blissfully cohabited for 50 years.

The next decade marked a distinguished career in poetry and drama. His life turned to political commitments, as he endorsed the rising Napoleon II as one who could unite Germany and Russia with France. Hugo now seeks a liberal humanitarian socialism, which falls short of the dreams of both utopianists' and radicals' dreams.

In 1840, he comes to the Place de la Bastille to greet the German princess and pleads with the crowd, whose passion for justice he shares. But Republicanism is in the air, *le deuxieme republic*. To Hugo's delight, the new government suspended imprisonment for debt, abolished the tax on salt, recognized universal suffrage, and abolished the death penalty and slavery. He was elected to the national assembly on a moderate platform the summer of 1840. But the forces of revolt of the masses were mounting. Hugo, the sympathetic man of law and order yet advocate of the poor and oppressed wrote:

> Before the barricades I defended Order. Before dictatorship I defended liberty. In imprisonment Louis Napoleon wrote of his own deep concern for *les miséres*—passions he shared with Hugo. The revolution of 1848 followed the revolt of the people of Rome against the Pope. France moved militarily against the mob. Hugo was torn on two issues—destruction of the printing presses and public relief for the poor. Yet his sentiments go to the side of the poor. "I am not one of those who believe that suffering can be suppressed in this world; suffering is a divine law; but I am one of those who think and affirm that poverty can be destroyed."[12]

In 1849, Hugo joined in the World Peace Congress that met in Paris. On the anniversary of the Massacre of St Bartholomew's Day, his speech spoke of the end of war and torture and the beginning of a day of joy, conviviality, arts, commerce—all under the purview of divine providence.

---

12. Diary, quoted in Elliott M. Grant, *The Career of Victor Hugo* (Cambridge: Harvard University Press, 1945), 149.

This did not sit well with the Pope in Rome, who exerted his influence on Louis Napoleon to not be so magnanimous.

Liberal in government, secular, and anti-clerical, Hugo's concord with the government was strained. He spoke out against the withdrawal of anti-exile laws, universal suffrage laws, and anti-guillotine laws (1850) and eventually concluded a famous speech extolling Charlemagne, Francis I, Henry IV and "Napoleon the Great" with the words "must we now have Napoleon 'Le Petit?'"

Little Napoleon proceeded to suspend the constitution and the Assembly and the barricades went up. December 4 witnesses bloody scenes and a massacre near Porte St.-Denis, which Hugo chronicled in his *Histoire D'un Crime*. An arrest warrant was issued. Hugo was protected for weeks from the Napoleon police by friends and Juliette. Disguised as a *clochard*, he escaped on a midnight train to Belgium. When his writings, *Histoire D'un Crime* and "Napoléon le Petit," became embarrassing to the Belgian government, Hugo exiled himself to England, and his works were published there.

A long exile in England extended to 15 years. It is at this point that Hugo›s genius as a prophet and witness emerges as in the late 1850s and early 186›s he is formulating his master work—honed now by life and death, love and hope—all on the tableau of a splendid classical and contemporary artist. He has become the mature theologian of human life. Three works: *La Légende des Siècles*, *Dieu*, and *La Fin de Satan*, not published until after his death—are composed in the period prior to completing *Les Misérables*. In the preface to *La Légende des Siècles*, he clarifies the insight he seeks:

> . . . expansion of the human race from century to century, man mounting from darkness to the ideal, the paradisiac transformation of the earthly hell the slow and supreme birth of liberty, with rights for this life and responsibility for the next; a kind of religious hymn with a thousand stanzas enclosing a deep faith and manifesting a lofty prayer; the drama of creation lighted up by the visage of the creator; that is what this poem will be when terminated, if God, the master of human existence, consents (and of the connection with *Dieu* and *La Fin de Satan*) . . .

> . . . a long poem that reverberates the unique problem of being in its triple aspect. Humanity, End, The Infinite, the progressive,

the relative, the absolute, and what one might call three cantos: *La Légende des Siècles, La Fin de Satan, Dieu*.[13]

Though these works, even *Les Misérables*, do not measure to the grandeur or epic quality of Shakespeare's *Macbeth*, Goethe's *Faust*, Milton's *Paradise Lost*, the Bible, or even the *Aeneid* and *Odyssey*. They fathom the *Akedic* mystery, the anthropology, theodicy, and ethic, the ways of God and man—in intimately humane, modern, and global terms with seldom witnessed and unparalleled grace and force.

LES MISÉRABLES

His theological masterwork, gestating for over thirty years, culminates in *Les Misérables* (1862), a work that finally embraces the full depths of human suffering, the gentle and outgoing love of God to the poor—*la misère*—and the final victory of the redemption. It charters a transformative ethic for human existence from 1830 when "man condemned" and Jean Valjean and Javert rivet the human ordeal of poverty made crime, both involved with stealing bread to feed one's family. Here we deal with the divine/human quandary of human's stealing the glory or prerogatives of God and of humanity by so dehumanizing one another and reducing persons to poverty so that one is forced to inhuman envy and theft.

In the great *kenosis* passage of Phil 2, the condescending Son of God does not crave or grasp divinity but "empties himself, taking the form of a slave—obedient unto death." Here the moral architecture for human desire and anxiety is exposed and a new world of plenteous provision, justice, and generosity is proposed to be tested in real life through faith. This is the historic theological ethos of the French tradition—reenacted at the dawn of the modern world.

In contrast to Javert's slavish idolatry of the law and punishment, Bishop Myriel embodies a new justice where "pardon" (forgiveness) displaces even expectation and "right." If people demean one another as the rich concentrate wealth in themselves while others go hungry, the culture of theft inevitably arises—now in the "Mystère de la Pauvre et de la Riches» (Calvin), the sin of the privileged.

The 1828 experience of Bishop Myriel of Digne—who took under his wing an ex-con Pierre Maurin who had stolen a loaf of bread and

13. Victor Hugo, *La Légende des Siècles* (Paris: L'Harmattan, 1859).

spent five years in prison, transforming him into an honest man—personified and clarified for Hugo this divine-human drama.

The 1845 manuscript *Les Misérables* was finally removed from the trunk in Guernsey in 1860. He visited Belgium and the site of the battle of Waterloo. Volume I, "Fantine," appeared just as the entire work was completed on May 18, 1862. It was a work critiquing inhuman law.

The women in *Les Misérables* are the women in Hugo's life who represent the counterpoint and complementarity of humanity. They are heroines, no longer temptresses or subordinates as in preceding literature. Cosette becomes Adèle Foucher, the needy child, the beautiful adolescent, the *jeune fille française*. Cosette I marries Marius on February 16, 1833 the night that began Hugo's liaison with Juliette Drouet, his companion and protector for 50 years.

The work is a hymn to the triumph of grace within the agonies and ecstasies of human existence. It touched, transformed, and molded the French soul. The great celebration held in Hugo's honor on the avenue d'Eylau on February 27, 1881 and the funeral on June 1, 1885—when he was laid to rest in the Pantheon beside Voltaire and Rousseau—were a tribute to a France that in his lifetime had been transformed from a brutal, oppressive regime into to a free and democratic nation and as with France so the modern world, or so it was hoped.

PAUL RICOEUR

"Why Ricoeur?" asks British philosopher-literature scholar Karl Simms.

> . . . the most wide-ranging thinker alive in the world today. Although nominally a philosopher his work has also cut across the subjects of religion and bible exegesis, history, literary criticism, psychoanalysis, politics . . . sociology and linguistics.[14]

A "philosopher of faith" rather than "suspicion," he is widely considered the greatest living philosopher in France (step aside Derrida). Born in Valence, south of Lyons in 1913 (my father's birthday), he turned early to an interest in philosophy. Studying at Rennes, focusing on classical languages, he wrote an M.A. thesis on "the problem of God." To this day, he characterizes his work to be on "the relationship

---

14. Karl Simms, *Paul Ricoeur* (London: Routledge, 2003).

between philosophy and biblical faith."[15] With him as model, this author has striven to be a hermeneutic and kerygmatic philosopher and, like him, a "public intellectual."

At the Sorbonne in 1934, he met his intellectual mentor Gabriel Marcel, who coined the word "existentialism." From 1935 to 1940, he taught philosophy at various high schools and published pieces on Christian socialism and pacifism.

Enlisted in the French Army in 1940, he was captured and spent five years as a prisoner of war in East Germany. Despite harsh conditions, he helped establish a university in the "prison camp" and studied and taught Husserl, Jaspers, and Marcel.

His work embraces that classic French impulse of encyclopedic wisdom, of synthetic interest in theology and the sciences, of the conjunction of the spiritual and the political. Although a member of the *Eglise Réformée*, his work is fundamental in the *Institut Catholique*, as well as in Jewish and Muslim circles. His library has been given to the Protestant faculty in Paris, where I work on this section in the Ricouer Room and a teaching room honors his life here in my other home, the *Institut Catholique*.

As he told me at his 90th birthday party, he had been blessed to live two lifetimes. His alert mind and speech were still active in 2004 (he died in 2005). After teaching at Le Chambon and Strasbourg, he became chair and his project on the philosophy of the will appeared in seven parts. *Fallible Man, The Symbolism of Evil* and his broader teaching was celebrated in Paris and throughout France. Thousands of students thronged to his lectures. Along with other great public intellectuals of the post-war European world—Emmanuel Levinas and my other teacher, Helmut Thielicke, as well as Jürgen Moltmann, Hans Kung and Karl Rahner—he has supplied inspiration and theological/philosophical to generations to follow. Our work in this time will be particularly challenging because we live in an intensely faith-driven and interfaith milieu as well as an unashamedly secular age. In my sabbatical in Paris (Spring 2011), I have resolved to devote some time to exploring how his philosophy of kerygmatics can provide foundation for our interfaith age.

15. Ibid., 3.

In 1967, Ricoeur left the Sorbonne because of a conviction that education was deserved by working-class students and not just the elite. He came to Nanterre (now Université Paris X Nanterre), where the student revolt of the late 1960›s brought an end to studies as it had to most European education. He then became an itinerant scholar in Belgium (Louvain), the U.S. (Chicago), and Canada (Toronto).

In the 1980›s, *Hermeneutics and the Human Sciences* and *From Text to Action* were succeeded by the three-volume *Time and Narrative*. In the 1990s, he published *Oneself as Another* and *The Just* and held the Paul Tillich University professorship at Chicago. How do his ideas and spirit provide continuity to what I am calling the French ethos?

His work focuses on philosophy (theology) and ethics—belief and action. He relives and remakes the ancient synthesis of Genevieve and Clovis—of the sacred and the secular. He is known and loved among Jews in Paris and Muslims at Nanterre, a revered thinker among the Jesuits and Catholics of France and, of course, the favorite son of the *Eglise Réformée*.

Like Thomas or Pascal, he is as at home in the scientific and philosophical world as he is in the religious. Taking in hand Hegel and Heidegger, Marcel and Merleau-Ponty, Aristotle and Kant, he refines intellectual tradition to meet today's crises and challenges—political, psychoanalytic, legal, and literary. He is the preeminent hermeneuticist of the contemporary world, translating ultimate (theistic) and normative (moral) parameters into the understanding speech and action of contemporary life.

He is a biblical thinker. His phenomenology is never abstract. It is personal, narrative, word, action and life-focused, existential—having to do with suffering and justice, living and dying.

He sustains the Aristotelian and Thomistic heritage of Paris in taking epistemology and ethics—both rational and revelational—toward a comprehensive and post-modern theory. His pioneering work extends Heidegger's penetrating insights on being and time to a new level. Like Pascal, he probes the self, finding the person an admixture of necessity and contingency on the one hand—and freedom, will, and decisive action on the other. Two other public intellectuals who resonate his wisdom are Hannah Arendt, who spent eight years in Paris working with Jewish refugees before the venom of the French Vichy state became pronounced and she fled to the U.S. where she joined fellow Bultmann scholar, Hans Jonas at the New School. Jürgen Habermas, who taught at New School and then Northwestern (where I joined him for a seminar of Kierkegaard in the early 2000s), was also a kindred spirit. These all follow the ethos of Heidegger and Husserl.

Beginning with the five years he spent as a prisoner of war in East Germany, where under the severest health conditions and total surrender of material freedom, Ricoeur fashioned a cultural world of ideas and activities much like that of the interned Japanese in American concentration camps.

Creating a prison university and collaborating with Michael Defrenne on work on Karl Jaspers, he encouraged the inmates to teach the fields of their expertise. Much of the historic genius of the medieval Sorbonne is thus renewed in the work of Paul Ricoeur.

Here his anthropology begins to take shape with the inherent ambiguity of conditioned bodily constraint, material history and circumstance, the force of the exigencies of life on the one hand—as these are transfigured by creativity of concept and will—and eventful willing and decision-making and the awesome power of care, pardon, responsibility and hope on the other.

Building on Calvin›s (Institutes, Book 1) insight that knowledge of self and of God (including reality/truth) are reciprocal, Ricoeur contends that subjectivity and objectivity intertwine in the unconsciousness. Actually, he is so steeped in Kant that pure and complete objectivity and subjectivity are impossible, so that intersubjectivity or relationality with the "other" colors and illumines all perception and understanding.

The body (materiality), mind (subjectivity), and relationality (Heidegger: *Miteinandersein*) together form a matrix of consciousness that then conveys itself in language. Narrative is the exposition and expression of the person. Here again is the synthetic sense of reality which we find in Thomas, Calvin, and Pascal—the answer to Descartes' skepticism and demarcation of consciousness—the ancient genius of Paris.

Ricoeur is also realistic about the tragedy within life. With his Parisian mentor—Calvin—he affirmed the glory of human origination and destination, finitude and failure. Just as Calvin is acutely aware of the fallen human condition, and Pascal and Hugo trace its aggression/transgression into the human soul and human interactions—yielding to radical grace and the necessity for humanness—Ricoeur ponders the symbolism of evil, the parameters of justice and on justice, fallibility, finitude and the secret grace discovered within these limitations.

Ricoeur is also profoundly the child of Victor Hugo, conveying his sense of compassion for the vulnerable into modern existence. Ricoeur's book, *Oneself as Another*, and his fascinating formulations in dialogue with Emmanuel Levinas on *l'autre*, recall *Les Misérables'* "to love another is to see the face of God." In this heritage, the French political penchant of seeking a humane socialism, strongly marked by liberty and all the while avoiding the shoals of communism and Vichy fascism, is embodied by Ricouer.

EMMANUEL LEVINAS

Equally honored in France today is another non-conformist, Emmanuel Levinas, whose biblical and *Talmudic* approach to philosophy, theology, and ethics is close in kinship to my own and to that of Ricouer. In a eulogy on Christmas Day, 1994, the day Levinas died, Jacques Derrida acknowledged that his friend had effected a monumental revolution in the intellectual life of France by introducing phenomenology from Husserl and focus on the "other" from Heidegger in the light of existential ontology. The follower of the argument of this essay will recognize the deeper springs of the cultural wellspring of consciousness and the particular rivulets of very specific dispositions in French history, which had made possible the society for which Levinas introduced following the 1930s. At that demonic time, most of his Lithuanian family was murdered by the same German culture that had germinated these intellectual refinements.

What ideas and ideals had Husserl and Heidegger conceived that, when transformed into Levinas' Jewish, Rabbinic, Biblical and *Talmudic* system of thought would save the integrity of those same French and German cultures? And why had those same cultures in their diabolical captivity sought to extract those very threads of color from the fabric of public life? Only Bonhoeffer in Germany and the faithful Christian communities around Meaux, Strasbourg, and the deep southern cities of France like Chambon, were able to see the insidious, anti-human ideology that was arising and mustered "holy resistance" to preserve the soil for what Levinas brought to Paris and through Paris—the world.

Phenomenology is a mode of knowing, thinking, expressing and valuing reality, which is Hebraically (Prophetic) and Hellenically (Socratic) iconoclastic, stripping culturalism, nationalism, and egoism, destructive of the self and the other, from its enjoyed popular currency in the emerging cultures of destruction and death. It seeks to know and honor the authentic phenomenon arising from things in themselves rather than attributing to these entities ultimacy (idolatry) or penultimate loyalty (injustice).One immediately senses the resonance of such iconoclasm with one who reasons and believes from the guidance of biblical and sacred texts. Levinas is recultivating the soil first turned by Irenaeus, then Pascal.

The connection with Heidegger is more complex, given his reluctance to repudiate Hitler, Naziism, and the Holocaust. Derrida claims that Levinas introduced a viable ontology and axiology (ethics) beginning in 1930. "He changed the landscape in a place without a landscape of thought."[16]

The radical renovation he brought into France took him back 2000 years to the time when the eruption of Christianity into world history brought the "Here I am" of Hebraic thought into cultural contact with the Greeks and the ontological legacy of Socrates, Plato, and Aristotle—then appropriated that heritage forward into the 20th century "through the thought of Emmanuel Levinas in a way that was clear, confident and calm and modest."[17]

The ethos of contemporary France with its elements of truth and justice, freedom and the quest for integrity owes much to the three tenors, the three Parisienne philosophers—who have become salient world thinkers and public theologians for our time.

Ricoeur, Levinas, and Derrida have reestablished respect and mutuality with northern and deep French colonial Africa (e.g., Algeria and Senegal) and contact with new-world France in North American and global political and economic justice—all within solid frameworks of human rights and clemency. All this is their forthright and fervent commitment.

16. Jacques Derrida, *The Work of Mourning*, Pascale-Anne Brault and Michael Naas, eds. (Chicago: The University of Chicago Press, 2001), 208–9.

17. Ibid., 209.

CONCLUSION

We have viewed a short parade of *Prophètes Parisiennes*. Like watching the victorious Tour de France cyclists conclude their grueling ordeal as they ride down the Champs Elysees, these men and women have finished the race and carved their names into the soul of this monument-conscious country. Now it is a living monument, not Mozart's vengeful *Commendatore*, but the Creator-Lord of all life. But even more, these prophets have woven their exemplary witness into the soul of this and all nations. Like a great line of British leaders—Wyclif to Wesley—with predecessors and followers, our world has been enriched by their feats amid adversity. They may rest in the pantheon, but their abiding place remains in the hearts and minds of those who recall the noble heritage and live it.

VIII

Diary After Late Spring 2011—The Present

May 4, 2011 (The Louvre)

I BRAVED THE TENS of thousands at the Louvre today to catch the exhibition of Rembrandt's "The Face of Christ." I also renewed my acquaintance with the *Egyptian Book of the Dead* from the permanent Thutmose III collection. Then I resorted to the 16th century Italian masters, including Titian and Tintoretto's version of the Jesus Meal, either Emmaus or some sort of follow-up on da Vinci's "The Last Supper." After all, his "Mona Lisa," in her bullet-proof **insouciance**, is just down the hall.

The exhibition is about a single mystery; in the artist's words, this is "painted from life." What could this cryptic reference mean? Had he actually seen or been visited himself by the enigmatic visitor who joined the travelers on the road to Emmaus? That café stop has become the paradigmatic hospitality scene in humanistic lore, as well as the preeminent theistic event as it becomes the coalescence of the meal-instruction-disclosure event of the body of Jesus tradition. This tradition would embrace resurrection, "empty tomb," and appearances of *Logos*, Messiah, Mahdi, Emmanuel, Emmaus, yearning, expectant and ready humanity—spearheading the hope of the world. It also distills multiple signature events of the nascent church as it encapsulates the activity that busied the primitive witnessing community, which persisted in prayer, the apostles' teaching (*Didache*), and in the "breaking of bread" (Acts 2). Actually in (Tiziano Vecellio, 1488–1576) Titian's **"Tisch"** (1530) at Emmaus, which seems to be in a café with several waiters, a dog under the table, perhaps a Syro-phoenician hound waiting for scraps, we find decanters of wine, plates of red-tipped lettuce, Italian baguettes, yellow Fuji apples, and the *pièce de résistance*— crystal salt-dish, in other words, a living, contemporaneous event, with the ever-present companion.

Rembrandt's Jesus is celebrated as a break with the Hollywood, glorified tradition, now to a Millet, David, or Van Gogh-like realism in the museum's accompanying write up, a young Amsterdam Jew, a town so Judaophilic that even Bibi Netanyahu would be welcome at one's table. Actually Titian's Jesus is also a "young Jew' or Veronese look-alike, one who would be a natural walk-on in Pier Paolo Pasolini's (1922–1975) film, *The Gospel According to St. Matthew (1964)*. In that film, the reader will recall, a normal mountain village in Tuscany becomes Palestine, Galilee, Jerusalem, and the Jesus company and entourage. In a book I've just scanned in the *Institut Catholique*, the author describes a "Jewish Jesus," which now captivates the American scene in keeping with our Judaophilic and Islamophobic ethos. As Rapture is about to break on the lands of Michele Bachmann, Sarah Palin, and John Boehner, we may find out what's going on in *Terra Sancta Americana* and if *Civitas Terrena* is about to rapture up to *Civitas Dei*.

But this is the very mystery. Jesus is now "real life," family, friends, disciples, crowds, all bewildered by confused vision. Who can this be—a hitch-hiker, a hanger-on who needs lodging for the night so he doesn't have to sleep in St. Mary's gaited side-niche in a cardboard box? "Have you not heard the confusing gossip up around Golgotha, Bethany, and Bethphage, the tombs and burial gardens?"

Rembrandt, as Visser 't Hooft has shown on the artist's Jesus work, is searching for universal, interfaith, humanistic, down-to-earth meaning, and that is the blazing dazzle, the "light from above." The original on paper, big screened at the exhibit, 18-foot-square, shows a blaze of radiation glory in the black, charcoal sketch.

The truth that Rembrandt, the Protestant, wanted to show was the same as his teacher, Rubens (Protestant papa and Medici Catholic mom), that Jesus alive is a living corpse or should we say *Corpus Christi*. To be credible, he had to communicate Scripture to his bible-memorizing, Dutch viewers. Thomas is accommodated, the touchy-feely Thomas. Descartes, the materialist, is devoid of Descartes the mystic. But there is a better way, the way of Jansenist, Blaise Pascal. Georges Bernanos

(1888–1948) is very much like his film follower, Robert Bresson (*Diary of a Country Priest*, 1951; *Au Hasard Balthasar, 1966)*. That way is the biblical doctrine of Word, living, written, preached, listened, lived. This is Augustine's visible Word, the mass has been transfigured into message— body is now communicated among His followers, Jesus-Yahweh, His Friends, His Testifiers, His confused, bewildered yet willing to speak up, act out and live and die for the world of people. Biblical research is now showing the connection between Yahweh, the "I Am," the "I will be who I am becoming, I'm going on are you coming?" And the Son of Man, Jesus' self-designation and Son of God, research on Mark 1. Both are hauntingly human figures, one walks quietly in the garden, one looks over Jerusalem then and, we suppose now, weeps. All sit on a splendorous radiant throne, Exodus, Ezekiel, Daniel, and Mark's Son of Man, the sapphire throne.

On Holy War, America, and the Middle East—yes, I'm hopeful that the end has come for the attack-counterattack war on terrorism with its "garden of Eden, Cain, and Abel" etiology ("you started it," "no you"/"your attack, my revenge, simple justice"). The violent Navy Seals blow-away of Osama bin Laden—then dumping his long, rich, fanatic, and debili-tated torso to the sharks in the Indian Ocean—is macho-mania stands in a long tradition of American violence. Now is time for repentance and reconciliation all around, *Jihadist* and Christian right extremist, Israel, Pakistan, The U.S. and ever-patriotic France. Can a new theology of death and resurrection body finally emerge in the world? Perhaps on some road to Emmaus, right now?

May 10, 2011

I'm speaking tonight to the 50 pastor/spouse teams of American church pastors in Europe. They come from Paris, Bonn, Vienna, Hague, Stock-holm, Strasbourg, Middle East, East Europe, Turkey, Uzbekistan,, even a few from Africa. My talk will excerpt a little piece I've been crafting, *Prophètes Parisienne*, which finds a thread of universal theological history developing right here in Paris. The essay goes from Genevieve (419–512) to Clovis and Peter Abelard (1079–1142), through Aquinas, Calvin, Pascal on to the great catholic minds of the 50s and 60s at *Institut Catholique, de Lubac*, Yves Marie Joseph Congar (1904–1995), Pierre Teil-hard de Chardin (1881–1955), then out Rennes Boulevard to the *Institut Protestante de Théologie*, and Paul Ricoeur, thought to be the foremost philosopher and theologian in France in our time. My talk tonight will focus on Aquinas and Calvin, Victor Hugo, and Ricoeur. The talk flubbed or bombed, take your choice; too much for a weary after-dinner speech. I should have just focused on Aquinas, with lateral reference to the others, perhaps related to their trip to Chartres today, using Henry Adams, from Mont St. Michel to Chartres. Actually, I might better have spoken of Schweitzer, Bernanos, and more Alsatian Francophones; they seem so much more Protestant than the Catholic Parisians.

This afternoon, I visited *Musée Rodin*, here on the east side of the great Napoleonic headquarters, now the *Hôpital les Invalides*. This is one of the great sites in Paris. The garden monument is profoundly moving, a block-mass of solid bronze weight from which the torso, head, and hand of Victor Hugo emerges. I gave him a low five, dealing with my frustration of not being able to touch, you know museums—*ne touche pas*.

On the Van Gogh paintings, I confess that I have started to touch a few of the perhaps 100 pieces I have seen in Amsterdam, *Musée d'Orsay*, and now here at Rodin, an Arles piece on a viaduct. Rest assured I withdrew the hand in time, except for Rodin, who welcomes the touch. Almost everyone wants to caress or hug "The Burghers of Calais," and they love it in their frozen but ever-living living. My thought on this masterpiece is prompted by another Rodin masterpiece, Jesus (on the cross with Magdalene) clinging to his fallen or toppled head. In this twilight of Easter, I thank God for the (single and sufficient) burgher of Calais, one who saved the whole people, not only of France, but of the world.

Sunday May 15, 2011

A *tour de force* at the American Church in Paris. An amazing worship service, first of all—a sterling message from Mark Labberton, our teacher this week from Fuller Seminary. Today from Isa 58 and Matt 8, worship as life. I wished him Godspeed as he "straddles the evangelical-para-church world and the mainline Protestant-Scriptural world of social justice." Fred Gramman's music was about the best scripted church service I have heard in many years. As prelude, Fred played "Toccata in D Minor," then a fine clarinetist played Mozart's "Concerto for Clarinet," First Movement; Phil

Glenister sang George Herbert/ Ralph Vaughn Williams, *The Call*, and Fred played Bach's "Fugue in G Minor" as postlude.

Following the service was a spectacular dinner by the Filipino community in the church. A moving conversation followed, with a couple who had ministered in Zurich and throughout the world—an exceptional pair. It was a thrilling day. I was really able to minister at some depth with these 55 pastoral- teams of International churches, Antalya, Turkey, American Protestant, The Hague, American Protestant in Bonn, International Church of Strasbourg, Bratislava, Immanuel International, Stockholm, American church in London, Berlin, Geneva Lutheran, International Protestants of Zurich, Lutheran in Nairobi, Westlake in Nyon, Luzern. I thank Scott Herr for this privilege.

Tuesday, May 17, 2011

I have not yet commented on the decision last week by the Presbyterian Church in the U.S. to return to a policy where it gives no explicit directive as to whether an ordained officer (elder or deacon) can be homosexual. Being posted in Europe on my sabbatical, I must acknowledge that the matter does not rile the French, Dutch, or even English the way it does Americans. Actually, we feel right at home and I feel I am back at Garrett-Evangelical Theological Seminary where we have long been committed to an inclusive church, even on the question of ordination and the performance of marriage or commitment services. Again, in our view (Sara and myself, the ministry team), we believe that marriage is about what the signal biblical material, the Book of Micah and Christ and His Church, contends, cherishing and committing, analogies to the character of God.

The reader should know, also, that my involvements have caused the church much grief on this question. I wrote the 1978 document for the Presbyterian church in America which created the atmosphere for a harsh exclusive and restrictive policy, which ensued in the 1997 amendment to the Book of Order which guides the polity action of organs of the church—local church sessions and congregations, Presbyteries, which are the Calvinist-democratic substitute for bishops, synods and the general assembly, the prototype of American political order.

In that groundbreaking committee, appointed at General Assembly in 1976, I was asked by the conservative-leaning minority committee to seek conciliatory language from my teacher, Helmut Thielicke, the most forceful evangelical voice in the Christian world, to heal the bitter *Zerris-enheit* (tearing apart) of Christ's body by this matter. My grounding draft of the position, which was eventually adopted by the General Assembly in 1978, sought full civil rights for gay persons, inclusion within the life of the church extending even to sacred orders under the conditions of chastity and monogamous fidelity. That proved to be the hitch, and the eventual lynch-pin (by which I mean the pin which causes lynching).

My convictions on the issue, drawn now 35 years ago, were that monotheistic and Christocentric faith stressed man-woman, monogamous marriage, family, the nurture of children, and the sustenance of a generally "normative" view of this familial life-style. (The gay life was discountenanced, to say the least, or if we consider the American Missionary model in Uganda, hounded down and killed.)

This ethos I sought then was found in Evangelical and Protestant Christianity, in Eastern Orthodoxy and Roman Catholic practice, in Pentecostal expression, the most rapidly flourishing version of Christian faith in the world, as well as in Judaism and Islam, which I see as hermeneutically corroborating faiths to the Christian faith and life. The family life, man-woman model was also a preferential norm in African, Hispanic, and Asian cultures. This all convinced me and my teacher, Thielicke, that while a new life-style diversity might come to prevail in autonomous and free-spirited Europe and America, globally another ethos, one more traditional, was deeply embedded in the rest of the world.

The 1978 position of the Presbyterian Church sought to recognize in this way "what God was doing in the world" (Paul Lehmann and H. Richard Niebuhr). Little did I know that the "Tea Party," "Presbyterian lay committee," Methodist "circuit riders," and a thousand Carl-Rove protégés were waiting in the wings. I agreed with Halford E. Luccock (1885–1961) at Yale and his comment on his Methodist compatriots, "I'd like to see those fat-guys on a horse."

So what has changed? As I have confessed in my writings over the last 30 years (in recent books such as *Jew, Christian, Muslim, Journey into an Interfaith World*, and *Ministry at the Edge*), I now know that gays and lesbians are perfectly as able of cherishing and committing their love-lives as are we heterosexuals, who have watched our own indices of violence and divorce rates sky-rocket. I have known countless men and women of LGBT sexual preference worthy of Holy orders and fine-tuned in

Christian piety and pastoral sensitivity. God not only accepts the witness of this community, but also needs it. And it is not the "woman-taken-in-adultery" admonition: "go and sin no more" (John 8:11).

The achievement of a majority vote of a majority of presbyteries in May of 2011, good representative processing of the democratic political mode of decision-making, is not only called for at long last as a matter of justice and kindness but also may even be an expression of the wishes of the One God of the universe, The God and Father of the Lord Jesus Christ.

My assertion here is tentative, since we are not in-the-know Gnostics, the heresy of most Christian evangelicals and militant Muslims, but rather travelers with the Emmanuel God of Moses, the Emmaus Companion, *Panis Angelicus*, and One, whom a colleague minister at the American Church in Paris rightly says is the unknown God, the "in-a-glass-darkly-God," a God who is bigger than any particular religion.

So, in sum, we are back to square one, to Jesus and Augustine, but not Tertullian, to Aquinas and Calvin, but not John Knox, to Barth and Thielicke, but not Pastor Hagee. Silence, this policy is golden, let's fleece it for all it's worth (see also my sermon later in this diary on December 1, 2011).

May 24, 2011

Paris continues to unfold her treasures and pleasures onto the Algerian carpets and the swift-footed-*gendarme*-escaping carpet-baggers. This past week against the *ciel d'orange* (Van Gogh's threatening sky in Auvers-sur-Oise), the wrath of heaven radiating relentlessly earthward, was graced by Terrence Malick's brilliant and resplendent film, *The Tree of Life* (2011), as it won the *Palme d'Or* at Cannes.

Global skies are still El Greco's "View of Toledo," dark and ominous, as Egypt reverts into injustice, Syria blithely sprays gunfire on her own citizens, Libya slogs along with a madman at the helm, and from blessed *Al-Andalus* to European Barcelona, social chaos erupts in another fast-becoming-third-world country, Spain. Little pity rises for the President, even as 7 million jobs have disappeared in America during the Bush II / Obama-watch since 2007.

Just at the moment when the world is at sixes and sevens, Malick's gorgeous treatise on Kierkegaard, Buddhism, and Polish catholic liturgy, *The Tree of Life*, opens in Cannes along with Woody Allen's *Minuit à Paris* (2011), with its poster of Van Gogh's "Starry Night." Meanwhile, the Dardenne Brothers' *Le Gamin au Vélo* shares top prize with Malick.

What does the former teacher of Kierkegaard's philosophy at MIT have to say about theology and theodicy, even as the sun smiles for the third straight month on *la belle Paris*?

I woke before dawn, in my room at 48 rue St. Placide, thinking of Malick. I have just finished my first draft of *The Ministry of Vincent Van Gogh in Religion and Art* and am surrounded by our landlady's art, Marianne de Vaux, like me, an offspring of Pere Jean de Vaux, curé de *l'église Saint-Eustache* (c.1300), where St. Saens used to play. A frequent teacher in Arles, the room is surrounded by scenes of bullfights in the Arles coliseum. With Spain in turmoil, I realize the symbolism of the toreador as he deftly taunts, wounds and evades the raging bull until he himself dies through goring heroism or boring retirement—*c'est la vie et la mort*.

In the "Ballad of the Rose" in Bizet's "Carmen," we sense the poignancy of fragile and fickle life and love. Both Carmen, the cigar rolling, man-taunting , whirling Flamenco/castenada (dance) of love, and the toreador's sweeping illusion and side-step are parables of the drama of life and death in God's "creation" or our "godless' world (1Cor 15:19).

And so, Malick's five-volume works: *Badlands* (1973), *Days of Heaven* (1978), *The Thin Red Line* (1998), *New World* (2005), and now *The Tree of Life*, searches out the redemptive mystery. In "The Tree of Life," among other themes, he enunciates the "grace of life, the sacred gift of the creation, the drama of guilt and new beginnings and the sacrament of life, together, within, and beyond the cosmos.

Early in the film, we see the knock at the door of their suburban 1950s home in Waco, Texas and the delivery of a telegram announcing that a beloved 19-year-old son has died. Breathless grief grips the young mom and dad, sucking the gasp of breath from their very being. Malick's familiar haunting voice from the background, foreground, overground, and underground, speaks of the ubiquitous presence of grace, *tout est grâce*, as Bernano's/Bresson's *"Journal d'un curé de campagne,"* (Diary of a Country Priest), would have it. Paul the Apostle spoke of the "All sufficiency of grace" (2 Cor 9:8), amid disease and death, ship-wreck and discouragement, failure and loss of all things. Bible testimony sees amid all vicissitude that we are surrounded and confronted with the inexplicable "grace of life" to which we are heirs as the "children of God."

Down under, within and out beyond this mystery (*sacramentum*) is the ever giving and taking, creating and destroying, tempting, saving and damning, intention and action of God within and without the creation. Our response to this prevalent, prevenient (Wesley) and highly particular gifting and loving presence all around us enables us to "be more than conquerors" in "all things" through One who Loved us and gave Himself (Rom 8) for *peccata mundi*, the fallen yet being-redeemed "cosmos" (realm of iniquity/ raptured in grace).

Much of *The Tree of Life* is a flashback on the drama of the love and betrayal, duty and forgiveness, striving and gratitude, that is the life of this microcosmic family, all portrayed against the enfolding macrocosm of unfolding creation both in her interiority and exteriority, her appearance and essence, her ancient beginnings and future destinies. Our corpuscular, Cambrian-ancestral and cosmic beings and bearings do not escape Malick's searching and scrutinizing lens.

The environment or theatre (Kierkegaard after Calvin) of this veil of thrill, terror, triumph, and tragedy is the watch, the post, we are given here and now. What do we do now with who we are, what is our *lebenswelt* and what we do with those lives that have been entrusted to our precarious and passing attention is the realm of salvation and damnation. His message is the ancient wisdom of Gilgamesh, that we cherish the one who lies on our breast and the tiny hand placed within ours. The other who transects our path is also *Deus incognito*, another in whom is the Other (Levinas). From the dawn of creation, the wonderful Tyrannosaurus Rex who decides not to stomp on a little transgressor on his turf, we know what is of God and human accountability. It is self-evident.

As for now "we do not yet know who we are or who we will become," we see only the vague and opaque shadow of God and even ourselves as is seen in the ancient vanity mirrors in the exhibit cases in the Egypt section of the Louvre, "through a glass darkly." All we know for sure is that we will only know there and then when we shall see Him as He is and we shall at last know even as we have been fully known.

While I Have Being

June 6, 2011

Today was a wonderful day with Mitch and Nancy Bruski, our dear neighbors in Evanston—soul brother and sister in matters political, cultural and philosophical. We did the Duffy Exhibition at *Musée Marmottan Monet* in La Muette, these brothers brilliantly taking the impressionist Van Gogh brothers, into the mood of avant garde. Then we metro-ed across to Centre Pompidou and the riveting and inspiring "Chagall and the Bible" exhibit at the Jewish Museum of History. Charles Tompkins finished the day playing the great organ of Notre Dame for 1000 people promenading through. It reminded me of a preaching engagement at Fourth Presbyterian, Chicago, when I was a candidate for the dean of chapel position at Princeton University. Bloomindales had just opened across the street, and thousands of curious shoppers wandered in and out of Cram's splendid sanctuary. Ironically, he had also built the great chapel in Princeton. I began my message with the quip from Socrates, *vis à vis* the "shop till you drop" liturgy at Bloomies dueling with ours, "Never have I seen so many things I didn't want."

For the theologically curious, Charles played four movements from Messiaen's "*Méditations sur le Mystère de la Sainte Trinité*," a pondering of the *Summa Theologica* portions where St. Thomas worked through the relationship of God's identity and existence, "*Dieu-est et Dieu est immense*," ripe for the full volume and virtuosity of Messiaen's sound and scales, ending in the sublime "*Dans le verbe etait la vie et la vie etait la lumiere*." The one-hour, pre-Vespers concert was followed by the hymn "*Veni Creator Spiritus*" and the celebration of the seventh Sunday of Easter, a preparation for Pentecost. Then we liturgically begin the long season of ordinary time, better known as the seven-week summer holiday of French civil servants, at which time they resort to the bikinis and beaches, and Ken and Sara will return to Chicago to face another winter on Lake Michigan.

This gets me back to the theological story-line which is the leitmotif of this diary. What of the Trinity and doctrine of spirit, or what of our at once "restless" and "holiness" world probably would now rather call "the movement of the Spirit?"

Olivier Messiaen (1908–1982) follows closely the logic of Thomas Aquinas in the *Summa Theologica*. This classical orthodox heritage is kept intact by Eastern Orthodoxy, Protestantism, Evangelicalism, and

Pentecostalism, the major impulses of Christian faith and life from Christian beginnings into our own history. Messiaen also ponders the mysteries of Judaism and Islam which, one author here at the *Institut Protestante* calls the "Mystery of the Cross of Christ." This is the quintessential mystery of the One and Unique God and His ever-quizzing humanity. To capture the theological genius that makes him the best-theologian-composer since Bach and Mozart, we must join the *"Méditations sur le Mystère de la Sainte Trinité"* to the well-known "Four Songs for the End of Time."

These secular songs were written in a German concentration camp, and they have taken their place in the concert repertoire alongside Brahms's *"Deutsches Requiem."* When Messiaen was sent to the *Konzentratioslage* on the fall of France in 1940, he composed the *"Quatuor pour la Fin du Temps"* for the guards and his fellow prisoners, using the only four instruments available: piano, cello, violin, and clarinet. One scholar we know has analyzed this work in the terms of *Nausea* by Jean Paul Sartre, France's greatest philosopher of the time. To my mind, it resembles more the composer's meditations on the mystery of the Trinity or Sartre's lesser-known works on the phenomenon of crucifixion and resurrection. To this author, *"Quatuor"* also resonates with Messiaen's music on colors or birds, even caged-birds or coal-mine birds, whose song can still be *joi d'vivre* or a *todeslied* admonition to humanity.

In the *"Méditations sur le Mystère de la Sainte Trinité,"* which is closely related to an organ work called *"Messe de Pentecote"* (which we may hear this coming weekend), we see that Spirit arises in the world in the uniqueness and unity of divine being, in creation, continuing creation and consummation, as an intimation of the Triune God. Trinity is necessary, in other words, to fathom humanity and divinity. Or to put the same truth in the words of Calvin as influenced by Aquinas, humans can only be known in God and God only in humans. God is the *Christos* of Bonhoeffer, the "man for others." In Messiaen's introduction, he quotes Aquinas: ". . . the angels communicate with each other without the constraints of time and space." In the Government of the Creatures, (Summa, Part I), Question 107, entitled the "language of the angels," Thomas writes, "If the angel by his will commands his mental concept with a view to communicating it to another then immediately the latter takes cognizance of it."

Lest we find ourselves at this point counting the number of angels on the head of a pin, this simply means that language or speech is commensurable with the will, Word, or command of God. At Pentecost, "they each heard in their own language," and the word came through as *Shavuot*, the festival of the giving of the law, Sinai, command—and they were summoned to believe and follow. Babel had been reversed. Comprehensible speech, *verbum Dei*, is the gift of Pentecost Paraclete, the comforter, or in biblical meaning, the strengthener.

Messiaen's mystery of this Trinity or Triune God unfolds in eight movements, which we list here:

- The Father of the stars or the Father ungendered (so much for male and female from the beginning).

- The Holiness of Jesus Christ (the salience of association/ "no togetherness without holiness").

- The true relation to God is actually identical to the Spirit.

- I am that am.

- God is, God is immense, maybe the child's "God is great/God is good," but certainly not the "ludicrous twaddle" of the praise song, "God is good all the time, all the time, God is good." That's Jane Russell's God as "cosmic sugar daddy" and even worse, "This is the best of all possible worlds, I love sinning, God loves forgiving," etc. "God is eternal, immovable, unchangeable," and that other blithe chatter of 18th-century Protestant orthodoxy. Much better, Messiaen continues is "the breath of the Spirit, God is Love." This is Mozart's *perdone contessa perdone*, as the count sinks to his knees in "*La Notte Di Figaro*" or in "*Don Giovanni.*" In the forgiving spirit of life, the statue of *Commendatore* comes to life as the promiscuous Don Juan is condemned to judgment. Pentecost rules and reigns in the world for God is righteous and given to Repentance—*perdone*.

- The Son as Word and light.

- The Father and the Son love through the Holy Spirit, themselves and US (get that? "US?").

- God is the unique and only, "Hear o Israel, the Lord our God is One," "Have this God and none other"/"Father let them be One as You and I are One"/The *Shema*, High Priestly Prayer, El *Shahadah* (God is God).

There you have it, the charter and geography of the Godhead, Pentecost and Trinity, through the tones, tunes and textures of Olivier Messiaen.

To now exegete the great doctor, we now turn to the revelation and reason about Pentecost/Easter. His revelation is Scripture, but also living and preached concomitants to written Word. His reason is Judaic/Islamic corroboration, Maimonides, and Avicenna.

Scripture roots Pentecost in *Torah*. The festival where Peter preaches is *Shavout*, the celebration of the Law or way of God. Pulses of wind, flames of fire, tongues deciphered and conviction and contact established, it's all Numbers Chapter 11. Moses is distributing the Spirit, truth and counsel, admonition and encouragement, commission and companionship to the seventy elders, the Paracletic entourage. There's too much pain and need in the world; Moses and Jesus must be multiplied, *Lapidim*, gifts of Spirit must rest on 70, and 70 times 7.

Now it is Jesus' ambassador, the same Spirit that hovered over creation's waters, inflamed the prophets and descended on his baptism. She falls on the 70 nascent Christians, though they do not recognize that designation yet, for now they only proclaim and live out what Paul calls, "The Gospel of God," NEWS! *Torah* Way, the Law of Christ, seems to simply be the "Way of Righteousness."

Let's take Isaiah 11 as Pentecost *midrash*, The Spirit of the Lord is upon me, the Spirit of wisdom and understanding, the Spirit of counsel and might, the Spirit of knowledge and the fear of the Lord. That sounds like Numbers 11 and Acts 2. Scriptural *midrash* goes back and forward into interfaith corroboration. The fast and feast I have chosen writes Isaiah 58, is to "loose the bonds of oppression, to break every yoke, to take bread to the hungry, bring the poor into your house, cover the naked, preach good news . . ." To receive Paraclete's wind is to know life's course in knowing its giver, and to set sail into that needing and blessing world. The blessing of the season is to be "righteoused" with God by Christ's indwelling Spirit and triune life (The Tree of Life) as we repent of our idolatry and injustice and are set on a new journey of mercy and reconciliation, a witness in the world.

Though biblical doctrine has trouble documenting Trinity just as monotheism has trouble accommodating polytheism, the doctrine of a dynamic, saving and spirited God is replete in Scripture, *Torah*, Prophets and Wisdom, Gospels, Epistles and Apocalypse.

The 13th-century Muslim poet Rumi, probably the most celebrated poet in the world today, is revered by all persons of faith. He writes that "Spring is Christ."

Everyone has eaten and fallen asleep. The house is empty.
We walk out into the garden to let the apple meet the peach,
to carry messages between rose and jasmine.
Spring is Christ,
raising martyred plants from their shrouds.
Their mouths open in gratitude, wanting to be kissed.
The glow of the rose and the tulip means a lamp
is inside. A leaf trembles. I tremble
in the wind—beauty like silk from Turkestan.
The censer fans into flame.
The wind is the Holy Spirit.
The trees are Mary.
. . . The scent of Joseph's shirt comes to Jacob
A red carnelian of Yemini laughter is heard . . .
We talk about this and that. There's no rest
except on these branching moments.

(Jalal-ad-Din Rumi, "Spring is Christ," c. 1258-1273)

July 8, 2011 Homecoming

Tough days in Antwerp. Our little family in diaspora seems to be edging toward a *modus vivendi* of blame, misrepresentation and mutual castigation. Matters seem to be spiraling out of control where no interventions can get through. This is all disheartening to this dad, father-in-law, and grandpa who also was the attending pastor at their wedding. I'm reading C.S. Lewis, *The Four Loves,* and learn again that *eros*, affection, friendship, commitment, and self-giving forgiveness and love, *agape*, often break like a single glass so opaque and dark. Yet we hope with Mozart for the surprise of pardon, reconciliation, and new beginnings even in this God-forsaken world, where our little slips slide into a cascading avalanche of bitterness and the lawyers laugh all the way to the bank with the family's few carefully-garnered resources.

For our part, the three-month sojourn in Paris came to an encouraging point with hope for future activities abroad as Sara found a friend in an associate of Clint Eastwood, who promised to see that he received the November publication of *The Ethical Vision of Clint Eastwood* (Eerdmans Press, 2011) and my sabbatical book on *Vincent Van Gogh's Ministry in Religion and Art* coming to happy fruition with some hopes for a publisher.

My ongoing research and development on theological foundations for "interfaith" work finding impetus at the Paul Ricoeur Library at *Institut Protestante* and toying with the tantalizing possibility of ongoing pastoral work was given a hearing at the American Church, Paris.

For now, it is back to getting the Garry Wills essays project back on track, preparing the fall teaching materials, fulfilling backed-up obligations for baby-sitting grandchildren, planning a family reunion and 70th birthday party for Sara in Pennsylvania and generally taking stock of this important moment of retirement and our own new beginnings.

July 18, 2011

The Wills' essays are all in and off to Northwestern University Press. Hard copy has gone to Garry Wills and Martin Marty (commentator at the November reception). My Van Gogh book is finished and off to Eerdmans for a read and hopefully a publication. The *au revoir* to France is complete as I copy Van Gogh's "Wheat Field with Cypresses" *"Ciel d'orange,"* one of his last paintings at Auvers-sur-Oise, for my urologist, whose good hands have given me a new lease on life. I have also enjoyed painting a copy of DeLaney's "Towers of Laon," (1911), a quasi-cubist masterpiece, reminiscent of his master Cezanne and his contemporary, Pablo Picasso.

We have been greeted by a sweltering U.S., even Chicago. The weather is what it was in Texas 50 years ago, steaming heat and stultifying humidity and the explosive rain-storm once a day. Dallas is in the midst of some 50 straight days of 100 degrees Fahrenheit. Our life has returned to the old normal—lively grandchildren, yard chores, and frantic planting to sneak in a few fruits of summer, even mid-stream. Our gorgeous arboretum at 1615 Ashland sweeps around our newly-roofed "small Victorian," two Pennsylvania hemlocks and a stately black hickory from our old family homestead in Pennsylvania. The yard is also ringed by memorial fruit trees for former parishioners, Mary Duff, Carol Hettinger, two McIntosh apples, and a long-needle green pine.

America, Libya, the European Union, and Syria continue to perplex the world. The U.S. has transferred 2 billion dollars of frozen Libyan funds to the rebels along with space in its Tripoli compound. Parishioners at the Anglican Church there continue to pray for peace as two more of Colonel Qaddafi's sons are killed by NATO bombing. Meanwhile, deposed President Mubarak appears in court in a cage and hospital cot to answer for his war crimes of killing 800 persons at Tahrir Square while Syria hopes that the same justice will catch up with President Assad in Damascus. The world wonders whether and how these events, like those thousands of years ago, will be enfolded into the meaning of biblical history for the world. I remain committed to the government in exile reflecting the learning and wisdom of the religious leaders, philosophers, professors previously mentioned in this narrative. I especially want to know whether my forerunner in the Cambridge Interfaith Program, Aref Nayed, succeeded in his confrontation with Qaddafi before he took refuge in Saudi Arabia.

In July and August, other tumultuous events would transpire. The killing of 70 persons in Oslo and a youth camp in Norway by a crazed religious fanatic, egged on by American Islamophobic bloggers, offering his life to resist the multicultural commitments of that great nation and people. The "debt ceiling" crisis followed in the U.S., with the accompanying uncertainties about a viable political structure. The U.S. continued to expend 50 percent of its discretionary national wealth for militarism and security, even though it has become evident that the focal enemy, *al-Qaeda*, may only be a phantasmal projection of America's Manichean imagination numbering only a few dozen persons.

August 6, 2011

Standard & Poor's has lowered its estimate of America's credit-worthiness, and world bond and financial markets are worried. For the first time in history, we are not at the very top of the community of nations in the perceived reliability of holding our debt. Citing two points, the "debacle" of the debt-ceiling fiasco and the rapid crescendo of the national debt as a portion of the total economy, Standard & Poor's, despite the lack of credibility in misleading the country in the critical economic crisis of economic collapse in the final years of the Bush II administration and the early months of Obama, have decided to throw the world's bond markets into a crisis, shattering an already precarious American and international market.

In America, two parties, who will now turn to a committee of 12 persons and a trigger backdrop of automatic cuts should the absolutely predictable result of stalemate occur, find themselves diametrically opposed on every issue of philosophy and strategy. The president and the Democrats believe in investing in the now four-year-old faltering economy, bringing the "very wealthy" cohort of Americans who have been excused from participation, into the sacrifice now requiring their participation along with the myriad tax loopholes allowing corporations like GE (20 billion dollars earnings and no taxes) into responsible involvement. They seek to maintain Medicare, Medicaid, and Social Security as a floor of support for the sick and aged. In sum, they believe in the religious vision of justice where the strong support the weak, rich, the poor, and the healthy, the sick.

Republicans, spearheaded by the "Tea-Party" remain firmly committed to defense and security as the main responsibilities of government with "no taxes," no new spending, and the eventual balanced budget, even a constitutional amendment, where the deficit is eliminated and every public expenditure is assured by a revenue-income source. The undergirding belief and value operative is that liberty of action, private sector predominance, and shrinking of government is divine mandate. As the fiscal drama works its way out, the faith drama is enacted in Houston's coliseum congregation and God is entreated to redirect, morally and spiritually, this wayward nation and world.

Freedom and community, dialectical truths and values in our finest philosophical and theological traditions. There is merit in some synthesis of such altruism and autonomy. Standard & Poor's has long warned that it would need to see at least 4 trillion dollars cut over the next decade to affirm its belief in keeping the nation whose "business is business" at the *crème de la crème* of nations. Meanwhile, the common working people starve and suffer as they do in Somalia or South Carolina and robber elites, Saba or hedge-funders, steal the people's bread.

August 23, 2011

Tripoli has fallen to the rebels. Colonel Qaddafi has disappeared with most of his family. The Transitional National Council (TNC), a government in exile, now *in situ*, grass-roots and constitutional, secular, humanistic and theistic, receives the accolades and deserves the pride of the world. NATO policies, with leadership and inspiration provided by President Obama and U.S. power and influence, has deposed-Qaddafi, yet all, at the end of the day, was achieved by the witness, by the blood and toil, suffering and courage of the devout Muslim patriots of Libya, *Allah Akbar*, martyrs against the unjust orders, idolatrous and unjust, structures propped up by 60 and more years of Western endorsed "strong men," authoritarian in funding and policy, diametrically opposed to the hopes and dreams of the poor, the religiously devout , the school teachers and shop-keepers, the simple people of faith and justice.

An age of interfaith freedom and social justice has upended an authoritarian and violent rule. America, now an interfaith nation along with Europe, also with an interfaith and interreligious commitment, have helped facilitate a new world order in this remarkable Spring and Summer of spiritual and moral revolution, one of historic dimensions such as the world has not seen since the Prague spring and the beginning of the end of the communist empire, which would culminate in the 1970s with Vaclav Havel and Lech Walesa.

In America, we can be as proud as we were when Dr. King and Peter, Paul and Mary condemned racism, contempt for the poor, and a hegemonic war in Viet Nam. Now we can continue the revolution by rebuilding Iraq, Afghanistan, and Syria displacing a Prince-of-Peace agenda in place of our historic policy of vested interest, invasion and occupation. As the rebel troops stop firing and break the Ramadan fast for prayers, in America we can remember the caution of Peter, Paul and Mary who asked groups of racist haters, militarists, gay-haters, those contemptuous of the poor and immigrants as well as anti-Semites and Islamophobes, not to co-opt the singing of "this land is your land, this land is my land," as such groups diametrically oppose the spirit of their song.

Now, as in the day of Abraham Lincoln, we can seek to forgive, reconcile, and begin to build anew. This pained and anguished world, the beloved creation of the Lord God, the One God of all peoples on earth, needs to see a new birth of freedom and justice, sharing and mutual edification, a biblical *shalom*, where the strong serve the weak, the rich, the poor, the well, the sick rather than our prevalent ethos where we cry "you're on your own," "grab all the gusto you can," and "the needy be damned."

August 24, 2011

Tripoli is liberated, although pockets of Qaddafi loyalty and resistance still remain and he and his family and entourage have not been found. The insurgency was inspired by French President Sarkozy's and British Prime Minister Cameron's and President Obama's qualms of conscience when Qaddafi threatened to go door to door and "kill all the rats." It culminated in NATO's and the Coalition's "no-fly-zone," air support, and ongoing "ground-advisory" support from Britain, France, Qatar, United Arab Emirates, and Jordan. It seems close to succeeding.

This morning the surprising news at CNN is that Aref Ali Nayed, whom I succeeded as fellow in Interfaith Studies at Cambridge, is now spokesperson for the new provisional government in Libya. From his post as ambassador to the United Arab Emirates, he seems to be a leader of the emerging new government as he was for many months in the government in exile. A business leader in Tripoli, he seems to have confronted and had a falling out with Qaddafi, taking up exile in Saudi Arabia, he was a spiritual-political leader in the government in exile, formulating an important document called the "Free Ulema," which laid the spiritual/ethical foundations for a new society, writing a new constitution, and forming rules of engagement for the long and arduous freedom revolution in his homeland.

Before we elaborate on these features of his witness, let me declare the perspective from which I write and speak. I write as a theologian and moral philosopher. My research continues to focus where it has been for 50 years when, in Germany, I studied Judaism in search of what I now call a kerygmatical hermeneutic of interfaith work. My purview is simply that of a prophetic analyst, one who seeks to interpret what the "will" and "way" of God may mean in the activities of this world, how the history of God is impinging on the events of world history. Mine is the discipline of discerning the eruptions of the kingdom of God within the kingdoms of this world, as these are vouched-safe to the Scriptures of the monotheistic faiths.

Nayed, an engineer and business leader by vocation is, to my mind, the leading Islamic theologian and interfaith leader in the world. As I suspected, he has become a preeminent spokesperson for TNC now the functioning government of the Libyan nation. He holds a Ph.D. in hermeneutics from the University of Guelph in Canada, and his scholarly genius has been to see the hermeneutical and kerygmatical meaning of the three Abrahamic revelations. In this witness, he shows how the concerted message of Judaism, Christianity, and Islam is one where each revelation enhances the others conveying good news of faith, justice, and peace for this world which is the beloved child and creation of the One God. The *midrashic* (Scriptural) chain on Mary's Magnificat, for example, runs from 2 Samuel through the Gospel of Matthew into the *Qur'an*.

Nayed was an interfaith pioneer, an appellation applied to my own work beginning 40 years ago when I did my doctoral degree in Hamburg, Germany on the medical experimentation on and the devised extermination imposed on world Jewry. Nayed was a principal author and promulgator of the document *A Common Word*, which is now the major interfaith dialogue document used around the world. In a three-volume series with Stephen Kepnes and David Ford, he is contributing a study of the future of Muslim theology.

All this means that the provisional government, the legitimate authority in Libya, until elections can be held, is in good hands. These leaders are theologically sophisticated, ethically astute and they offer North Africa and the Middle East a fresh model of righteous leadership in this area of the world so morally bereft. As we approach the decade memorial of September 11th, the region faces horrific, tragic violence in Syria, stalemated renewal in Egypt, Tunisia and elsewhere and continuing uncertainty in the region's typhoon epicenter, Israel and Palestine. Hope is vibrant, but realism is sobering, as ever.

September 3, 2011 (Tripoli, Libya)

It appears that the American CIA was involved up to its eyeballs in Libyan torture chambers, sending its terrorism suspects to her for special care.[1] Obviously, we are not surprised, given the last 60 years of American policy and practice abroad. Latin America, the Cold War, the War on Terrorism, all allowed numerous instances of violence and violation of human rights, war crimes, kidnappings, water-boarding, assassinations, invasions, occupations.

1. Rod Norland, "Files Note Close C.I.A. Ties to Qaddafi Spy Unit," *The New York Times*, September 3, 2011.

All this illegal, sub-ethical and activity ultimately inimical to our self-interest is blessed by Vice President Chaney's lurid smile, "so what?" "what else is new," " that's the real world, stupid." His view is perfectly true in a Machiavellian world, one where only expediency rules. Here there is no God and therefore no moral order.

Idolatry begets injustice. Even the well-intentioned interim provisional government has moved from purity of purpose to sullied acts of extremism and exigency. "Dark skinned" brothers, mercenaries from Chad, Mali and Cameroon, who fought with Qaddafi, are treated harshly.

Today also America prepares to join a few other rogue nations to veto the admission of Palestine into the United Nations, further eroding our prestige and credibility within the community of nations, even as the world still suffers from the grievous economic crisis we introduced into world history whose peace, justice, and progress, we still threaten her with our hegemony and imperial neocolonialism. As I argue in *America in God's World*, the matter is not just geopolitical, it is theological, a matter of idolatry and injustice, of God and the world.

September 15, 2011

To me, it is a day of momentous significance. The "Jasmine" revolution or "Arab Spring" is now entering its golden autumn. Today, Prime Minister David Cameron of England and President Sarkozy of France, stalwart forces in the accomplishment of this remarkable freedom uprising, visit Tripoli and lay their hands of blessing on the new government forged in the crucible of that nation's suffering. These stalwart forces in the accomplishment of this remarkable freedom-uprising pledge their support to the Transitional National Council, (TNC), and the world takes heart.

At the same time, the new government in Tunisia pledges itself to the same kind of religious-democratic state as in Libya.

As a fellow at the Interfaith Program at Cambridge University in England, I succeeded in that role the famous Islamic theologian and Libyan businessman, Aref Ali Nayed, who is now the coordinator of the TNC's stabilization team, the Tripoli businessman and ambassador to the United Arab Emirates. When I worked in Cambridge this winter while on sabbatical, our program, through our team leader David Ford, conferred with Nayed in forming the new constitution, writing guidelines for "just-war" tactics in the rebel freedom campaign against Qaddafi's tyrannical regime and exploring and recommending political, ethical, and religious values for the emerging new nation.

The New York Times today reports on the meeting of the wealthy Tripolitans who helped finance the revolution. Everyone asks, "will the Islamists or the democrats win the battle for the soul of Libya?" Nayed, the staunchest of the religious and interreligious democrats, says that the revolution, with its 30,000 to 50,000 martyrs, "will not accept anything but a democratic society." The day has been won, it appears, not by intensivists, who have that frightful fanatical belief that non-Muslims are apostate and must be eliminated but by secular-pluralistic religionists. As in Tahrir Square in Cairo they see devout, Muslim martyrs, faces to the ground on the day of prayers, ringed by the circle of Christians, arm in arm, affirming their cause.

Following tactics of non-violence, non-revenge and non-retaliation, learned in the campaigns for freedom in Dr King's revolution in America and Nelson Mandela's in Africa, truth and reconciliation efforts will win out as the only way to go. The kerygma of Christian Jewish and Muslim martyrs, those who in Daniel Boyarin's words were prepared to "die for God, has transformed revenge into resurrection. As throughout Africa in preceding decades, strong men, propped up by western oil and capitalistic values are yielding to freedom and a gentle, altruistic, women affirming *Sharia*, and Jews and Christians, prompted by the cognate biblical impulses are at their sides. The greed-driven materialists of both the West and Middle East have, in the Spirit of the Living God, been driven out. Nayed, like his exemplars in the American civil rights, South American, African, and Asian liberation theologies refined his faith by his reading of Karl Barth's bible-centered church dogmatics. Scripture again has tolled the bell of Liberty, justice and peace.

Thursday, September 23, 2010

Today seems to be a momentous day in world history. Brooklyn settlers in Israel are seeking to agitate the Palestinian aspirants for their own state as they demonstrate against the barriers and walls in the occupied West Bank. In Zambia, Christians are made to feel unwelcome in the Muslim markets. Israel's belligerence and America's solidarity with her, even to the underwriting of weapons and bulldozers, is not going down well in the world. Today I excerpt several of the speeches to the U.N.

EXCURSUS: FALL MEETING AT THE UNITED NATIONS

Text of President Ahmadinejad's speech at the United Nation

United Nations, New York, September 24, IRNA. The following is a partial text of President Mahmoud Ahmadinejad of Iran's speech delivered to the 65th annual meeting of United Nations General Assembly in New York on Thursday. The striking theology, ethic, and rhetoric demands our close attention as do the more measured but equally provocative words of President Obama of the U.S. and that of Israeli Prime Minister Bibi Netanyahu.

Mr. President, Excellencies, Ladies and Gentlemen, I am grateful to the Almighty God who granted me the opportunity to appear before this world assembly once again.

In the past years, I spoke to you about some of the hopes and concerns, including family crises, security, human dignity, world economy, climate change, as well as the aspiration for justice and lasting peace. After about one hundred years of domination, the system of capitalism and the existing world order has proved to be unable to provide appropriate solution to the problems of societies. I shall try to examine the two main causes of this failure and picture some features of the ideal future order.

Attitudes and Beliefs

As you are well aware, the divine prophets (Moses, Jesus, Mohammad) all had the mission to call everyone to monotheism (adoration and service to the One God), love, and justice and show mankind the path to prosperity.

They invite men to contemplation and knowledge in order to better appreciate the truth and to avoid atheism and egoism. The very nature of the message of all prophets is one and the same. Every messenger endorsed the messenger before him and gave glad tidings about the prophet to come, and presented a more complete version of the religion in accordance with the capacity of the man at the time. In opposition to that, the egotist and the greedy stood up against this clear call, revolting against the message. Nimrod countered *Hazrat* (messenger). Abraham, Pharaoh countered *Hazrat*, Moses and the greedy countered *Hazrat*, Jesus Christ and *Hazrat* Mohammad (Peace be upon them all). In the recent centuries,

ics and values have been rejected as a cause for backward-
re even portrayed as opposing wisdom and science because
infliction on man by the proclaimers of religion in the dark
West. Man's disconnection from Heaven detached him from
f.

Man with his potentials for understanding the secrets of the universe, his instinct for seeking truth, his aspirations for justice and perfec-
tion, his quest for beauty and purity and his capacity to represent God
on earth was reduced to a creature limited to the materialistic world with
a mission to maximize individualistic pleasures. Human instinct, then,
replaced true human nature. Human beings and nations were considered rivals and the happiness of an individual or a nation was defined
in collision with, and elimination or suppression of others. Constructive
evolutionary cooperation was replaced with a destructive struggle for
survival. The lust for capital and domination replaced monotheism which
is the gate to love and unity. This widespread clash of the egoist with the
divine values gave way to slavery and colonialism. A large portion of
the world came under the domination of a few western States. Tens of
millions of people were taken to slavery and tens of millions of families
were shattered as a result. All the resources, the rights and the cultures
of the colonized nations were plundered. Lands were occupied and the
indigenous people were humiliated and mass- murdered. Yet, nations
rose up, colonialism was alienated and the independence of the nations
was recognized. Thus, the hope for respect, prosperity, and security was
revived amongst nations. In the beginning of the past century, nice talks
about freedom, human rights, and democracy created hopes for healing
the deep wounds of the past. Today, however, not only those dreams are
not realized, but memories, even at times worse than before, have been
recorded. As a result of the two World Wars, the occupation of Palestine,
the Korean and the Vietnam's Wars, the Iraqi war against Iran, the occupation of Afghanistan and Iraq as well as many wars in Africa, hundreds
of millions of people were killed, wounded or displaced. Terrorism, illicit
drugs, poverty and the social gaps increased. The dictatorial and *coup
d'etat* governments in Latin America committed unprecedented crimes
with the support of the West. Instead of disarmament, the proliferation
and stockpiling of nuclear, biological, and chemical weapons expanded,
putting the world under a bigger threat. As a result, the very same old

goals of colonialists and the slave masters were, this time round, pursued with a new facade.

The Global Management and Ruling Structures

The League of Nations and, then, the United Nations were established with the promise to bring about peace, security and the realization of human rights, which in fact meant a global management. One can analyze the current governance of the world by examining three events: First, the events of the 11 September, 2001 which has affected the whole world for almost a decade. All of a sudden, the news of the attack on the twin towers was broadcast using numerous footages of the incident. Almost all governments and known figures strongly condemned this incident. But then a propaganda machine came into full force; it was implied that the whole world was exposed to a huge danger, namely terrorism, and that the only way to save the world would be to deploy forces into Afghanistan. Eventually Afghanistan, and shortly thereafter, Iraq were occupied. Please take note: It was said that some three thousand people were killed on the 11 September for which we are all very saddened. Yet, up until now, in Afghanistan and Iraq hundreds of thousands of people have been killed, millions wounded and displaced and the conflict is still going on and expanding.

I wish to announce here that next year the Islamic Republic of Iran will host a conference to study terrorism and the means to confront it. I invite officials, scholars, thinkers, researchers and research institutes of all countries to attend this conference. Second is the occupation of the Palestinian territories.

The oppressed people of Palestine have lived under the rule of an occupying regime for 60 years, been deprived of freedom, security and the right to self- determination, while the occupiers are given recognition. On a daily basis, the houses are being destroyed over the heads of innocent women and children. People are deprived of water, food, and medicine in their own homeland. The Zionists have imposed five all-out wars on the neighboring countries and on the Palestinian people. The Zionists (Jews and Christians?) committed the most horrible crimes against the defenseless people in the wars against Lebanon and Gaza. Even the renowned Jurist Goldstone accused his own Jewish people of "crimes against humanity."

The Zionist regime attacked a humanitarian flotilla in a blatant defiance of all international norms and lost the support of its allies, Turkey. This regime which enjoys the absolute support of some western countries regularly threatens the countries in the region and continues publicly announced assassination of Palestinian figures and others, while Palestinian defenders and those opposing this regime are pressured, labeled as terrorists and anti Semites. All values, even the freedom of expression, in Europe and in the United States are being sacrificed at the altar of Zionism. Solutions are doomed to fail because the right of the Palestinian people is not taken into account. Would we have witnessed such horrendous crimes if instead of recognizing the occupation, the sovereign right of the Palestinian people had been recognized? Our unambiguous proposition is the return of the Palestinian refugees to their home land and the reference to the vote of the people of Palestine to exercise their sovereignty and decide on the type of governance.

Ladies and Gentlemen, Very recently the world witnessed the ugly and inhumane act of burning the Holy *Qur'an*. The Holy *Qur'an* is the divine Book and the eternal miracle of the Prophet of Islam. It calls for worshipping the One God, justice, compassion toward people, development and progress, reflection and thinking, defending the oppressed and resisting against the oppressors; and it names with respect the previous Messengers of God, like Noah, Abraham, Isaaq, Joseph, Moses and Jesus Christ (peace be upon them all) and endorses them.. They burned *Qur'an* to bum all these truths and good judgments. However, the truth could not be burned. *Qur'an* is eternal because God and truth are everlasting. This act and any other act which widens the gap and distances between nations is evil. We should wisely avoid playing into the hands of Satan. On behalf of the Iranian nation, I pay respect to all divine books and their followers. This is the *Qur'an* and this is the Bible. I pay respect to both of them.

Ladies and Gentlemen, I announce clearly that the occupation of other countries under the pretext of freedom and democracy is an unforgivable crime. The world needs the logic of compassion and justice and inclusive participation instead of logic of force, domination, unilateralism, war, and intimidation. The world needs to be governed by virtuous people like the divine Prophets.

Response

What interests me in this now semi-annual address of Ahmadinejad, always hyperbolic and provocative is not the weaknesses. He believes in the sacred nature of the Persian state. Perhaps he can be forgiven, residing, as he does, in one of the three great holy states of antiquity, Persia, India and Afghanistan. His was the homeland of Zoroaster and the biblical savior figure, Cyrus the Persian.

The President's bizarre work and word commends itself for as a simple schoolteacher for he is the most strenuous advocate of the radical sovereignty of God among world leaders today, forthrightly interfaith, with a commendable compassion for justice and the poor. The vehement walkout of the United States accompanied by the "coalition of the willing"—Israel, the Jewish nation—and those stern partners, England, Britain, and the United Kingdom prompted the mendacious American Press to speak of a great general walkout rather than one of a few disgruntled folks under American coercion..

The world community of nations, some more than 200 sovereign bodies who stayed there with courtesy, disputes Netanyahu's mockery of the Iranian leader. In a perverse way the Israeli and Iranian leaders share a condemnation of the U.N. This is even creeping into the rhetoric of the U.S. again. Imagine Togo and Burkina Faso, China and India, we must ask, overriding the U.S. and Israel. It's like the American Presbyterians—2 million persons hanging by their fingernails, trying to call the shots with our 20 million confrers in Africa. Why should the destiny of Palestine lie in the hands of the "Jewish state of Israel", we should ask.

Text of Palestinian Leader Mahmoud Abbas' speech at U.N.

Ladies and Gentlemen, says the Palestinian leader, Mr. Abbas. It is a moment of truth and my people are waiting to hear the answer of the world. Will it allow Israel to continue its occupation, the only occupation in the world? Will it allow Israel to remain a State above the law and accountability? Will it allow Israel to continue rejecting the resolutions of the Security Council and the General Assembly of the United Nations and the International Court of Justice and the positions of the overwhelming majority of countries in the world?

Excellencies,
Ladies and Gentlemen,

I come before you today from the Holy Land, the land of Palestine, the land of divine messages, ascension of the Prophet Muhammad (peace be upon him) and the birthplace of Jesus Christ (peace be upon him), to speak on behalf of the Palestinian people in the homeland and in the diaspora, to say, after 63 years of suffering of the ongoing *Nakba*—enough. It is time for the Palestinian people to gain their freedom and independence.

The time has come to end the suffering and the plight of millions of Palestine refugees in the homeland and the diaspora, to end their displacement and to realize their rights, some of them forced to take refuge more than once in different places of the world.

At a time when the Arab peoples affirm their quest for democracy, the Arab Spring, the time is now for the Palestinian Spring, the time for independence

It is a moment of truth and my people are waiting to hear the answer of the world. Will it allow Israel to continue its occupation, the only occupation in the world? Will it allow Israel to remain a state above the law and accountability? Will it allow Israel to continue rejecting the resolutions of the Security Council and the General Assembly of the United Nations and the International Court of Justice and the positions of the overwhelming majority of countries in the world?

Text of Prime Minister Benjamin Netanyahu's speech at U.N.

Mr. President, Ladies and Gentlemen. Nearly 62 years ago, the United Nations recognized the right of the Jews, an ancient people 3,500 years-old, to a state of their own in their ancestral homeland. (The actual decision of 1948, most political scientists contend, is the right of the Palestinian and Jewish peoples to live on the land with peace and security. It was a matter of days until Palestinians sought to expel Israel and the Jews began to cleanse the land of these indigenous Palestinian peoples.)

I stand here today as the prime minister of Israel, the Jewish state, and I speak to you on behalf of my country and my people. The United Nations was founded after the carnage of World War II and the horrors of the Holocaust. It was charged with preventing the recurrence of such horrendous atrocity . . .

Response

This Iranian regime is fueled by an extreme fundamentalism that burst onto the world scene three decades ago after lying dormant for centuries. In the past thirty years, this fanaticism has swept the globe with a murderous violence and cold-blooded impartiality in its choice of victims. It has callously slaughtered Muslims and Christians, Jews and Hindus, and many others. Though it is comprised of different offshoots, the adherents of this unforgiving creed seek to return humanity to medieval times.

Netanyahu's theology is not as profuse as Mahmoud Ahmadinejad's, nor as serene as that of Abbas. He accepts the myth of a divine biblical presentation of the ancient Holy Land to the modern state of Israel, which he has renamed "The Jewish State of Israel." This construction is accepted by very few modern scholars of the Hebrew Bible, though it is fanatically popular with the Christian and Jewish "right wing." Where his presentation commends itself is the earnest proffering of compromise and his acceptance of a two-state solution. Where his stance may fail on the cause of "self interest," as well as justice, is his readiness to allow Christians to all but disappear from *Haaretz Israel* and Palestine during his watch.

October 6, 2011 (Anwar al-Awlaki)

A cleric (Scripture scholar, imam, mullah, pastor, preacher, a minister, or a terrorist murderer?), al-Awlaki is revered in the Islamic world and reviled in America and Israel. On this day, he was hunted down and killed, along with many innocent bystanders and perhaps by another wanted terrorist suspect. As I write today, a Pakistani Task Force, investigating the assault of Bin Laden's home and his assassination has accused a doctor of aiding the CIA and feigning inoculations to the family to betray them to the CIA.

Al-Awlaki was called "bin Laden of the Internet." The Yemini-American was a high-profile suspect of American defense and homeland security programs. In the public mentality and media, he was pretty much evaluated in accord with Israel Prime Minister Bibi Netanyahu, as a "militant Muslim terrorist" to be brought to "ultimate justice" (Obama: as if that was a human prerogative and responsibility?) for his acts against America. In other words, he was charged with the same charge against the Pakistani medic who betrayed bin Laden to the CIA, Espionage. Who was the hero, and who the traitor—Grant and Sherman or Lee and Stonewall Jackson, the same conflicted historical appraisal? The obvious answer is that history and its imputed meanings belong to the victors, and right now we are not certain whom that will be.

Following just months on the heels of bin Laden's assassination, that of al-Awlaki was similarly fraught with ethical questions. Could we in the U.S. one day be accused with international crimes? This is surely one subliminal reason we don't want nation status for Palestine. We might be hauled in for the atrocity against the refugee camps or Gaza. It would be like being charged for "crimes against humanity" for the extermination of the Amerindians or complicit in the 100 million deaths of Africans in the "Great Passage" (W.E.B. Dubois). Assassinated by shock troops, only accusations, no evidence or trial, abrogation of all rules and rights of civil societies.

Were it not for the wide-spread hatred of Obama, there might have been gleeful macabre celebration in the streets, no sense of the holy, no *Kiddush*, no reverence of the body, bin Laden dumped to the sharks in the Indian Ocean and Pastor al-Awlaki, incinerated. And we wonder why the Muslim world hates and fears the U.S., like the bombers of September 11th, we simply lack the sense of the "holy" in human life and death.

Liberal Noam Chomsky and libertarian Ron Paul, from the poles of the political spectrum, objected to this action with conceptual and practical arguments. Fundamentally, the action was against the foundational tenants of free, democratic societies. The principle of "innocent until proven guilty" was not only totally ignored but also disbelieved. A U.S. citizen surely deserved the right to counsel and a fair trial and the precipitous action, in the middle of the night, smacks of cover-up from the outset. In sum, both actions, especially that with cleric al-Awlaki, were against all of the freedom principles we hold dear and fight for with our very lives in the world.

Practically speaking, such actions are against our self interest. Rather that deterring or preventing terrorism, they vitalize the movement, enhance recruitment, create religious martyrs and intensify global hatred against America, making us a more and more marginal player.

My take on these two assassination cases is that I'd like to know more. What kind of preacher was al-Awlaki? What was the substance of his message? Whence came his conviction that he operated within the divine will even though his actions were soaked in blood, especially innocent blood? Where was authenticity of character and validity of message to be justified? If we were to accept the party line (Tea Party line), the victim was to be seen as pure evil, the very validation of our Manichean construal and division of humanity into "good and evil" cohorts.

What are the alleged charges against him? He is thought to have masterminded three attacks inside the U.S. He trained three of the 9/11 hijackers, inspired the Fort Hood shooter, Nidal Malik Hasan, and assisted the Christmas Day bomber, Umar Farouk Abdulmutallab.

Now we'll never know who he was and what he was up to, which seems to be exactly what we want. He was thought to be the chief for operations for *al-Qaeda* in the Arabian Peninsula, which we can never be sure if that were our concocted designation or a real organization. The rapid vaporization of *al-Qaeda* may prove that it was more a figment of our anti-terrorist and Islamophobic imagination than anything real.

He was a scholar of Sayyid Qutb, of the Egyptian Brotherhood. Qutb espoused a very intense Islamic philosophy of war and peace, theology and ethics. The brotherhood believed in purifying and protecting the homeland. It believed in purging godless, materialist, and immoral presence from Terra Sancta. It also adhered to classical Islamic just-war theory, although it has expressed ambivalence about "suicide bombers," even in the destruction of innocents as "collateral damage." Al-Awlaki often read 200 pages per day of this literature. In the early 1990s, he was a pro-American, anti-soviet *mujahideen*. Today, as Muslims and Copts kill each other in Egypt, egged on by paid goons, we realize that any revolution, especially those of a religious nature, almost always deteriorate into ugly scenes of violence.

Al-Awlaki is such a conflicted leader, as are the heroic American and British (NATO) soldiers who brought him down. War in any form, as Augustine warned us, is never heroic; it is always terrible, terrifying, terroristic, nothing to celebrate.

The New York Times of October 9, 2011 appropriately concludes this diary entry. It cites a secret U.S. memo, which reflects on the justice and injustice of an officially sanctioned assassination of al-Awlaki. On the side of justifying and rationalizing the act, only in the case that taking him alive was unfeasible, was the argument that he was a central player in the war between *al-Qaeda and* America. This justification overrode the U.S. State Department's forbidding assassinations, the protection of the human rights of American citizens, a Federal law against murder, and protections against such actions in International Law and universal standards of human rights.[2]

October 10, 2011 (Reflection on Steve Jobs)

Steve Jobs died this week after an eight-year battle with pancreatic cancer. The national and international mourning was extraordinary. Why? I venture several explanations: His words to Stanford graduates in 2005 were simple and profound.

> . . . My third story is about death. When I was 17, I read a quote that went something like: "If you live each day as if it was your last, some day you'll most certainly be right." It made an impression on me , and since then, for the past 33 years, I have looked in the mirror every morning and asked myself, if today were the last day of my life, would I want to do what I am about to do today? And when the answer has been "no" for too many days in a row, I know I need to change something. Remembering that I'll be dead soon is the most important tool I've ever encountered to help me make the big choices in life. Because almost everything, all external expectations, all pride, all fear of embarrassment or failure—these things just fall away in the face of death leaving only what is truly important. There is no reason not to follow your heart. No one wants to die. Even people who want to go to heaven don't want to die to get there. Your time is limited, so don't waste it living someone else's life . . . Don't let the noise of others' opinions drown out your own inner voice, and have the courage to follow your heart and intuition. They somehow already know what you truly want to become. On the last issue of *The Whole Earth Catalogue* was a photograph of an early morning on a country road. Beneath it were the words "stay hungry, stay foolish." As you graduate, I wish that for you.[3]

2. Charlie Savage, "Secret U.S. Memo Made Legal Case to Kill a Citizen," *The New York Times*, October 8, 2011.

3. Commencement speech given by Steve Jobs, CEO of Apple Computer and Pixar Animation Studios, to graduates of Stanford University, June 12, 2005, Stanford, California.

Jobs call to everyone in the world is to search, to know, to communicate, to help, to do good. Steve Jobs did something to bring that about. He dropped out of Reed College in his first year since it cost his family their life-savings. Then he dropped in. He became the master of his own education. He reverted back to all education before the insidious modern spoon-fed fiasco, choose your mentor and follow her (e.g. Eloise and Abelard at medieval Paris).

He slept on the floor of his friend's rooms. He walked long-distance to a soup-kitchen for an evening meal. He took (audited) the courses he thought interesting—like Japanese calligraphy. Here he learned to write characters legibly, thus eventually the proto-personal-computer, the legible bits and bytes, with the flashing cursor. He had bitten the apple of awesome knowledge, and the new life it would portend. Jobs also showed the courage of greater and greater deeds of love even though threatened by death. He had discovered the Scriptural truth that faith (and care for others) can move mountains. He knocked and the door was opened. (Matt 7) Was Jobs an incognito Christian? Of course. Just as certain as Jesus was a prophet of Islam and Buddha.

Two pieces of knowledge confirm and corroborate this assertion, which exclusivist monotheists (Jews, Christians and Muslims) will dispute:

1.   In a new book, *Religion in Human Evolution*, Robert Bellah makes a startling claim about the pertinence and power of religion.[4] He singles out what he sees to be the four decisive religious developments in human evolution: Classical Greece, Ancient Israel, Indian Buddhism, and Chinese Confucianism. One may ask about the absence of the two movements, which now embrace more than half of the global human population, Christianity and Islam? Is he suggesting that these are offspring movements, which universalize Judaism, or even more controversially that these may be genocidal, even suicidal movements, which will burn themselves out in history, perhaps taking creation with them? On this point, I have a colleague at the seminary who feels that Christianity is symbiotically and irretrievably linked to genocide, the extermination of the Amerindians, the Great passage and racism (one hundred million Blacks extinguished), and Judaicide in the *Shoah* and Islamicide in the "war on terrorism."

4. Robert N. Bellah, *Religion in Human Evolution: From the Paleolithic to the Axial Age* (Cambridge, MA: Belknap Press of Harvard University Press, 2011).

This morning, dozens of Coptic Christians lie broken and mortally wounded in the morgue of Cairo, victims of the religio-military phalange.

2. In a just published work, psychologist-linguist Stephen Pinker of Harvard explores the topic of "the better angels of our natures."[5] Here he argues that modern faiths, far from being treacherous, are leading humanity into great leaps of betterment and human enrichment. We are advancing as a species in kindness, respect, justice, and understanding. For example, in 1300 the Mongol Hordes killed 50 million out of a global population of 1 billion. While in 1900, Christian hordes killed 50 million of a total population of 7 billion, a factor of 7. Scarce comfort, but in statistical abstraction perhaps a breathtaking moral advance.

Steve Jobs and his ilk (Bill Gates, Jerre Stead, Warren Buffett, et al.) have nudged the world toward knowledge, justice, righteousness, and the counter-kingdom of God, while the Wall Street demonstration against the kingdoms of this world march on.

October 16, 2011 (Washington Mall, Dr. King Memorial dedication)

President Obama's words are autobiographical as he honors Dr. King's return to a niche where this nation and humanity itself will find perpetual memory and inspiration on the Washington mall. As freedom fighters across Africa and the Arab world, throughout Europe and America strive for justice and peace, and for the end of inequality and greed, violence and war. As the President gracefully and rationally, forgivingly and resolutely, faces reviling, even death wish, in his frustrated wish to realize Dr. King's dream, he speaks of failed schools, stagnated quality of life, absent jobs, failed health care, persistent war, and a deadlocked government and crippled global order.

As I listen again to the August 28, 1963 "I Have a Dream" speech, I think of several nightmares despoiling that dream:

5. Steven Pinker, *The Better Angels of our Natures: Why Violence has Declined* (New York: Viking, 2011).

1. In the last 50 years, millions of blacks have been disenfranchised by partisan gerrymandering of election districts and unjust apprehending and jailing, just as Dr. King predicted in his speech that blacks in the South will not be able to vote as those in New York will not have anything to vote for. Still he asks that we will "let freedom ring, from the New York Mountains to Stone Mountain, Georgia."

2. As with Viet Nam in Dr. King's closing days, now terrorism and wars wrack the earth. Prophetic critique of such immoral wars is as absolutely forbidden, even in the light of Dr King's highly patriotic version of American exceptionalism, as it is today, as U.S. troops move into Uganda, Somalia, Congo and elsewhere to combat groups of *al-Qaeda* and other "terrorist Muslims." The Manichean enemy, once communists is now "militant Islamists," and not American and Judeo-Christian violence and hegemonies. Will history again reverse our renditions about who are the "good and bad guys?"

3. With reference to jobs, dark-skinned families now seek to escape police surveillance and seizure in "illegal" hounding and hunting Alabama creating a new "underground railroad," flight by night heading north. As Dr. King stated, "the governor of Alabama's lips were dripping with vilification and degradation." I remain proud that the sponsoring church of my seminary, Garrett-Evangelical, has forbidden use of the word *illegal* as a blasphemous appellation.

Still Obama evokes, even implores for, hope, grounded in the goodness of God. The president knows where the only hope for faith and hope, love and justice resides, in God and our own steadfastness in God's will. So we press on and keep marching and singing, we shall overcome.

November 1, 2011

All Saints, Halloween, coming up on retirement lecture (Van Gogh) and the Garry Wills *Festschrift* event, and the haunting fear that one so compulsive about productivity (like my dad) will not do well in retirement. Teaching Sunday by Sunday in the church, in a course called *Book of Life, Tree of Life*, allows me, and Sara, on occasion, to traffic between the Scripture of the day and the daily newspaper, certainly my penchant. Wouldn't it be nice if someone, a church or school, would employ me to do just this? When I pastored at Second Presbyterian and wrote frequent, Jonathan Swift-like "moral essays" in the *Chicago Tribune*, this was the essential rhythm of my life—wonderfully satisfying.

Qaddafi has been blown away in the disgraceful, *Kaddish*-less way (deprived of all of the holiness required by sacred thought as well as international law). This is the third such event in the span of this diary, so satisfying to gun-slinging Americans but ethically, so reprehensible. It's like our *capitalismus savage*, predicted exuberantly by Max Weber, which continues to threaten world peace and provision for the poor. And the "powers that be" crack down on the "Wall Street" occupations as the "strong men did in the Arab Spring and now throughout the world." Meanwhile, Greece wants a referendum on the "cut the budget, austerity, measures required by Germany, France, and Belgium in return for ongoing bailout and debt-forgiveness.

December 1, 2011

I've given my last lecture, last sermon, and last supper. All that remains of the tenure at Garrett, the capstone of my academic career is grades for two classes and farewells at what has been to me a heart-warming final post. A year after the confusing and frantic reports at the beginning of this diary, my health is restored, worrying still about our children and the pains they are experiencing with the economic crisis and family issues and settling into a kind of unsettled gratitude and vague expectancy as we enter another Advent. So I bring this diary to a close.

EXCURSUS: LAST SUPPER AND SERMON

Yesterday I offered the following meditation at Garrett Chapel, co-celebrating with my pastor and friend, Ray Hylton.

The voice of one crying in the wilderness,
prepare the way of the Lord, make his path straight.

(MARK 1 AFTER ISAIAH 40)

Since the world began no one has opened the eyes of the blind, If this man were not from God he couldn't do it (John 9: 1-41, vv. 32-33).

Today in Eucharist we greet the promised One of the prophet as our Advent midday guest. The voice crying in the wilderness points to Word and *Logos*, the light in the eyes of one born blind, Lord and Christ, Maranatha.

The Prophet who cries speaks from and for Godself, the One.

The Prophet foretells and forth-tells, hope and truth.

The Prophet is forerunner and follower, presence fore and aft, alpha and omega.

We don't know whether to open or shut our ears and eyes to the prophet; his word is decisive, commanding our attention; it is disturbing.

We all know *The Prophet* by Khalil Gibran, a study of the Christ and of the generic prophet—Lebanese: Christian and Muslim, He sees One being, over and beyond all faiths, the One God, Lord and Christ, Word and Wisdom, mediated by the captive tongue and eyes, speech and sight, being mediated by the Prophet.

We also remember another prophet who rode on a night journey from home in Mecca, to God's earth home in Jerusalem, and then on into the heavenly home of eternity.

This prophet was on a great white steed, transporter and trans-positioner, reminiscent of Jesus in Rev 19, on that white horse rode one faithful and true, wielding righteousness into the world. This Christ-ride of a prophet is foundational to the Scriptures of Christianity and Islam, perhaps alluding to the soaring of Ezekiel or Enoch in our common Hebraic heritage.

The true Prophet arching through Judaism and Christianity is now the faithful "suffering servant," One who delivers his people from provenance to the transcendent. His is the way of sorrows, acquainted with grief.

And so in this mood we welcome the Bethlehem visitor from eternity to earth with whom we now await communion and companion as He breaks to us presence and bread.

That other prophet beams over Arabia to Jerusalem then up, through the seven heavens, he comes to the level of Abraham and Moses . . . then John the Baptist and Jesus, true enough so far, but the journey then becomes more fantastic and apocalyptic, something like "Star Wars." The real journey, the journey of Way, *Torah* and Gospel, **Taurut** and **Injil**, the biblical way is from God to galaxies, down into the earth, landing at Bethlehem

To preserve rightful vision among plausible and imaginary visions, our lectionary this first week of Advent also layers on our tale the story of one born blind in the architectonic narrative of John 9. This passage exhibits the other Islamic vision, "then will the eyes of the blind be opened . . . and the tongue of the dumb shall speak" (Isa 29:18).

In a world before his appearance on earth, one born blind is cursed not wounded, someone is at fault, in the world view most common before Jesus' we ask, "who sinned, him or his father?" But in this "new being," atoned, *Yom-Kippur* world, Messiah is found sitting at the gate with the blind, the sick, the deaf and dumb and lepers. Now the Son of Man name becomes interchangeable with Yahweh, God, right here with us—Emmanuel. Here one who has borne our iniquity and healed our diseases makes his abode, pitches his tent with us.

Who opened your eyes protests the anti-prophet, the prophet killer. "He is a prophet" cries the stumbling one, and as light streams in he cries in thanksgiving, "one thing I know I was blind, now I see." But Pharisee holds his course, the prophet must be driven from the synagogue. "If he says He is the Christ he must be banished," banned now and forever. As Jack Miles showed in his book *Christ*,[6] the suffering One of God is colored *pathetique*, in Menotti's words in "Amahl and the Night Visitors," the humbled color of earth is transfigured into the triumphal color of wheat and dawn. And as the curtain between outer world and inner sanctum is torn, that dark afternoon on Golgotha, the darkness and green laser radiance and illumination of God in the Holy of Holies becomes the light of the world.

Today, in this second week of Advent let us try to fathom together what this prophetic kingdom is about. To do so, let us juggle two balls: red for AIDS, green for Advent.

First, today is international AIDS Day and we honor this challenge of our history now in our daily lectionary. We learn that there are 30 million new cases of AIDS in the world this year. Holding steady at multiple millions annually in Africa, the accelerating volume of cases is now in Asia and Eastern Europe.

I was designated to preach and preside at this chapel, I assume, because I've thought and written a lot about HIV. In 1981, I convened the first medical conference on the matter in Chicago with the help of

---

6. Jack Miles, *Christ: A Crisis in the Life of God* (New York: Alfred A. Knopf, 2001).

the CDC. No one, even at the medical schools and hospitals, knew much about it.

I've also pondered the cognate issues of sexual and homosexual ethics. I was part of the team that wrote the Presbyterian doctrine and policy 40 years ago. With the churches, at least Anglican, Congregational, Lutheran and now Presbyterian and the U.S. Chaplaincy in the intervening years, I changed my beliefs from one firm on civil rights on secular issues and hesitant on matters like ordination and ecclesial celebration of marriage. Now I have seen the light and come to a position of affirmation of gay rights in both state and church. As God is One, we in the human family all have received the grace of life.

As AIDS incidence moved from a disease afflicting homosexual persons to one that tracked poverty and became a matter of social justice, I found decisive mandate for this challenge in biblical teaching on the poor, especially in regard to women and children.

I also came to see that **arsenokoitai** in Romans and Leviticus (LXX) did not refer to homosexuality as we understand it today, lifelong and faithful covenants, but to the Penn State disorder—pederasty and pedophilia. Coming into the seminary from the medical world I discovered that gay persons were being called in large numbers to lay and clerical ministries and that God in Jesus Christ was calling them.

From the influence of my dear wife and children and the G-ETS community, I grew toward tolerance believing that we are all accepted and that the church must learn inclusivity. Since there will always be two licit readings of Scripture and there will always be pro and con communities of belief, the church must remain a broad and welcoming fellowship. To become an evicting, banning and banishing community would be to resist the Holy Spirit of God and the dominant direction of Scripture.

A particular input in my own career as an interfaith biblical scholar and theologian, one especially perplexing, has been the persistent reservation on the matter by Jewish, Evangelical Christian and Muslim faiths. I've learned that the only straight and gay to be known in the church is the *Torah* Advent Way made straight on the highway through the desert by the ever coming Messiah King. The Advent table waiting expectantly for that King is ever open to the poor and rich, the well and not well, the dignified and the derelict, persons of all manners of sexual preference and identity. What God hath joined together man must never tear asunder.

So much for that zinger. Let's go to the second Christmas ball of Advent. In my two decades at Garrett, I've often preached at Advent. Some perennial students will remember my last Colbert Report on the voice crying in the wilderness entitled "Here's Johnny!" I'm not sure why I'm always invited to do John the Baptist. Is it my wardrobe or my diet?

This season affects me deeply. We're often at hand at Kings College Cambridge for readings and carols. The ancient lectionary is awesome— the com-forte of Christ the King, the fury of John the Baptist, the topsy-turvy Magnificat, the gentle German forest of *Stille Nacht*, and the little town of Bethlehem nestled in rolling, snow-clad Vermont hills, all soon to be disturbed by Herod's infanticidal madness, all down here in *Haaretz* Israel, *Haaretz* Palestine, *Haaretz* Syria, *Haaretz* Egypt, the coming, then and again is about our world. It is a haunting season, which causes us "to ponder in our hearts," the vexation of this ever coming may be the reason we scurry to Black Friday sales and couch potato on NFL games.

The theological orthodoxy we ought to ponder is built around the three foci of creation, incarnation, and final coming. The latter theme is most complicated. Discontent with Jesus' admonition that it is not for us to know the time or place for end time, which even he doesn't know, we pour in our own frightful time-lines, agendas, and geographies. Especially in the malpreaching of American dispensationalist churches and the radio and TV charlatans: rapture, tribulation, 1948, tearing down *al aqsa* mosque in Jerusalem, rebuilding *the* Jewish temple of Zion –only to soon take them out at the scene of the Christian uptake, millennium, the left-behind selection and final separation and reaping of the Son of Man.

Totally misunderstanding this **Hashem /Shema,** this One Name, **Ben Adam** now cuts off sheep from goats, no longer righteous judge and savior, the Lord of the way home, but now the grim reaper. For good evangelical authority on these matters read Don Wagner, Gary Burge, and Barb Rossing, all whom, incidentally, serve with Dr. K.K. Yeo and myself on the evangelical-Muslim consultation.

When I first studied Isaiah 40 with Durham's CR North, we approached this servant song in the rigorous hermeneutical method known to John Wesley: Hebrew bible, Septuagint and King James English Bible, the Koine Greek text, and the *Qur'an* as side reference. I learned that in 40 verse 3, crying was imperfect, ongoing crying, *parakaleiten* in LXX. The voice continues crying to this day.

The times were just like ours. In Abraham Heschel's *Prophets*, it was the waning of the Babylonian empire to be replaced by the Persian. King Cyrus of Iran was God's deliverer and messiah for his people—who had been punished for sin, idolatry, immorality, violence, and injustice.

The nations and the peoples of the world were dispirited, anxious, and vulnerable. Destructive wars and security apparatus had left all nations especially the aspiring empires on the brink of economic collapse. The sin was national, economic oppression, contempt for the poor and weak, unemployment, land seizure, concentration of wealth, foreclosure, civil deadlock.

The judgment proffered in the exile is about justice for all, that American value so prized yet so obliterated in our history. Acute inequality is tearing our world to shreds. The image in Isaiah and Mark is pure *Torah* and Law of Christ, rough places plane, crooked straight, valleys elevated, mountains cast into the sea, glory revealed and all see it together as the scales of blindness are lifted.

A servant messiah has come and will come. This One will speak comfort to God's people that her warfare is accomplished and iniquity is pardoned. This penultimate deliverer is glimpsed and foretold by a wylie desert Nabi, a desert seer, a baptizer, one who doesn't know when to stop preaching, as witnessed by Caravaggio's sobering painting—remember the dance and the platter.

Government henceforth will be on the shoulders of a child. Warfare will henceforth be hidden beneath the endless history of wars and rumors of wars and this conquering hero will not be drenched in blood, but he will be called wonderful counselor, prince of peace. His government will never end while ours come and go, King of Kings and Lord of Lords, until he has brought all governments and peoples under his thrall.

I love Gian Carlo Menotti's depiction of the color of this child in "Amahl and the Night Visitors":

> Have you seen a child the color of wheat, the color of dawn?
> His eyes are mild, his hands are those of a king as king he was born.
> Have you seen a child the color of earth, the color of thorn?
> His eyes are sad, his hands are poor as poor he was born.
> Incense gold and myrrh we bring to his side and the eastern star
> is our guide.
>
> (Gian Carlo Menotti, "Amahl and the Night Visitors," 1951)

CONCLUSION

At the beginning of this journal, I wrote of the persistence of hope and new vistas of service even in the face of various and sundry weaknesses of the flesh and weariness of spirit. At the end of my "Last Sermon and Supper," I responded to the stock-in-trade question, "What are you going to do now?"

While the question seemed as absurd as the one we used to ask our Amish neighbors in Pennsylvania, whom we assume are also agonizing of whether to deep drill into the Marcellus Shale on their property, destroying water table and stream and spring water as well, "what are you going to be when you grow up?" As if there were myriad options.

I suggested blithely that I might drive an 18-wheeler on Pennsylvania Route 80, bind books, go trout fishing, if the streams still support life, or sit back, like Scrooge McDuck, counting my gold coins from gas revenues. I continued responding in the above sermon in this sardonic way speaking of my impending retirement: ". . . In my favorite Peter Sellers film, "Heavens Above!" the bishop and archdeacon are in the luxury car of the train to London commiserating on how to rid themselves of the Vicar Smallwood, who had been appointed to an uppity Church of England parish by a clerical mishap and had now turned the "well to do" parish into a haven of the poor and mischievous by taking Gospel justice seriously and giving over the hallowed halls of Orbiston Parva to the scallywags. At the climactic moment when the decision to send him packing has been made ("the church must stick to politics and not get involved in religion"), the porter cries as the train enters a dark tunnel "final call for the last supper." Amen, so let it be.

> As a stranger I arrived
> As a stranger I will leave
> I can't choose the season
> To depart from this place
> I won't delay or ponder
> I must begin my journey now.

(Franz Schubert, "Die Winterreise," 1828)